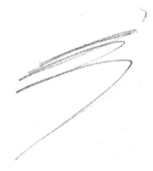

W9-AGY-665

WITHDRAWN

Machine Gun Kelly's
Last Stand

❖ ❖ ❖ ❖ ❖ ❖ ❖ ❖ ❖ ❖ ❖ ❖ ❖ ❖

Machine Gun Kelly's Last Stand

Stanley Hamilton

UNIVERSITY PRESS OF KANSAS

© 2003 by the University Press of Kansas

All rights reserved

Published by the University Press of Kansas (Lawrence, Kansas 66049), which was organized by the Kansas Board of Regents and is operated and funded by Emporia State
University, Fort Hays State University, Kansas State University, Pittsburg State University, the University of Kansas, and Wichita State University

Library of Congress Cataloging-in-Publication Data

Hamilton, Stanley, 1934–
Machine Gun Kelly's last stand / Stanley Hamilton.
p. cm.
Includes bibliographical references and index.
ISBN 0-7006-1247-5 (cloth)
1. Kelly, Machine Gun, 1897–1954.   2. Criminals—United
States—Biography.   3. Outlaws—United States—Biography.   4. Criminal
investigation—United States.   5. Kidnapping—United States.   6. United
States. Federal Bureau of Investigation.   I. Title.
HV6248.K414 H34 2003
364.15′23′092—dc21   2002154124

British Library Cataloguing in Publication Data is available.

Printed in the United States of America

10 9 8 7 6 5 4 3 2 1

The paper used in this publication meets the minimum requirements of the American
National Standard for Permanence of Paper for Printed Library Materials Z39.48-1984.

Contents

❖ ❖ ❖ ❖ ❖ ❖ ❖

Kidnapping is as bad as murder, if not worse. There is no greater menace in the country today.
—U.S. Judge Edgar S. Vaught, Western District of Oklahoma

Mankind knows no crime as base and as vicious as kidnapping. It is an offense all the more savage because it pits brute force against the innocent, the unsuspecting, the helpless.
—J. Edgar Hoover, director, FBI

And he that stealeth a man, and selleth him, or if he be found in his hand, he shall surely be put to death.
—Exodus 21:16

Illustrations

❖ ❖ ❖ ❖ ❖ ❖ ❖

Preface

❖ ❖ ❖ ❖ ❖ ❖ ❖

Melvin Purvis, who was arguably the most fabled and admired agent in the early days of the FBI, said of the drama Machine Gun Kelly set off, "There is probably no case in the history of crime as interesting from the standpoint of mystery as that of the kidnapping of Charles F. Urschel, of Oklahoma City." Purvis was right. So was the managing editor of the *Daily Oklahoman* of that city when he wrote, "In my experience in Oklahoma, the Urschel case was the most interesting, the most exciting, best suspended crime mystery since statehood. It was a newspaper natural." Purvis wrote his words in 1936, three years after the famous kidnapping, and Editor Walter Harrison penned his in 1954. If only they could have known that there were still more intriguing and unique developments to come.

As noted in the telling, I became intrigued about the case through conversations years ago with a now-deceased uncle who, but for a quirk of timing, would have been a major player because he was not only a business partner in the oil wildcatting business with the victim, Charles Urschel, but also a close friend. Some parts of the story have been told, often with errors. The instant telling adds elements not told before and explores others in closer detail than heretofore published.

One difficulty encountered was that even though contact was made with some descendants of the principals at the time, none accepted my invitation to provide information. Their reluctance to do so is fully appreciated and respected; it can only be imagined how many others have bothered them with similar prying requests for one reason or another over the years. A *San Antonio Express–News* article of April 25, 1971, reporting on the Urschels' estate sale, revealed their feelings on the matter: " 'The family is sick of people resurrecting the kidnapping,' a friend said. 'That's the one thing they wanted to forget the most.' A relative said the Urschels 'did everything in the world to ward off publicity—the whole family did, in fact.' "

Thus, the pages that follow here are a dramatic rendition, based on extensive use of primary research and secondary sources, providing a reconstruction of the main events and sidelights of the long-running drama. The narrative is based on newspaper reports and investigative documents, court transcripts, literary accounts, and the best recollections of participants at the time others interviewed them. When "conversation" or "thoughts" are employed, it is noted in each case that they represent what might well have taken place.

Still speaking of sources, the various FBI written versions of the case and the 8,748-page file about it at the agency's headquarters in Washington, D.C., were revealing both in what they contained and what they did not. For instance, some agency documents cited, quoted, or even reproduced elsewhere were absent. Some data in the files repeated errors long ago corrected. And, even some seven decades after the crime itself, great numbers of names were still blacked out—names, for example, of policemen and writers of letters or internal government memos.

Mention should be made as well of an example of the convoluted thinking that the federal bureaucracy sometimes produces. Attempting to find the kidnap victim's World War I service records, I corresponded with the Department of Veterans Affairs Records Management Center in St. Louis. The first answer indicated they had "probably" been destroyed in a devastating 1973 fire. This use of "probably" led to a second request for any information available. After several more months came a reply saying my letter was being forwarded (for some unexplained reason) to the veteran's last known address—even though I had noted that he had died some thirty years earlier. My next letter pointed this out once again and said there obviously was a record of some kind if his last address was in the files. There ensued another reply that no records could be found. Then I solicited the services of Senator John Warner of Virginia, who was chairman of the Senate Armed Services Committee. Amazingly, within a matter of days of the senator's intervention, the full army records arrived. They are referred to at some places in the text.

There needs to be a brief note on the spelling of "kidnapping" and "kidnapped." A majority of the printed reports in the 1930s used a single "p," whereas in recent years two are more common. Therefore, except in referencing book titles that had the old spelling, the double version is used throughout for the reader's convenience.

Many fine friends have stood with me from day one on this project.

In no particular order, and with the hope that no one is inadvertently omitted, sincere appreciation is extended to them. There absolutely would have been no book without my two indefatigable researchers, Carol Welsh in Oklahoma City and Pam Patteson in San Antonio. The Hon. Ralph G. Thompson, chief judge of the U.S. District Court for the Western District of Oklahoma and an expert on the Kelly trial, provided invaluable assistance and leads. Susan Connor Beal of Portland, Oregon, made outstanding editorial improvements. So did Washington, D.C., author and book reviewer John Greenya. Paul Dickson, prolific author and good friend, was a wealth of tips and introductions. Ed Kelley, editorial director of the *Daily Oklahoman*, graciously opened the newspaper's old files to me. At the National Press Club in Washington, my cheering section was led by Bill Hickman of the American Petroleum Institute; Allan Cromley, retired bureau chief for the *Daily Oklahoman;* Naaman Seigel, a former Agriculture Department officer; and Bill Buff of Strat@comm Strategic Communications.

There were other good friends upon whom I prevailed to give up their leisure hours to read parts of the raw manuscript or who helped in other ways: Betsy Moniz, Carole Cones, Peter Kirley, Mike Thomas, Jim Boren, Bill Hill, and Joan MacLeod. Good input about the area where the kidnap victim was held captive came from Rosalie Gregg, chair of the Wise County (Texas) Historical Commission; her equally convivial colleague, Shirley Zedaker; and LaDarla Keith, local historian of note. The fascinating revelations about the education of the Kelly daughter came from Mrs. W. Rowland Denman of Edmond, Oklahoma, granddaughter of the judge who presided in the case. Data in great quantities about the kidnap victim's early days came from Mrs. Wanda Pohlman, a member of the Fostoria (Ohio) Lineage Research Society, and Leonard Skonecki, a freelance writer in the same city. James C. Leake, the delightful owner of KTUL-TV in Tulsa, Oklahoma, dug up much useful information plus a tape of a documentary he had produced about the kidnapping.

Hillary M. Robinette, communications director of the Society of Former Special Agents of the FBI, granted access to his files at the society offices in Quantico, Virginia. Dr. Ray Miles, author of a fine book about Tom Slick, the *King of the Wildcatters*, turned up new material that is included in this narrative. Nina Graybill of Graybill and English in Washington, D.C., merits special thanks for valuable initial guidance. Judith Michener, archivist and assistant oral historian at the Oklahoma Historical Society, was most helpful. Colleague Brian Kelly produced the map indicating where most of the action took place. Others who went out of their way include Randy Falkofske at the John Marshall Library in Alexandria, Virginia, and Susan Bleistein and Soon Williams, interlibrary loan staffers for the Fairfax County (Virginia) library system. And then there is Nancy Scott Jackson, acquisitions editor for the University Press of Kansas, to whom there cannot be enough thanks for steering this work into print.

Finally, any errors are the sole responsibility of the author, who dedicates this book to four fine offspring: Susan, Rob, Jennifer, and Art.

1

Prologue

❖ ❖ ❖ ❖ ❖ ❖ ❖ ❖ ❖ ❖ ❖ ❖ ❖ ❖ ❖

Oklahoma City, Oklahoma
Saturday, July 22, 1933
11:45 P.M.

There was no moon to spotlight them. No streetlights. Not even a light on the porch of the house that was their target. Nothing that might reveal, to anyone out for a late-night stroll, the presence of the two men trying to be invisible in the bushes at 327 N.W. 18th Street, a substantial home situated prominently on a large corner lot. Any observer would have been extremely alarmed to see that one of the men now stealthily approaching the porch at the side of the house was carrying a submachine gun and the other a revolver.

Their escape car was positioned for the same kind of fast getaway the two men had made in the numerous small-town bank holdups for which they were wanted in a number of states. This night, however, there was nothing small-time about their undertaking. This was to be a really big-time job—a spectacular kidnapping that they hoped would produce an enormous sum of money.

Silently the two of them crept, slowly and deliberately, up the four steps to the screen door. In hopes of enticing any hint of a breeze on this hot, muggy summer night, the occupants had conveniently left the inside door open and the screen door unlatched. Thus the gunmen could easily see and faintly hear the two couples huddled around a card table, under a slowly rotating overhead fan, taking turns speaking in soft monosyllables, bidding in words probably to this effect:

"One club."

"A diamond."

"Pass."

"Two diamonds."

"Two hearts."

Confident from their earlier, if rather perfunctory, surveillance that no guard was on the premises and watching to be certain no one passing by might inadvertently disrupt their plan, the two nervous gunmen waited for the opportune moment to pounce. After checking their weapons one last time to make sure they were ready to use, if necessary, they looked at their watches and saw it was almost midnight. Finally, ready as planned, they nodded to each other. All business, they stepped quietly into the house, brandishing their weapons.

"Don't any of you move! Don't make a sound, or we'll blow your heads off!"

It was all over in less than ninety seconds. They made off with the two mute and unresisting men as their prisoners, leaving the petrified women with a stern warning not to notify the police if they ever wanted to see their husbands alive again.

This was no isolated small-time crime. Within hours it would explode into an event commanding national, even worldwide, attention for three frenetic months, and then surprisingly resurface intermittently over the next quarter of a century and beyond.

With the abduction of their two wealthy hostages and their carefully calculated flight south to a desolate rural hideout in north-central Texas, the gunmen unwittingly set in motion a chain of events that would have lasting historical and national significance. Their crime conferred instant celebrity or, in truth, infamy on the leader of what was in fact only a three-person team of amateur kidnappers. He is still remembered in criminal lore for pulling off the most lucrative kidnapping of his time— a sensational crime that remains unique in the annals of crime solving, jurisprudence, and journalism.

Just as the normally placid, well-to-do neighborhood in this frontier-city-gone-modern of 195,000 citizens would never be quite the same again, neither would the entire country. This high-profile kidnapping would prove to be a major impetus in a wide and suddenly growing mood swing among Americans. Before this crime captured headlines everywhere, ordinary people were rather bemused and entertained by the criminal antics of small-time gangsters. An isolationist, anti–big government view prevailed, opposed to the idea of any kind of national police force.

Kidnapping certainly was by no means new in the United States. The difference was that abductions had mostly been underworld hoodlum-against-hoodlum crimes, gangs capturing members of rival gangs in the name of debt collection or payback. As often as not, the victim was roughed up or killed to send a strong message. Confined to the underworld, such kidnappings rarely aroused the public's anger.

But by the early 1930s, alarmed at the increasing numbers of innocent victims taken for ransom, Americans were beginning to come around to the idea of the necessity for a federal presence to combat kidnappings and other outrages, such as arrogant gangsters skipping back and forth across state or county lines avoiding pursuit. Such a force already existed within the U.S. Department of Justice, but on a very small scale and with limited manpower and jurisdiction. J. Edgar Hoover, thirty-eight at the time of the kidnapping, had been with this force since 1917 and had served as its director since 1924. He had reformed a moribund bureaucracy and made it a truly professional force. Yet he was hampered by the fact that his agents would not obtain legal authority to carry arms or even make arrests until 1934.

Even so, Hoover responded immediately to the Oklahoma kidnapping by boldly stepping forward to coordinate what, in 1933, was the biggest, most intensive, and most widely publicized nationwide manhunt in the country's history. The result was a stunningly rapid closeout of this high-profile case through local law enforcement's newfound cooperation with Hoover's emerging agency, soon to be renamed the Federal Bureau of Investigation, or FBI. Hoover would continue for nearly five decades as its powerfully effective yet aggressively self-promoting crime-busting director.

Although fascinating and unique in their own right, the kidnapping, the ensuing nationwide manhunt, and the legal outcome were really a microcosm of this bleak period in American history. July 1933 was the midpoint of a brief and intense crime-ridden period in which the country seemed to be cursed with a series of titanic natural, economic, and social catastrophes. So great was the onslaught of bad news that many demoralized citizens feared that the American dream of democracy and capitalism was in danger of crumbling. This iconic case, breathlessly followed by a fascinated public, was so quickly and effectively concluded that it was largely instrumental in bringing about the end of the short-lived but intriguing time in America known as the Gangster Era.

2

The War against Crime

❖   ❖   ❖   ❖   ❖   ❖   ❖   ❖   ❖   ❖   ❖   ❖   ❖   ❖   ❖

The summer of 1933 was a grim time in the United States. Little more than a decade had passed since America had been the dominant military force in winning the Great War. Now, however, the nation was mired in the grip of not only the Gangster Era but also the Great Depression, the ravages of the Dust Bowl, and the utter failure of the misguided moral crusade known as Prohibition.

More than thirteen million desperate, despondent people, a full quarter of the nation's workforce, had lost their jobs as a result of the worldwide economic collapse. Most were willing to do just about anything more or less legal for food, for shelter, for a dollar or two. Simultaneously, tens of thousands more were driven out of the Great Plains of the Southwest and the Midwest because millions of acres of their land had fallen victim to the Dust Bowl.

Just a distant historical footnote now, the Dust Bowl was a devastating, monumental, ecological and agricultural disaster. It was brought about by a combination of three factors—a century of ranchers overgrazing their livestock, farmers then abusing the originally lush land by plowing up the natural grass cover to plant wheat year after year, and finally some eight years of sustained severe drought. Starting in 1931, the rains all but stopped. The desolation eventually spread out over some one hundred million acres of the panhandles of Oklahoma and Texas, western Kansas, eastern Colorado, and northeastern New Mexico. Hearing, then seeing, one of the monstrous rolling dust storms—"black blizzards," which could tower higher than seven thousand feet and stretch several miles wide—tearing across the barren land directly toward them, people would hastily soak towels, rags, or whatever was available and stuff them around windows, doors, and fireplaces. Cribs were draped with wet sheets or strips of damp cheesecloth to protect infants as best they could. Their efforts had only minimal success.

Some of the storms raged on for two, even three days. When they finally passed and the dust was taking hours to settle, houses and barns had to be swept or shoveled out to remove the thick layer of dirt that had forced its way in. With no moisture to hold the soil and few trees to serve as windbreaks, the dust invaded the lungs of livestock, fowl, even people, sometimes fatally. Wells and creeks were choked with it. Automobile and tractor engines were clogged. Sometimes the winds kept right on carrying residual dust as far east as the capital in Washington and into New England, even to ships as far as two hundred miles out in the Atlantic. Each big blow meant more of the rich vital topsoil was swept away, forever, and with it the farm families' very equity, the collateral for their loans. When the farmers had no crops to harvest, pinched merchants finally had to shut off their credit. And eventually the detested banks had to foreclose on their defaulted mortgages and auction off thousands of unproductive homesteads. Or their resigned families, pushed over the edge of financial disaster, simply shuffled away from the barren land, often without even shutting the doors behind them, rather than suffer the indignity of being evicted. As the population dwindled, churches and schools and even some towns simply closed up.

John Steinbeck's gripping 1939 Pulitzer Prize–winning novel *Grapes of Wrath* summed up the depressing times vividly: "Car-loads, caravans, homeless and hungry; twenty thousand and fifty thousand and a hundred thousand and two hundred thousand. They streamed over the mountains, hungry and restless—restless as ants, scurrying to find work to do, to lift, to push, to pull, to pick, to cut—anything, any burden to bear, for food. The kids are hungry. We got no place to live. Like ants scurrying for work, for food, and most of all for land." The motion picture of the same name as the book, starring Henry Fonda in what some critics consider his finest dramatic role, played to shaken audiences when it premiered in 1940 and ran for years afterward. Many of these "Okies" and "Arkies" (Oklahomans and Arkansans) trudged west, to the Promised Land of California. Some hardy and determined others, however, did elect to stay behind and persevere, clinging precariously to the dream of the way of life they hoped would return and praying fervently for rain.

Prohibition (formally known as the Volstead Act) was called the "greatest social experiment of modern times" by President Calvin Coolidge. In reality, it was the openly violated "Noble Experiment," a sad public joke soon to be mercifully ended by repeal after thirteen and a half tumultuous, lawless years. Easy profits were still being made in 1933 by the illegal sale of alcoholic beverages (defined as anything more than one-half of one percent alcohol) to the segment of the thirsty public that could afford them. Rampant bootlegging led popular humorist Will Rogers to quip, "Prohibition is better than no liquor at all."

From Washington, as part of President Franklin Delano Roosevelt's New Deal aimed at pulling the country out of the Depression that followed the "War to End All Wars," came the Agricultural Adjustment Act of 1933, a "temporary" emergency measure introducing the concept of federal subsidies and low-interest loans to prop up the farmers in difficult times. It would be too late, however, for some. Those included the ones who took the lawless route, becoming the gangsters.

In the especially hard-hit Great Plains—the gritty, dreary Dust Bowl— a new breed of hit-and-run criminals like "Pretty Boy" Floyd, Bonnie Parker and Clyde Barrow, "Baby Face" Nelson, "Creepy" Karpis, the Ma Barker Gang, and "Terrible" Touhy roamed the landscape, sociological by-products of the tough times. Newspapers, Sunday rotogravure sections, the radio, news wire services, magazines, and newsreels actually romanticized them, all but extolling their daring exploits. Many people looked on these small-time gangsters with a sort of admiration; they provided escapism and a welcome diversion from the despair of the Depression. They captivated and enthralled the public with their derring-do, approaching a certain celebrity status like motion picture stars and athletes. These freelance gangsters differed from the structured, disreputable big-city mobsters and syndicate racketeers, such as Alphonse ("Scarface Al") Capone, Charlie ("Lucky") Luciano, and Benjamin ("Bugsy") Siegel. They seemed more like reincarnations of the not-so-long-ago flamboyant and equally glamorous Wild West outlaws like Billy the Kid, Jesse James, and the Dalton gang. In fact, the pair of western lawmen most famed for hunting down and capturing outlaws had died only a few years previously—Wyatt Earp in 1929 and Bat Masterson in 1921. Cole Younger, the last rider with the train-and-bank-robbing James gang, who reputedly killed seventeen men and was himself shot no fewer than thirty times, lived until 1916, dying a natural death at the age of seventy-two.

A *Kansas City Star* reporter astutely examined how the exploits were exaggerated and even fabricated during the Gangster Era in a feature article written half a century later: "America's newspapers, even those far from the victimized heartland, quickly recognized the folk-hero aura surrounding these men and women, and exploited it to the fullest. Every criminal move was chronicled, including moves that they never made at all. Reporters with no facts felt no compulsion to skip a deadline. They simply made something up."

The reason for this tolerance, and even admiration, for the freelance desperadoes was that banks, the major victim of their crimes, weren't exactly the most beloved institutions in the heartland. Public opinion held them as cold enemies of the poor and downtrodden; they foreclosed on delinquent mortgages and auctioned off the homesteads of third- and fourth-generation families for whatever pennies on the dollar they could recoup. So as long as the organized crime underworld characters were just kidnapping and killing one another, and the small-time underdog gangsters were winging an occasional banker or shooting up the place in the course of a robbery, it was looked upon as a sort of interesting sidelight during otherwise drab times. Such events actually provided a vicarious thrill of sorts for much of the public. It served the blood-sucking banks right! The aforementioned Alvin ("Creepy") Karpis, bank stickup man extraordinaire, told an illustrative story. When he was intending to commandeer a North Dakota farm family's motorcar for a necessarily hasty getaway one afternoon, the sympathetic owner summed up the widespread resentment against bankers as he voluntarily handed over his car key: "You robbed the bank, did you? Well, I don't care. All the banks ever do is foreclose on us farmers."

Another contemporary bank robber of some well-deserved infamy, James ("Blackie") Audett, stated it a little differently in *Rap Sheet: My Life Story*, an autobiography that a ghostwriter helped him compose between the second and third terms he served in Alcatraz in the thirties, forties, and fifties:

Whenever a bank was robbed we used to kind of listen around afterward and find out what the public thought. That way you could tell whether you was just hot with the police or hot all over. Sort of helped to know that in planning your next move. Like a politician taking a poll. We would go to restaurants and places right after a job and lots of times we would hear people talking about it. Many's the time I've heard people sitting right next to me in a restaurant saying, "Well, they didn't hurt nobody. I kind of hope they don't get caught." Maybe that ain't the proper attitude to take toward a bank robber, but that's the way we found it, many's the time. Well, times was mighty hard here in the early thirties and people didn't care much whether the banks got robbed or not. Maybe some of them sort of hoped they would. You take some family that's just been kicked off their place by the bank and lost everything they worked all their lives for, well, they ain't going to be too hostile, maybe, if you want to hide out in their haystack. Sometimes they might even sneak you a fried chicken. Once or twice when I was on the hideout like that I've even had them suggest that such and such a bank down the road might be a good prospect and might deserve to be took.

It's a funny thing, but people in general ain't, as a rule, too hostile to bank robbers. That is, they ain't if you never hurt anybody in the heists. If you was halfways a gentleman in the robbery, people kind of was on your side after it was over. The bankers felt different about it, of course, and so did the FBI. But people in general, they never got too het up. . . . They didn't feel that way about it if anybody got killed, though.

Homer Cummings, the frustrated but astutely publicity-minded new attorney general of the United States, employed deliberately exaggerated rhetoric to demonstrate that Roosevelt's newly installed administration was moving firmly and swiftly to combat the crime wave. Cummings called this dark period of American history "a war that threatens the safety of our country—a war with the organized forces of crime." He was just getting warmed up to the subject: "It is conservative to say that there are more people in the underworld carrying deadly weapons than there are in the Army and Navy of the United States."

He took particular aim at an alarming new type of criminal extortion racket centered largely in the Midwest and Southwest—the kidnapping of rich and socially prominent private citizens for ransom. These differed from the somewhat commonplace (and often fatal) kidnappings of bootleggers and other criminals by one gang or another, generally for purposes of intimidation or "territory." But looking at the new "citizen" kidnappings, Cummings went so far as to suggest a set of "rules" he urged families of the victims to follow. One was to "avoid publicity at all costs, for news of the crime would give notice to the kidnappers that the authorities had been appealed to, with the result that the hostage might be killed."

The journalistic standard–setting *New York Times* bestowed national stature on these new crimes by instituting a regular page one feature. Its day-by-day label headlines varied: "Progress of Kidnap War," "The Drive on Crime," and "The Kidnapping Situation." These were running summaries much like the baseball box scores, recording the status of the most newsworthy cases. Twenty-seven "major" ones made the newspaper's list in 1933, including the following four prominent ones: Mary McElroy, the young and tragically impressionable daughter of the city manager of Kansas City, Missouri; Charles Boettcher II, the grandson of a millionaire Denver entrepreneur; August Luer, a wealthy retired farmer-banker from Alton, Illinois; and St. Paul brewery company president William A. Hamm Jr.

Twenty-five-year-old Mary McElroy early on came to empathize with her kidnappers, who got only half of the $60,000 they'd demanded from her father, Judge Henry F. McElroy. After the capture and conviction of her kidnappers, Mary convinced the governor of Missouri to commute the ringleader's sentence of execution to life imprisonment. Having spent many days visiting them in prison, she agonized to a reporter, "It was my testimony that convicted these men. I have nightmares about those men and the fates they brought on themselves. I was a part of the drama that fixed their destiny." Six years after the crime from which she never mentally recovered and four months after her father died, she fatally shot herself, leaving a tragic suicide note: "My four kidnappers are probably the only people on earth who don't consider me an utter fool. You have your death penalty now—so—please—give them a chance."

Young Boettcher's frugal grandfather in Denver at first told the newspapers he wasn't of a mood to pay a single dollar of the $60,000 ransom demanded. "What right do these men have to make demands? The boy will come back all right. The men who have taken him will use common horse sense and send him back without harming him." However, it was announced that the money would be paid after the release of the thirty-two-year-old heir, and it was done. The kidnappers were soon caught.

Illinois farmer and retired banker Luer was seventy-seven years old and in ill health, so feeble in fact that his family pleaded publicly with the kidnappers—five men and a woman—not to give him any coffee and "only the mildest of cigars." Equally concerned about his health, the kidnappers freed him after five days when no ransom was forthcoming. Amazingly, they sent him a note a few days afterward demanding $16,000. This was the last clue authorities needed to nab them.

Hamm, the thirty-nine-year-old owner of the Hamm Brewing Company, was snatched in Minnesota by Alvin ("Creepy") Karpis and friends, who collected the staggering sum of $100,000 for his safe return, setting the record for the most ransom ever received to that time. They, too, were soon apprehended.

The consortium of "names" at Lloyd's of London shrewdly took note of this growing epidemic across the pond by introducing the concept of insurance for ransom (it being a felony in Britain to pay ransom). Lloyd's reportedly did a good business. Purchasing this coverage and employing very visible bodyguards became something of a status symbol, particularly in celebrity-conscious Hollywood, where Bing Crosby and Marlene Dietrich were among the first big motion picture stars known to do so. As for the new kidnapping and ransom insurance, Lloyd's went into the business of underwriting policies of up to $100,000 (U.S.) for adults, charging a premium of three-quarters of 1 percent. Arrangements were conducted under conditions of utmost secrecy. Only applicants of "unquestioned reputation" were considered for coverage. They had to have been free of any involvement with "shady or undesirable characters." Finally, if accepted, their identities were kept confidential in order not to provide an invitation to kidnappers to come and get them.

The Lindbergh case investigation wasn't winning law enforcement any kudos in mid-1933. For seventeen embarrassing months, there wasn't a solid lead as to who in early March 1932 had stolen and brutally murdered the twenty-month-old son of Charles and Anne Morrow Lindbergh, he the world-renowned pioneer aviator and she the equally famous author. In fact, it wouldn't be for another fourteen months, until September 1934, that the alleged kidnapper/murderer would finally be identified and run to ground.

Then came the bloody Kansas City Union Station Massacre of June 17, 1933. Met by two local officers, four lawmen (including an FBI agent) were returning a bandit under a twenty-five-year sentence for armed train robbery to the federal penitentiary in Leavenworth, Kansas. Three gunmen ambushed them; in less than two minutes the FBI agent, the prisoner, and three officers were savagely gunned down and the two others wounded at 7:20 on a Saturday morning in full view of breakfast diners entering and exiting the Harvey House, a dozen or so porters and redcaps, and hundreds of terrified travelers in the vast parking plaza fronting the city's massive railroad terminal.

When children and respected law-abiding private citizens became victims, stolen from their homes and sometimes murdered, the amusement and the glamour went out of the game. Now even those who had followed the gangsters' daring exploits wanted the whole crime wave brought to a swift end and the criminals put out of business. The Lindbergh kidnap-murder and the Union Station Massacre triggered a rapid mood swing in a previously apathetic public and its rather bemused attitude toward free-lance gangsters. The folk hero image was starting to tarnish, and they began to look like the common criminals they really were.

Newly inaugurated President Roosevelt directed Cummings and his Department of Justice to conduct a quick and intensive probe into this new wave of kidnappings. The radical possibility arose of creating a supranational police force, perhaps patterned after Scotland Yard, to battle the crime wave. Deftly, Cummings continued to keep the subject on the front pages. He told the press, "We know there is too much crime. That is all we need to know. What we want is action. We intend to spend as much money as needed, and when needed, to fight kidnapping and punish criminals."

As the first step, J. Edgar Hoover was promoted to lead the battle. Journalist Rex Collier reported this turn of events in a front-page *Washington Evening Star* article on July 30, 1933, dramatically headlined "U.S. Crime War 'Supreme Command' Filled with Appointment of Hoover Division Head." Collier wrote:

> Plans for the crusade, the scope of which will exceed anything ever before attempted by federal authorities, have in view the spreading of a coordinated web of federal, state, and local detective forces from which few criminals may hope to escape. . . . Although young

in years, the keen-eyed director of the Justice Department's new investigative arm is a pioneer in the modern school of scientific crime detection and a recognized authority on criminal identification.

His force of special agents—scattered over the country in 23 strategic field offices—are lawyers or accountants who have been graduated also from Hoover's novel training school here for investigators—popularly called his "Crime Detection University."

Both the Lindbergh tragedy and the Union Station Massacre were proving to be frustrating and drawn out, with no easy solutions. The pressure was bearing down on Hoover, who had been sent—uninvited, unwanted, and against his own better judgment—to the scene of the Lindbergh kidnapping in New Jersey as the president's personal representative.

The so-called Lindbergh Kidnapping Law had been hastily enacted by an alarmed and angry Congress and quickly signed by President Herbert Hoover in mid-1932 in reaction to the murder of Charles A. Lindbergh Jr. and the wave of "public citizen" kidnappings. It decreed that taking a hostage across a state line or using the U.S. Postal Service, radio, or telephone for communicating ransom demands or conditions was now a federal crime, subject to a maximum punishment of life in prison. This penalty applied not only to the kidnappers themselves but also to anyone else found guilty under the loose definition of complicity. It made no difference whether any ransom was ever collected or if the victim was released unharmed. (The death penalty for kidnapping would be added to federal law in mid-1934.)

Before the Lindbergh Act and the related federal legislation that followed, kidnappers and other roving gangsters had little reason to fear apprehension or severe punishment if caught. There was little mutual cooperation or coordination among law enforcement agencies when it came to the matter of who had authority when political or county lines were crossed. How could there be, since there were 3,096 counties in the United States, most with their own sheriffs of widely varying competence and honesty? Only eleven states (Oklahoma not among them) even had state police forces.

Law enforcement agencies simply didn't have the advantages of communication and detection tools that would be routinely taken for granted many years later, such as direct long-distance dialing (every call then requiring the time-consuming assistance of one or more switchboard operators—known as "centrals"—depending on the distance and inter-connections involved), faxes, cellular phones, caller ID, conference calls, television, videos, satellite tracking, call tracing, copy machines, DNA analysis, computers, e-mail, the Internet, and so forth.

In those early 1930s, the latest in law enforcement communications "technology" included one-way radios (police officers in their cars could hear their dispatcher, but in most cities and towns they had to locate and pull over to a public telephone or call box and get out to respond), the old reliable Western Union telegraph, upright manual typewriters with their inky ribbons and erasure-marred or x'd-out carbon paper copies, slow and messy mimeograph machines, rotary or wall-mounted crank telephones, and the fairly new fingerprinting identification system, introduced three years into the new century.

Furthermore, the gangsters were usually able to outrun police pursuit easily because they could afford bigger, faster, more powerful automobiles—"gangster whitewalls," so-called for the distinctive style of their tires. Even when the gangsters were picked up, there was no such thing as the polygraph, or lie detector, for breaking alibis. There were no Social Security numbers for tracing; that federal program wouldn't come about until 1935. And, of course, there could be no trailing of people's movements through their use of credit cards ("plastic money"), a dubiously beneficial creation of the 1950s.

Philosophically, a strong isolationist sentiment about crime investigation remained in the country. Looking back with the retrospective advantage of seven decades, the early 1930s seem to be a rather quaint, ineffective age in which the Forces of Good tried to counter armed desperadoes who were rapidly becoming more daring and successful criminals.

Into this void moved Hoover. When he took over the FBI, it had only 650 employees of varied experience and ability. He soon culled out those he rightly deemed deadwood and set up rigid standards. He quickly did away with automatic promotion based on seniority and inaugurated the radical practice of annual performance reviews based on "Efficiency Rating Sheets." New agents had to be males between twenty-five and thirty-five years of age, physically fit, and with experience in the law or accounting. Each had to undergo a thorough check, his college record and entire background examined for any possible character flaws. After acceptance came formal training courses in areas including federal law, finger-print science, crime scene searching, interviews, and photography. And, while it was never formally spelled out, the newcomers quickly learned to emulate the director's personal dress code—dark suit, white shirt, neu-tral tie, polished shoes. They took their oath of office very seriously.

3

Charles Urschel

❖ ❖ ❖ ❖ ❖ ❖ ❖ ❖ ❖ ❖ ❖ ❖ ❖ ❖ ❖

In July 1933, Charles Urschel was a wealthy and rather high-profile res-
ident of Oklahoma City. Although unpretentious and averse to publicity, he was described by one local business editor as "a silent mystery
man of the oil fraternity."

He was born on March 7, 1890, near Fostoria, Ohio, and spent his first
nineteen years toiling on the family farm. Wanting to break away from
that seven-days-a-week, dawn-to-dusk drudgery, he put himself through
business college, then taught for a few terms in a country school. After
switching to a job as an accountant for a harness-making company (a
declining industry), he became intrigued by reading about the up-and-
coming oil business. He enlisted in the army when America entered the
Great War. Discharged as a sergeant, he took his mustering-out pay and
small savings, packed his few belongings, and headed to distant Oklahoma to try to put his talents to productive use in the oil fields. Fortu-
itously, he landed in the boomtown of Cushing. The town—in which a
canny oil prospector by the name of Thomas Baker Slick was the major
player—was a burgeoning hotbed of speculative drilling. Derricks and
producing wells stood side by side in ragged rows almost as far as one
could see. The men, and a few women, lived in two- or three-story clap-
board buildings. Saloons and other forms of entertainment proliferated.
Occasional devastating fires sparked by lightning or, more likely, by an
errant cigarette stub dropped by a drunken roustabout would rage frighteningly out of control for days.

Calm, dispassionate, and quick to learn the oil business, Urschel soon came to the flamboyant Slick's attention. Impressed with Urschel's mature, deliberate reasoning, keen analytical mind, and single-minded devotion to business, Slick quickly embraced him as a partner in the business, making him his "inside" financial detail expert. Soon Urschel met his bride-to-be, Flored, better known as "Flo," who was Tom Slick's younger sister visiting from Pennsylvania. After the newly married couple relocated to Oklahoma City to run Slick's operations there, fellow oilmen grudgingly said that Urschel could be "pretty hard-boiled." He was an exacting worker and a rigid but fair stickler for detail. The oil editor of the *Daily Oklahoman* described him as "dogged," a man who "never moves in a hurry." As Slick's most trusted partner—his cautious "inside man" and buffer for ten years—Urschel had banked a considerable sum of money himself from the freewheeling, high-risk oil and natural gas exploration business in Oklahoma, Texas, Kansas, Louisiana, and Mississippi ($2 million of which, the *Kansas City Star* reported, Slick presented him in a single check for closing a big deal).

Known by all as the "King of the Wildcatters," the appropriately named Slick had owned under various names the world's largest independent oil operation. At one time, the usually tight-lipped Slick uncharacteristically let it be known that he had more than 500,000 acres of land under lease. His wife, Berenice, was the strong-minded daughter of the general superintendent of the St. Louis–San Francisco Railway. Loyally sticking by her husband through good and bad prospecting times, she took their young children along to ramshackle boardinghouses in the oil boomtowns in the early days and even did the family laundry in galvanized buckets.

Tom Slick died unexpectedly in 1930 at the age of forty-six, leaving an estate that, after inheritance taxes, legal challenges, and various other fees and expenses, netted somewhere between $6 million and $23 million, depending on which published account one chose to believe. A "council of three"—Urschel, Berenice, and her brother-in-law, attorney Arthur A. Seeligson—controlled his vast estate.

The two partners were so close professionally and personally that Slick directed in his last will and testament that "Charles Urschel shall have the final say as to when and upon what conditions any of my property, either real or personal, shall be sold, conveyed, encumbered, leased, or invested, in any manner whatsoever, and that unless the said C. F. Urschel agrees, no transaction relative to any of my property shall be executed and carried out." Under terms of the Slick trust, Urschel was made the legal guardian of the three Slick children, Betty, Tom Jr., and Earl. After Slick's death, Urschel consolidated the numerous interests and properties into various new firms, including Tom Slick Properties, Slick-Urschel Oil Company, and Transwestern Oil Company.

Shortly after Slick's demise came the death of his grief-stricken thirty-eight-year-old sister Flo. Two years later, Charles Urschel and Berenice Slick were married in a private ceremony in St. Louis, and after a honeymoon in Europe returned to Oklahoma City. There, almost every day, weather permitting, Urschel would briskly walk the eighteen blocks to and from his downtown office. Oblivious to any possible danger, he and Berenice frequently took leisurely evening strolls around their neighborhood, stopping to chat with neighbors. A public figure because of his business prominence, but by choice a private person, he assiduously shunned publicity about himself and the two families, especially about their finances. Yet when his habit of hiking to and from work found its way into print, he proudly showed the clipping to friends for weeks.

This was the man marked for kidnapping. Based only on the plotters' rudimentary "research" of the few published financial details, they chose Urschel from a pool of other possibilities: a Texas banker, a Missouri brewer, and two Oklahomans, one a bank president, the other a dry goods merchant. They enlisted as their lone accomplice a seasoned bank robber who, like themselves, was also a novice as a kidnapper. The would-be kidnappers hadn't taken the time to find out much about Charles Urschel except for a few newspaper mentions. They knew nothing about his character; they didn't even know what he looked like. They didn't know, they couldn't know, what a physically and mentally strong individual they were targeting.

Charles and Berenice, now Mr. and Mrs. Urschel, were sharing with several members of the two families what had been the Slicks' home in the Heritage Hills section of the Oklahoma capital. Prudently, they'd originally retained the security guard Tom Slick had employed because of rumors that either he or his daughter Betty was a possible kidnap target. Imprudently, because the guard had a tendency to take frequent naps on the job, the Urschels had dismissed him—and had not hired a replacement. In addition to not having a guard, they had no burglar alarm sys-

Berenice and Charles Urschel. (Copyright July 27, 1947, the Oklahoma Publishing Company)

tem. That didn't seem to concern the Urschels, whose preferred way of socializing was spending quiet evenings at their elegant home, entertaining good friends, often playing bridge or poker for small, friendly stakes.

Unguarded, they were doing just that after a leisurely dinner on the fateful night of Saturday, July 22, 1933, sitting around a card table on their screened-in sunporch with their friends, Mr. and Mrs. Walter Jarrett. Having arrived home an hour earlier in the evening, sixteen-year-old Betty Slick had said her hellos and good-byes and was upstairs in her room. Away from the house, in Mexico with relatives on a fishing trip, were sixteen-year-old Charles Urschel Jr., Tom Slick Jr., who was seventeen, and his twelve-year-old brother Earl Slick.

The warm evening was getting late; it was a little after 11:30. At that point, Mrs. Jarrett—Clyde—suggested to Walter that they ought to be heading home, some ten blocks distant. But he prevailed on her and their hosts to sit for one more rubber of bridge so he could try to recoup some of his losses. This decision inadvertently set the stage for the horror that was about to follow.

Several hands into the game, as bidding was progressing around the table, a pair of most unwelcome party crashers in shirtsleeves, ties, and hats, but without masks, burst through the unlatched screen door, waving their weapons. The two women would have no difficulty recounting for police the terse one-sided conversation, the ultimatum.

"Keep your seats, all of you," one of the intruders commanded roughly, moving closer. "Don't any of you move. Don't make a sound or we'll blow your heads off! We mean business! We want Urschel. Which one's Urschel?"

No response.

"Did you hear us? I said we want Urschel! Which one is Urschel?"

In their hasty plotting, the kidnappers had relied on a few newspaper articles but had done nothing more than make several superficial swings around the neighborhood by car for a couple of nights. They'd never even glimpsed their tall, ruggedly handsome intended victim—who had been away on a business trip most of the time—nor had they ever come across a photograph of him.

The four stunned card players sat mute, frozen in place, staring numbly at the guns the nervous intruders swept menacingly back and forth.

"Damn it, we asked you twice, which one's Urschel?"

Slowly, silently, their intended victim stood up, hoping against hope that Jarrett would follow suit: *Keep still*, Urschel must have silently prayed. *Don't make any quick moves. Don't spook them. Do exactly what they want so they won't panic and harm the ladies.*

To Urschel's immense relief, Jarrett slowly rose to his feet as well, also saying not a word. The stare-down continued. Getting no answer or hint from any of the card players as to which one was Urschel, one of the nervous and angry gunmen barked, "All right, we'll just take both you guys. C'mon, c'mon! Let's go! Hurry it up!" As they prodded the two men out the door with the barrels of their weapons, they turned back and threatened the wives: "Don't move 'til we're outta the driveway. Don't go to that telephone, either. Make a move and we'll blow your heads off. We mean business!"

Leaving nothing to identify themselves other than the brief glimpses the two terrified wives got of their faces and the sound of their gruff voices, the gunmen sped off in their dark two-door sedan, headlights and tail lights off—Urschel and Jarrett huddled in the back, their eyes riveted on a wavering submachine gun pointed at them. Finally stopping some minutes later on a deserted rural road, the kidnappers confiscated the men's wallets in order to figure out which of the silent pair was the man they wanted.

All right, they no doubt were thinking, *now we know which one's Urschel. We've got our pot of gold. But who's this Jarrett guy?*

Unbeknownst to them, Jarrett was also a well-to-do businessman. Had they thought to inquire, they might have been able to double the eventual stakes. Instead, after relieving Jarrett of the sixty dollars in his wallet, they put him out of the car and tossed him his empty billfold—plus a "refund" of ten dollars for taxi fare. They gave Jarrett, as he told police, a stern warning: if he or the two wives talked to the law, they could forget about ever seeing Urschel alive again. They cautioned him, "On your word that you won't talk, we're gonna let you out. Don't tell anyone what direction we took or where you got out. Don't tell anybody anything, or we'll come back and get your scalp." Jarrett nodded obediently and whispered to Urschel, "Don't do anything that'll endanger your own safety. We'll get you back." To which Urschel said, "Tell Berenice I'm O.K., and not to worry about me. I'll get along all right."

Leaving Jarrett marooned by the side of the road, the men raced off with Urschel to start on a deliberately circuitous route toward their eventual hideout near the small town of Paradise, Texas.

During the earlier short ride from the Urschel home, the gangster in the front passenger seat had kept the submachine gun trained on the two oilmen, ordering them: "Shut up, and stay shut up, back there."

Did Jarrett follow that command? "I certainly did," he would recount to police with a shudder. But did he have time to look closely at the weapon so he might be able to identify it later? "That's all I had to do," he would remember. "They didn't say a half-dozen words to me." Then, almost as an afterthought: "They behaved like gentlemen, if you overlook taking my money. Oh, yes, as we drove along, the shorter man took out

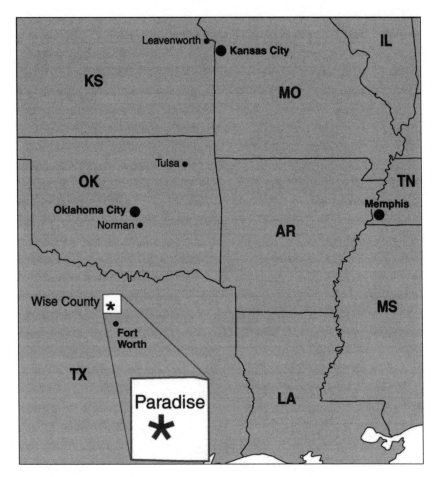

The locations of Urschel's hometown of Oklahoma City and Paradise, Texas, where he was held captive, along with other places that were important to the case.

a cigarette and told the other guy, 'Gimme a match, Floyd.' His name may have been Floyd, but he isn't the Pretty Boy Floyd whose picture I've seen in the papers, if that's the game they were trying to play with us. Neither of them looked any more like the notorious bandit than you or I."

As soon as the two wives were certain the gangsters had driven off, they hurried frantically upstairs to a bedroom. Automatically, Berenice locked the door. Ignoring the gunmen's parting threat, she grabbed the telephone and rang up the county sheriff and the city police chief. Both assured her they would immediately set up roadblocks and have men at the house within minutes. The chief also advised her to call the number of a special national emergency telephone line that the FBI had set up with much fanfare in Washington just a few days earlier specifically for the instantaneous reporting of these types of kidnappings. She did so, placing a call to NAtional 8-7117 in the capital with the assistance of long-distance operators, thereby becoming the first person in the nation to make use of what was an early version of modern-day hotlines.

A startled clerk, not accustomed to hearing the phone ring, quickly switched her call directly to the row house a stone's throw from Capitol Hill that J. Edgar Hoover would share for forty-three years with his widowed mother Annie. Abruptly awakened—it was 1:00 A.M. Washington time—an instantly alert Hoover took Mrs. Urschel's urgent report, doing what he could to calm and reassure her. Your husband will be all right, he promised her. These new "citizen" kidnappers don't generally harm their hostages; they collect the money and let them go. He'd see to it that Oklahoma City agent-in-charge, Ralph Colvin, would be at her house in short order to cooperate with the local lawmen to do everything possible to get Charles and Mr. Jarrett back quickly and safely.

It was shortly before 1:00 A.M. Sunday, Oklahoma time, not two hours since the bridge game had been aborted, when the shaken Jarrett reappeared at the Urschel home. He explained that after knocking at the doors of a couple of farm families, none of whom had automobiles or telephones, he finally managed to hitch a ride back to town.

"They let me go about ten miles outside of the city and took Charlie with them. No, he's not hurt," Jarrett related to police about the kidnappers. And, to Berenice, "They said they'll be in touch with you."

A loose cordon of police cars had already been thrown up throughout the city. Deputy sheriffs had been called back to duty to patrol the roads. Numerous peace officers had congregated in and around the house, but their search of the grounds and surrounding area yielded nothing. No fingerprints on the screen door or the doorknob. No shoe prints on the lawn, either. No tire tread marks in the driveway or on the street, not so much as a cigarette stub. Inside, the officers were in the process of setting up a command post. Ignoring threats the kidnappers would make, one or more top-ranking officers would surreptitiously remain for the duration—listening in on every call, monitoring all telegrams and mail, and observing various characters who presented themselves at the door.

At headquarters downtown, police showed Jarrett and the two women several hundred photographs from their rogues' gallery. It didn't take long for one mug shot to be identified as possibly one of the two unmasked abductors. If that indeed was the main villain, an officer remarked, they were after "one of the most vicious and dangerous criminals in America," the leader of "one of the worst and shrewdest gangs of criminals."

All of them except Jarrett were taken back to the house, which from this point on would be sealed off from the public for the duration. Nobody could or would even try to sleep for what was left of the night. Instead, they would agonize for the rest of the dark morning, consuming pots of coffee. They stared glumly at the mute telephone, as if wishing it to ring with news, trying to bolster one another's morale. The phone didn't cooperate. Meanwhile, Jarrett led police to the place outside the city where he'd been let go. Using flashlights, they found shoeprints and some suspicious tire tracks in the dirt road. They followed these tracks for nearly four miles until the trail went cold on a single-lane road over which other vehicles had since traversed.

Back in the city, it didn't take long for word of the crime to get out. Reporters, photographers, and newsreel cameramen, plus some assorted thrill-seekers, were already beginning to congregate near the Urschel house on Eighteenth Street in the early morning. A startled paperboy who came by soon after sunup on his regular route to deliver the Sunday papers found himself unceremoniously escorted around the corner by police and questioned for ten minutes. Had he noticed any strangers in the neighborhood recently? Any suspicious traffic, different automobiles? Sorry, no, he couldn't provide any help. As the day wore on, bicyclists, pedestrians, and automobiles filled with gawkers streamed by. Police tried to keep the traffic moving as best they could. At the same time, other officers fanned out for blocks around, asking the same questions of the neighbors that had been put to the newsboy. It was the same discouraging dead end. Nobody had seen or heard anything. The pair of kidnappers had done their job professionally.

With the number of newsmen outside the house swelling, the family and the police agreed it would be good strategy for Mrs. Urschel to meet with the press and issue a statement, and she bravely did so. Somehow holding her emotions in check, she asked that the reporters help by passing on a carefully crafted message—in full—so both the kidnappers and "my husband will see it if he is allowed to read the newspapers":

> I am in no way interested in your capture or prosecution. I care only for the safe return of my husband. To facilitate this I have had police withdrawn from my house, and there is no one here now except our family. We are sitting beside the telephone waiting for you to call.
>
> We, just our family, have made preliminary arrangements to negotiate with you speedily and confidentially. Arthur Seeligson, my husband's closest friend, will be in charge. You can trust him. The welfare of my husband, and his immediate return, is my only concern.

In an aside, she told a couple of the reporters, "I'm not afraid for Charlie. He's resourceful and sensible."

By then far from his home, Urschel's captors would never let him hear about this interview, with its obvious secondary purpose of trying to convey that the warning to Jarrett had been heeded and that no lawmen remained on the premises. The fact that officers were continually on the scene would be carefully covered up throughout the crisis.

The rest of Sunday dragged by with agonizing slowness, and no hint of Urschel's whereabouts or fate was forthcoming. Monday brought the first wave of what would become a growing deluge of what Agent Colvin labeled as "nut notes and chiseling propositions"—fake letters, calls, and wires from cranks, extortionists, or demented hoaxers purporting either to be the kidnappers or people with possible leads. Most of the latter made it blatantly clear they expected a reward. A few even strode brazenly right up to the house, knocking at the front door to offer whatever assistance they could or to promote their schemes. None of the ransom demands or tips could be dismissed out of hand; one of them just might turn out to be the real one. Among the people newly arrived at the house was longtime family friend and business associate Ernest Kirkpatrick. Much of what took place within those walls and referred to herein he made public for the first time in *Crimes' Paradise*, published a year after the kidnapping of his colleague.

One of the more distinctive phony demands that arrived at the house was a crude letter postmarked in Venus, a burg south of Dallas–Fort Worth. Surprisingly addressed to Kirkpatrick by name, he reprinted it in his book exactly as composed:

Note you are the go between for the family of Chas. F. Urschel if so I can tell you where they are holding him. I will reveal the facts to you if you wish me to are either reveal them to the Dective Dept—but I would sujest you in as much as I thank you should no & then you could tell whom you wished. If you want this informashion signify same by run add in dallas Times herld & Ft worth star telegram 6-27 & 6-28 in classified dept run add in a small circle. Mr. F. Urschel is fairing well but don't sleep much a trifel nervous location of myself will be revealed in next notice after I see your deceshion in news paper. Mr. Urschel release can be secured at small cost and without BLOODSHED if you will follow my instructions. MAP etc I will enclose to you at once after I see your add. Fore 3 times only.

In another frightening example, a note the family received in the mail said Urschel hadn't been harmed—not yet, anyway—and would be released for $50,000 provided Mrs. Urschel delivered $1,000 in good faith that very night. Declaring it to be a cruel and obvious fake, the veteran FBI agent explained his reasoning: the $1,000 was far too small, just a pittance, and the writer had offered to produce no physical evidence such as his watch or business card to prove that Urschel was his captive. So on the vigil stretched.

Hopes rose for a moment when a letter that arrived on Tuesday directed Mrs. Urschel to journey to Kansas City, Missouri, board a certain trolley, and heave off a bag stuffed with $50,000 as the streetcar crossed a specific bridge. This ruse was also determined to be a hoax, but trying to convince the resolute but ever more anxious Mrs. Urschel not to pursue every lead she considered even marginally promising wasn't easy for the officers hiding in the house.

They weren't always successful at keeping her reined in. On one occasion, she rashly decided to face down a male caller who said that if she would hand over $5,000 as a "down payment," he would give her Charles's watch as proof he was his prisoner, then provide further instructions about how much more to pay for his release. She simply had to follow this one up. Despite the FBI agent's strong advice to the contrary, she thought it had the ring of legitimacy. To evade the officers inside and the press outside, Berenice waited until well after dark when everyone, she hoped, would assume she was asleep. Then she eased out a second-story rear window that was hidden from the street by tall trees and a high wall and scaled down a trellis to the two-car attached garage that opened on Hudson Avenue, the unlit side street. Then, lying on the back floor of the car, she was driven off to the rendezvous.

She confronted this purported kidnapper, who did not have Urschel's wristwatch, of course. He sped away after rudely grabbing the down payment at gunpoint—actually just $1,000 on top of a package consisting of dollar-size strips of paper she intimated was the rest of the money. Several hours later, a woman called the Urschel house and cursed Berenice for shortchanging them by $4,000. Unfortunately, calls couldn't be traced in those days, and the con man, or couple, got away at least $1,000 richer. On one other occasion, Berenice pulled off the same "escape" from the house and was driven to another rendezvous, but the contact proved to be equally phony.

There were other contacts, some even wryly amusing after years of hindsight. A "medium" offered to establish an "ethereal contact" with the victim so he could be located. Another person offered to produce a bunch of greyhounds, guaranteed to track down the kidnappers. Others merely said they would be glad to serve as the go-between to recover both Urschel and the money.

Following the attorney general's instruction, the fact that there were no developments was not relayed to the impatient press horde during this time. Still, it was felt that the reporters might be of some use in unwittingly misleading the kidnappers, so each day Mrs. Urschel called the reporters in and offered brief statements to give them a little something to write about and in hopes the kidnappers would read them.

For example: "I am interested only in the safe return of Mr. Urschel and not in what happens to the kidnappers after his return" (Monday). And: "I want them to believe me when I say we will make no effort to run them down or to prosecute. I want nothing but the return of Charles, unharmed" (Tuesday). With nothing else to write about, most of the reporters dutifully complied and printed these statements.

Inside the house, the ever more concerned family seriously considered the possibility of retaining a prominent criminal lawyer or even contacting a noted criminal connected with the underworld—Al Capone's still-powerful Chicago gang was mentioned by someone—to try to establish contact with the kidnappers. But on the assumption that Charles wasn't far from Oklahoma City and that the kidnappers would want their money as soon as possible, the family decided to hold off at least one more day. Berenice decided to make still another attempt to try to talk to the kidnappers through the press:

We have let the kidnappers know in every way we can that we are ready to negotiate with them. I want you to tell them that they can get in touch with any of the men here in the house. If they don't want to do that, tell them that I will deal with them myself. Tell them the officers will remain completely away from the case. Tell them they are not even keeping a secret watch on the house. They can safely get in touch with us. He must know it already, but I would like Charles to know that we are going about this as calmly and as quietly as we can. We are doing everything possible.

I want them to believe me when I say that we will make no effort to run them down or to prosecute. I want nothing but the return of Charles, and I want him unharmed. Meanwhile, the officers have given us every promise of cooperation. They have agreed not to spread any kind of net while we are dealing with the kidnappers. We have done everything we can. Now we are just sitting here waiting for them to make the next move.

4

Ransom Demand

❖ ❖ ❖ ❖ ❖ ❖ ❖ ❖ ❖ ❖ ❖ ❖ ❖ ❖ ❖

It remained ominously still at the house. Although the family members naturally were terribly worried, they weren't yet frantic. All were well aware of Urschel's sharp mind and his generally calm, even demeanor. As they all knew, Urschel was an astute poker player and bridge expert. Not only did he know how to calculate and take advantage of the odds quickly, but his timing, when it came to bluffing successfully, was also legendary. He could easily disengage any business adversary. In the rough-and-tumble wildcatting business, he was accustomed to carrying large amounts of important information in his head—this in the much simpler days before government regulators began requiring voluminous written records and seemingly endless layers of reports and paperwork.

Still, three days had elapsed, and this wasn't a friendly game of cards or an ordinary, civilized business deal. Nonetheless, as family friend Ernest Kirkpatrick would bravely declare, "We are not worried about Charles. We believe he can care for himself, for we know he is not going to do anything rash. He is too level-headed to be taken advantage of to any great extent." About that same time, the legendary Gus T. Jones strode onto the scene, sent by Hoover to take over the FBI's handling of the case after having been assigned to the Union Station Massacre. A former Texas Ranger, Jones was an anomaly among FBI agents. He sometimes sported cowboy boots and western clothes rather than shined shoes and the regimented white shirt and tie; because of his excellent record, though, Hoover overlooked these eccentricities.

Shortly after Jones's arrival there finally was a glimmer of hope, the first indication that the kidnappers hadn't killed their hostage. What turned out to be the contact from the real kidnappers arrived on Wednesday, but not at the family home in Oklahoma City. Rather, it mysteriously dropped out of nowhere that morning.

A stranger, the brim of his fedora pulled low, put the operation in motion by appearing outside the downtown Western Union office in nearby Tulsa. The stranger handed a surprised bicycle-riding messenger boy a cartwheel—a silver dollar—if the lad would deliver a large envelope to the home of one John G. Catlett, another oilman who was a good friend of the Urschels.

Never in his wildest imagination, or in his nightmares, had Catlett entertained the remote thought that he would be involved as the intermediary in a kidnapping. In point of fact, he wasn't even Urschel's first choice. But of course he had no knowledge of that as he stood shaving, leisurely getting ready to go to his office, ignoring the plain-looking package that had been delivered. After all, it had no postage stamps on it, just his scribbled name and house number, and no return address or anything else to indicate it as being of any particular import.

Finally, when Catlett did get around to examining the package, he was severely shaken to discover three smaller envelopes inside. Two short penciled letters, one to him and one to Mrs. Urschel, were in his friend Charles's easily recognizable handwriting. The third, a lengthy typewritten one, was without a doubt from the kidnappers. It was addressed to two other men who would have key roles in the outcome: Ernest Kirkpatrick and Arthur Seeligson. The latter was Berenice's brother-in-law from San Antonio, who along with her and Charles was the third member of the council of three for the Slick estate. Seeligson, who had been in North Carolina on business, was able to scramble back to Oklahoma City within days.

It is impossible to imagine the duress Urschel had to have been under when writing the two notes, particularly the one to Berenice. Despite his well-known resourcefulness and presence of mind, the anguish he was going through as well as the underlying fear are painfully evident in the letter to his wife, which concluded with the brave but pathetic sentence, "If the demand is too great, just forget it, it will be O.K. with me." *What will she think when she reads this?* he must have thought. *She's tough, yes, but how will she handle this? I wish I could tell her I'm doing all right, considering the circumstances.*

The message to his friend Catlett, which Urschel had been forced to write exactly as dictated, was a terse and even more chilling plea.

Dear John:

You undoubtedly know about my predicament. If Arthur has returned, please deliver the enclosed letter to him, otherwise to Kirkpatrick. Deliver in person and do not communicate by telephone. Tell no one else about this letter, not even your wife, and when you deliver it do not go to residence. Authorities must be kept off the case or release impossible and they cannot effect rescue. For my sake follow these instructions to the letter and do not discuss with anyone other than those mentioned. This is my final letter to any of my friends or family and if this contact is not successful I fear for my life. When in Oklahoma City keep out of sight as much as possible because you will probably be used later on in this capacity. I am putting all my dependence in you regarding this matter and feel sure you will take every precaution possible.

Best regards as ever,

Your friend,

C. F. Urschel

When later contact is made party will have my identification card. Please give enclosed letter for Berenice to Arthur or Kirk.

Not twenty minutes elapsed before the trembling Catlett, forced into the role of the unwilling go-between, was nervously speeding the hundred miles southwest toward Oklahoma City. Having strictly obeyed the instructions and on the chance he was being watched, he hadn't breathed a word to anybody. On arrival, though, he simply had to violate the instructions by going directly to the Urschel home, parking out of sight and slipping in the rear somehow without being surrounded and grilled by the reporters camped out front. This throng, which was increasing by the day, even by the hour, now included not only a large contingent of Oklahoma, Kansas, Missouri, and Texas reporters, photographers, and newsreel cameramen, but also national and international correspondents like James L. Kilgallen, the noted national correspondent for the Hearst newspaper chain's International News Service, and Sir Percival Phillips of the *London Daily Mail.*

Neither they nor any of the other reporters had any way of being aware, naturally, that inside the residence the family and the officers were anxiously examining the first contact from the true kidnappers. It was a strange and shocking typewritten correspondence they were reading:

The enclosed letter from Charles F. Urschel to you and the enclosed identification cards will convince you that you are dealing with the Abductors.

Immediately upon receipt of this letter you will proceed to obtain the sum of TWO HUNDRED THOUSAND DOLLARS ($200,000.00) in GENUINE USED FEDERAL RESERVE CURRENCY in the denomination of TWENTY DOLLAR ($20.00) Bills.

It will be useless for you to attempt taking notes of SERIAL NUMBERS MAKING UP DUMMY PACKAGE, OR ANYTHING ELSE IN THE LINE OF ATTEMPTED DOUBLE CROSS. BEAR THIS IN MIND, CHARLES F. URSCHEL WILL REMAIN IN OUR CUSTODY UNTIL MONEY HAS BEEN INSPECTED AND EX-CHANGED AND FURTHERMORE WILL BE AT THE SCENE OF CONTACT FOR PAY-OFF AND IF THERE SHOULD BE ANY ATTEMPT AT ANY DOUBLE XX IT WILL BE HE THAT SUFFERS THE CONSEQUENCE.

As soon as you have read and RE-READ this carefully and wish to commence negotiations you will proceed to the DAILY OKLA-HOMAN and insert the following BLIND AD under the REAL ESTATE, FARMS FOR SALE, and we will know that you are ready for BUSINESS, and you will receive further instructions AT THE BOX ASSIGNED TO YOU BY THE NEWSPAPER, AND NO WHERE ELSE SO BE CERTAIN THAT THIS ARRANGEMENT IS KEPT SECRET AS THIS IS OUR FINAL ATTEMPT TO COMMUNICATE WITH YOU, on account of our former instructions to JARRETT being DISREGARDED and the LAW being notified, so we have neither the time or patience to carry on any further lengthy correspondence. RUN THIS AD FOR ONE WEEK IN DAILY OKLAHOMAN.

FOR SALE—160 Acres Land, good five room house, deep well. Also Cows, Tools, Tractor, Corn and Hay. $3750.00 for quick sale. TERMS. Box # _____

You will hear from us as soon as convenient after insertion of AD.

The jarring up-and-down style may have been unusual in the extreme, but the message was clear. Two hundred thousand dollars (the equivalent of roughly $2,775,000 at this writing) for a life! In circulated twenty-dollar bills—ten thousand of them. Whether to pay was never an option in Berenice's mind. All business despite her husband's pathetic note to her, she didn't blanch or hesitate a minute at the outrageousness of the demand. As far as she was concerned, it wouldn't pay to be emotional. In effect, it was no more than a normal straightforward business deal—only this time, cash in exchange for Charles's life, even up. The question was how to put that much money together in such a short time.

Without hesitation, they rang up their banker. At the same time, Seeligson sneaked downtown to the newspaper's business office to place the nondescript classified. It appeared word for word, as instructed, in Thursday's editions, assigned Box No. 807. The next day, Friday, half a dozen legitimate purchase offers had arrived in Box 807. But among them was the "illegitimate" one hoped for—an airmail special delivery envelope postmarked Joplin, Missouri, and surprisingly addressed to Kirkpatrick by name. Typed on the same Remington typewriter as the ransom note, the letter was very clear:

In view of the fact that you have had the Ad inserted as per our instructions, we gather that you are prepared to meet our ultimatum.

You will pack TWO HUNDRED THOUSAND DOLLARS ($200,000.00) in USED GENUINE FEDERAL RESERVE NOTES OF TWENTY DOLLAR DENOMINATION in a suitable LIGHT COLORED LEATHER BAG and have someone purchase transportation for you, including berth, aboard Train #28 (The Sooner) which departs at 10:10 p.m. via the M.K.&T. Lines for Kansas City, Mo.

You will ride on the OBSERVATION PLATFORM where you may be observed by someone at some Station along the Line between Okla. City and K.C. Mo. If indications are alright, somewhere along the Right-of-Way you will observe a Fire on the Right Side of Track (Facing direction train is bound). That first Fire will be your Cue to be prepared to throw BAG to Track immediately after passing SECOND FIRE.

Mr. Urschel will, upon instructions, attend to the fires and secure the bag when you throw it off, he will open it and transfer the contents to a sack that he will be provided with, so, if you comply with our demand and do not attempt any subterfuge, as according to the News reports you have pledged, Mr. Urschel should be home in a very short while.

REMEMBER THIS—IF ANY TRICKERY IS ATTEMPTED YOU WILL FIND THE REMAINS OF URSCHEL AND INSTEAD OF JOY THERE WILL BE DOUBLE GRIEF—FOR, SOME-ONE VERY NEAR AND DEAR TO THE URSCHEL FAMILY IS UNDER CONSTANT SURVEILLANCE AND WILL LIKE-WISE SUFFER FOR YOUR ERROR.

If there is the slightest HITCH in these PLANS for any reason what-so-ever, not your fault, you will proceed on into Kansas City, Mo. And register at the Muehlebach Hotel under the name of E. E. Kincaid of Little Rock, Arkansas and await further instructions there, however, there should not be, If YOU COMPLY WITH THESE SIMPLE DIRECTIONS.

THE MAIN THING IS DO NOT DIVULGE THE CONTENTS OF THIS LETTER TO ANY LAW AUTHORITIES FOR WE HAVE NO INTENTION OF FURTHER COMMUNICATION.

YOU ARE TO MAKE THIS TRIP SATURDAY JULY 29TH 1933. BE SURE YOU RIDE THE PLATFORM OF THE REAR CAR AND HAVE THE BAG WITH MONEY IN IT FROM THE TIME YOU LEAVE OKLAHOMA CITY.

This strongly reiterated threat against bringing in "law authorities" caused renewed consternation in the house, where the various officers had been camped, yet staying well out of sight (they hoped) to preserve the fiction of their noninvolvement as well as being on hand to guard the rest of the family. To lay down a smokescreen, Seeligson called in the press and told them that "police and federal officers are cooperating to the fullest extent in keeping away to give us an opportunity to be available whenever contact can be made. They have promised to do this as long as we desire."

Furthermore, with the details and time for the money drop now specified, there was concern that one or more of the increasingly restive reporters—totally in the dark thus far about all these developments and chafing unhappily about it—might get wind of the plan and inadvertently spook the kidnappers into doing something desperate. So Berenice Urschel approached the newsmen, several of whom by now had established a temporary office of sorts in the street in the form of a tent with telephone stations. Would they please consider making themselves scarce for awhile? "We feel that the kidnappers may be holding back from making contact because you newspapermen keep so close a watch. We want to ask if all news agencies and papers will withdraw their reporters for a few days, just as the government has withdrawn its agents."

Their editors and bureau chiefs agreed unanimously, taking the humanitarian position that not endangering a life was much more important than a fleeting headline. The publisher of the *Daily Oklahoman* and *Oklahoma City Times* even generously offered unlimited time on WKY, the company's affiliated radio station, for a direct appeal to the kidnappers by Mrs. Urschel, who was described by the Associated Press reporter on the scene as being "nervous and apparently on the verge of collapse . . . plainly worried to the point of illness," when she had addressed the reporters.

Some months later, Kirkpatrick did have some kind words in his book, *Crimes' Paradise*, about the press, which under normal circumstances the family could barely tolerate:

> Be it here said to the undying glory of the entire army of brilliant
> newspapermen, who thoroughly covered the Urschel case (and it is
> conceded that the case was ably covered), that the demeanor of each
> individual reporter or correspondent was such that the sorely pressed
> and nerve-torn members of the Urschel clique always felt that any
> newspaperman out there in front would forego a scoop, or even risk
> his life, to assist in a successful solution of the horrible episode.

With the arrival of the ransom delivery instructions, Kirkpatrick was of two minds. He was relieved and cautiously optimistic on the one hand to feel that his friend had (apparently) survived so far, but his hopefulness was tempered by the fear of what Charles was going through. At the same time, he was extremely livid not only at the crime itself but also at all the vultures trying to prey on the family. As he would bitterly write later on after he was sure they were dealing with the real kidnappers and not opportunistic imposters, "What a temptation it was to shoot every chiseler on the spot and let him lie where he had lied. But these lecherous frauds were still treated civilly because we dared make no offensive move until Urschel was safe."

Insofar as the ransom was concerned, Hoover and his men overtly stood aside, in effect voluntarily tying their own hands, but unwilling to do anything to impede or endanger the return of the victim unharmed. Covertly, however, the agency was already engaged in intensive but discreet behind-the-scenes investigative groundwork—throughout the United States—based on descriptions of the two men, the mug shot identification by Jarrett, and other leads that were developing.

5

Down on the Ranch

❖ ❖ ❖ ❖ ❖ ❖ ❖ ❖ ❖ ❖ ❖ ❖ ❖ ❖ ❖

Receipt of the pair of ransom notes gave the first and only indication that the kidnappers apparently intended to keep Urschel alive, at least for the time being or until delivery of the money. Indeed, Urschel himself was supposedly going to retrieve the bag of cash pitched off a speeding train in the middle of the night somewhere in Kansas. But, if so, where was he? Everyone—family, friends, newsmen—was increasingly fearful about what might be happening to him ever since Jarrett had been freed early Sunday morning. Was their Charles being treated civilly, or might the criminals be harming, perhaps even torturing, him? Would they try to extort even more money after the initial ransom was paid? Might they come back and kidnap or hurt others in the family? Why did his notes sound so forlorn, so pathetically unlike him? Did he himself think they were eventually going to murder him? What further horrors might he face in the however many days or weeks ahead of him?

In the early moments of his abduction on Saturday night and early Sunday morning, Urschel somehow pushed aside the initial alarm and terror at the inexplicable event that had befallen him. Although obviously frightened and uncertain of his fate, he immediately began to work out a master plan, a shrewd counterscheme to try to get ahead, and stay ahead, of his kidnappers. If he were to get out of this alive, he determined grimly, he wanted to have as much incriminating evidence as possible to put these gangsters behind bars. As he then demonstrated, he would employ his excellent memory for facts and figures, use all his senses, his reasoning abilities, to remember everything he possibly could about his captors and his surroundings. *I will try,* he solemnly, if somewhat doubtfully, must have vowed to himself, *to commit to memory every scrap of information. Every possible detail. Everything I see. Every sound. Every voice. Every word that's spoken. Even what the weather's like—however long it may be. Wherever they take me, I will leave fingerprints and other identifying marks wherever I can, starting with this automobile. Alone or together, the prints might prove useful when they let me go—or even if they don't. Just stay calm, calm, always outwardly calm. Play humble. Don't do a thing to upset them in any way. So far, anyway, so good.*

The kidnappers, having released Jarrett in ignorance of his possible worth to them, were still well ahead of the ragged police dragnet that was hurriedly but ineffectually being put in place. They turned down a deserted back road some twenty miles from Oklahoma City. They'd just passed a large, brightly lit power plant, the last landmark the alert Urschel was able to recognize or would see, as it turned out, for many days. It was already night, but now absolute darkness, a total absence of light, enveloped him as they blindfolded him tightly with cotton and adhesive tape and, for good measure, stuffed cotton balls in his ears. *No way to escape.* Dejectedly, he no doubt thought, *Now what can I do?*

So much for his original master plan. Confronted with this dark, new, unforeseen state of affairs, Urschel calmly tried to think, to draw upon something in this darkness that might help implement his plan. *Think, think! Yes,* he may have said to himself, *what were those words Shakespeare put into Lear's mouth?* "A man may see how this world goes with no eyes. Look with thine ears." This would give Urschel's master plan a new dimension—if he would ever have a chance to use it to capture these hoodlums.

Still, from then on, he had no idea in which direction or how far they were traveling, making his plan immeasurably more difficult. This disadvantage gave the kidnappers a false sense of security, because the blindfold and rudimentary earplugs did little to impair Urschel's keen powers of "observation" and hearing during his journey in total blackness. He had to sprawl crookedly and painfully in the back of the auto for interminable hours as the kidnappers drove back and forth over unmarked, unfamiliar, narrow dirt and gravel roads (called "cat roads" by some on the premise that only cats could see well enough to negotiate them in the dark). "Oh, damn," came from the front seat. "Now what?" was the response. The car was bucking, gasping for fuel. It sputtered to a stop. The conversation can be imagined. "Why didn't you watch the gauge?" "Me? You've been driving. It was your job." They were in the middle of nowhere, in the dark, as they all exited the car. Urschel feigned that he hadn't overheard the exchange through his earplugs, and one of the pair led him into what seemed to be a field. They huddled in stony silence for what Urschel gauged to be about an hour, waiting for the other partner to return with gasoline. All Urschel remembered getting out of this delay was a lot of insect bites that would aggravate him for the rest of his captivity.

Their vehicle finally refueled, sometime in the early morning hours before daybreak they pulled into the Texas farm of one of the kidnapper's elderly relatives to switch to another motor car they'd stashed. They hoped the transfer would allow them to slip through any traps the law might have extended up to that point. They made such a racket, though, that they woke up the sixty-six-year-old woman. Struggling painfully out of bed, she shouted, "Who's out there? What are they doing?" Told that they had a kidnapped man with them, she slashed her cane back and forth. "Lord a mercy. Tell 'em to get that man away from here as quick as they can! Get off my place! Get out right now or I'll scream so loud it'll raise the whole settlement!"

Much later she would publicly repeat what she had said and would explain why she hadn't screamed at the time: "I was scared so bad I couldn't gather up that much power. I didn't scream, but I jumped out of bed and I was gettin' on my clothes and shoes and I heard the car leave while I was tryin' to get dressed. I don't know what I meant to do, but I heard the car pass."

Hearing the old woman's commotion, and alarmed at this unanticipated turn of events, the kidnappers quickly scrambled to obey. Back on the road within minutes and fearing what Urschel may possibly have heard, they sternly warned him once again that he'd better forget anything about the entire trip, the auto exchange, or the woman's conversation if he ever expected to see home again. He played it correctly: "I didn't hear a thing. I can't hear a thing except when you fellows shout like that."

They didn't want to harm him, they repeated for the fourth or fifth time, and they sincerely meant it, but still they threatened that they wouldn't hesitate a second to shoot if he resisted or made any move to escape or seek help. Obediently, Urschel nodded that he understood. At least now he wasn't quite so uncomfortable physically. This second vehicle had been specially rigged out, in advance, with a sort of bunk they'd prepared for him in the backseat. So now he could at least stretch out his painful joints, a small favor.

His kidnappers couldn't know it, considering their poor preparation, but the fact that they'd woefully underestimated Charles Urschel would be much to their later regret. They didn't reckon that their outwardly docile and seemingly cowed victim was continuing to do a lot of fast calculating despite his apprehension and their repeated warnings and threats. He refused to despair. Instead, in his methodical way he was crafting the subtle strategy he hoped would trap them—his excellent memory for detail. He had recognized the familiar power plant, the last thing he had seen. He'd been able to formulate educated guesses about the makes of the cars he was in by the sound of the engines and the way the drivers shifted through the gears. Exhausted and fearful though he was, he willed himself not to lose track of the minutes or the hours. He cleverly ascertained approximate times by noting the brief hushed conversations between his two captors. From the first, he began committing to memory their voices, their manner of speaking—*please keep talking,* he prayed—as well as the fact that at least one was a heavy cigarette smoker.

The onset of a brief shower led the kidnappers to demonstrate their ineptitude once again. Finding a filling station, they struck up what they'd intended to be a casual conversation that the female attendant providing the gas from one of the two tall bubble-top pumps would have no reason to remember. But someone else did. It apparently didn't occur to the gangsters that Urschel might be able to hear anything through the rolled-up windows and his earplugs. What he didn't hear was important as well—no other vehicles—which told him they were at a remote location. What he did remember hearing clearly was a short, stilted conversation:

"Think this rain'll do the crops any good?" one of the men asked the attendant as she was pumping the gas. "Nope, the crops around here's all burnt up," she replied. "But it may help the broomcorn some." Wash their windshield? Check the oil stick, the radiator? Thanks, no. They were on an important trip and were in a bit of a hurry. But they did purchase several bottles of Coca-Cola, which would be Urschel's only nourishment on the trip.

On the road again, the kidnappers engaged in minimal, very hushed conversation, although as Jarrett had reported, one always pointedly called the other "Floyd" in an apparent ruse to lead Urschel to believe (if he could hear) that he was in the company of the dangerously psychopathic murderer "Pretty Boy" Floyd.

Some time after filling up, and by now in another cloudburst that was

almost too much for the primitive windshield wipers even in early daylight, things turned worse. The drowsy driver of the moment lost control. The car started to skid on the slippery roadway. As to what perhaps
transpired: "Watch out! WATCH OUT, DAMN IT! Get off the brake! Turn
the damned wheel!" Too late. Frighteningly, the sedan did a 360-degree
turn, fishtailing down the slick roadway. Finally, it careened off the road,
bounced a few times, and sank into the red mud common to the area,
tires spinning to no avail, totally bemired. "Damn it, now what?" one
angry kidnapper shouted at his partner, not realizing that their prisoner
had been roughly slammed from side to side in the back (the 1930s pre-
ceded safety belts in cars). The spat took a few minutes to die down, and
finally one of them had to get out to shove the car back onto the roadway, getting himself thoroughly caked with mud. Farther on and still
unhappy with each other about the car problems, they totally lost their
sense of direction and had to stop and ask a startled farmer a question
laced with unconscious humor: "How do you get to Paradise?"

Actually, they weren't far away by that time, and thanks to the farmer's
directions, Urschel's painful, jolting trek finally came to a merciful end—
after fourteen hours with nothing to eat and only the one soft drink he'd
been given. He figured it must be early Sunday afternoon; when he
inquired, they confirmed that it was 2:30 P.M.

The three of them had arrived at a desolate 523-acre ranch—extremely
modest by Texas standards—four and a half miles from the hamlet of
Paradise. As the crow flies, they were thirty-five miles northwest of the
outskirts of Fort Worth in a largely agricultural area of Texas.

To reach the main ranch from Paradise itself, they had to follow a mean-
dering farm-to-market road—even today deeply potholed and poorly
paved, but then nothing more than a rutted dirt lane—then across what
was a wooden bridge over Rush Creek, and up a narrow county road.
Posts painted with white stripes on top guided the way the last quarter
mile to their goal: a spread farmed by longtime owner Robert ("Boss")
Shannon and his third wife, Ora.

Living a considerable stone's throw away on the same land were Shannon's twenty-one-year-old son Armon, his teenage wife, and their infant
daughter. It was to this unpainted, weather-beaten, rundown three-room
shack that Urschel was taken the next day to sweat out the rest of his captivity. Like nine out of ten rural dwellings in the nation at the time, it was not
wired for electric service, nor did it have inside plumbing or a telephone.

The entire time Urschel was there he had to live in a pair of borrowed pajamas. Sprawled uncomfortably on a threadbare quilt on the wood floor, he was handcuffed at night to a chain (attached either to a metal cot or a wooden highchair) with his arms extended over his head, an excruciatingly painful position, hardly conducive to sleep. On Friday, the cuffs were fastened to the end of a short chain that was connected to the front of a lumpy bed he was allowed to lie on for the rest of his stay, though he was still kept blindfolded at all times, day and night. *Well, so much for any hope of escape,* he no doubt thought ruefully. Despite his obvious helplessness, the kidnappers threatened that they wouldn't hesitate to knock him out with "hypodermic shots" if he made any trouble, although just how he could possibly mount any resistance was a mystery to him. Every minute, around the clock, he was guarded.

He became even more uncomfortable when one said, in a conversation that might have run like this, "I'm going to read the Oklahoma City paper to you":

CHARLES F. URSCHEL IS KIDNAPPED

TWO MACHINE GUNNERS
INVADE CITY HOME TO
SEIZE OIL MILLIONAIRE

Federal Men Take Up Hunt.
All U.S. Operatives Are Called Out
In Urschel Kidnapping Case Here

"So the negotiations are going to be more difficult and it may be a longer proposition than we figured. It may be a little more tricky, but we'll still get what we want. You just sit here and stay calm."

At first his abductors believed they were intimidating this outwardly passive victim of theirs with their threats; as he later put it, "I was not to see or hear anything; if they felt that I had seen or heard that I would never come back, that they would kill me." One of them did reveal to him that the unidentified ranch was a safe haven other outlaws occasionally used as a hideout. "He said the place was used as a stopover and that occasionally bank robbers would come to the house and stay a few days to cool off," Urschel remembered. "He said they usually gave the people two or three hundred dollars." That no questions were asked was hardly unusual among hard-pressed farmers who could always use extra money of any kind.

As is sometimes the case in kidnappings, an affinity, a sort of shared camaraderie, developed between perpetrators and victim. More and more, Urschel's kidnappers and guards grew to like their hostage, maybe even respect him a bit. Throughout, all of them always deferentially addressed him as "Mister" Urschel. In return, he was politely pleasant, extremely so, not wanting to do anything that might possibly irritate them. Lured into a false sense of security by his humble politeness and figuring Urschel was so literally in the dark that he could never be able to bring them down, they probably began reading other headlines and news items aloud, sometimes late in the evenings by the dim flickering light from a couple of kerosene lanterns: "California, West Virginia Vote to End Prohibition; 21 More States Required" or "Capone Indicted in Chicago Rackets."

One can imagine the gangsters' comments about that story: "The paper says they're charging ol' Scarface with, quote, 'conspiracy to stifle trade by bombings, acid throwing, sluggings, strikes and less violent forms of intimidation in the cleaning and dyeing industry, the laundry trade, among the distributors of carbonated beverages, and in the linen supply houses,' unquote. Capone's been in jail for a year and a half already—for what, tax evasion? What more can they do to him? We should be so lucky. Besides, who the hell pays income taxes? Except you, of course, Mister Urschel." Or words to that effect.

Greeted with further amused derision by his captors was a dispatch datelined Albany reporting that New York governor Herbert H. Lehman was going to ask the state legislature to put an "end" to kidnapping by forbidding payment of ransom to kidnappers under penalty of law.

As the duration in Paradise wore on, the kidnappers inadvertently began to let potentially incriminating details slip out. They boasted at length about the various armed bank jobs and other crimes they'd supposedly pulled off, particularly in comparison with the exploits of other "lesser" gangsters. The Barrow gang came in for particular derision as "just a couple of cheap filling station robbers and car thieves. I've been stealing for twenty-five years and my group doesn't deal in anything cheap," bragged one of Urschel's kidnappers, slurring and giving off what was a familiar strong odor of cheap gin.

Like the kidnappers, Urschel's guards Boss and Armon Shannon went to great lengths to try to mislead him as to his whereabouts and to camouflage the location of the ranch. They didn't volunteer it, but he was able to figure out the father-son relationship, having heard them referred to by the others as "Boss" and "Potatoes."

"They were decent but not talkative," Urschel recounted, and when they did speak they would refer to events or weather "way down south in Oklahoma or Texas." He had a hunch these seemingly forced comments were poorly disguised attempts to divert him, and so he discounted them early on. During all of their conversations, and every other waking minute, Urschel's photographic memory was continually clicking away, absorbing and storing an encyclopedic amount of incriminating information he was hearing and "observing" despite his blindfold.

Although condemned to total darkness, Charles Urschel was easily able to identify the various animals outside, plus other distinctive farm sounds and smells, because he'd grown up in a rural environment. And he was an army veteran, a sergeant. A college student. A former teacher. An astute businessman. A shrewd card player. With all this experience, he assimilated random, possibly useful, scraps of information that Armon and Boss let drop. *Keep them talking,* he reminded himself repeatedly. Without any reason apparent to his overseers, other than maybe boredom and making idle conversation to fill the time, Urschel offhandedly inquired as innocently as possible what time it was. This was no exercise in trivia. With the answers to those seemingly innocuous questions, Urschel engaged in a solitaire-like mind exercise with great willpower and with no watch, silently counting off the seconds, minutes, and hours to figure out when certain things occurred. His blindfold worked loose once or twice, allowing for some quick, furtive glances around the place. *There's the bed, the high chair. So that's what the father and son look like—the old man about five-foot-six but bent with age and hard work, the frail-looking son even shorter.* Both wearing baggy one-piece overalls that had seen better days.

Caught peeking, though, Urschel had his eyes quickly sealed again,

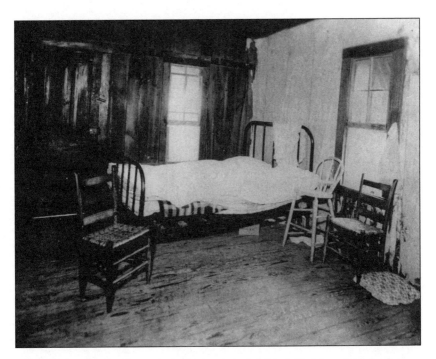

The room in Armon Shannon's shack where Urschel was held. (Copyright August 3, 1933, the Oklahoma Publishing Company)

more tightly and uncomfortably this time. But thanks to these two rather gentlemanly and almost apologetic guards, he could ascertain directions; they would move him, stumbling under his blindfold, from the west to the slightly less sweltering east room in the afternoons. Water, drawn from a well in a rusty bucket with a squeaky pulley, had a distinctly unpleasant bitter mineral taste, and it was given to him in what seemed to be an old cup missing its original handle or ladle. When escorted to what served as the privy or permitted to walk around briefly inside or outside the squalid shack, holding onto the arm of one of his guards, he would memorize details and distances by counting the number of paces. There was but a single step up to the front porch, for instance. It was so many halting strides to the well for a drink of that sour water.

With little else to do and nothing to see, he could hardly help but be aware of the weather. Hot? It was stifling and dry for six days running until near gale-force winds roared in from the south on Saturday. A morning-long rain followed—an electrical storm punctuated by rolling thunder, beginning around dawn Sunday. Every day, every chance he had, he surreptitiously scratched what he hoped would be telltale marks with his fingernails on the primitive furniture to which he was manacled. Cagily, he also planted his fingerprints every place he possibly could. ("I frequently passed through the cabin door, and each time I tried to leave my fingerprints, hoping they would come in handy some day.") He figured realistically that even if he ended up murdered, the FBI might use this relatively new scientific method of identification to prove where he'd been imprisoned and to identify the cars in which he'd been transported. He carefully noted the daily routine—when the others went to bed and when they arose, when the animals were fed, eggs collected, water drawn from the well for the livestock, mealtimes.

Those shared meals were adequate, but little more. Since his guards were fearful of giving any signs to neighbors that they were home, they laid only one small fire daily, well before daylight, using wooden kitchen matches to light corncobs rather than logs to avoid smoke. "We ate out of cans," Urschel said. "There wasn't much cooking done." The menus consisted basically of canned goods, tomatoes, baked beans, day-old bread, and fresh milk. No vegetables or fresh meat. Urschel said, "The only time they made coffee or anything was before daylight, in the morning."

Armon and one of the kidnappers shared preparation of the meals, such as they were, and it usually fell to young Armon to do the cleanup in addition to his routine farm chores, like feeding and watering the stock and doing the milking.

Urschel's guards did give him some small pleasure by sharing cigars with him. He noted, too, that every night somebody whose voice he never heard came to the shack and left a jar of refreshing ice water outside.

Early in the week came the time to set in motion the plan for collecting the ransom. When they couldn't locate Urschel's first choice for the go-between, because the nominee was away on business, the agitated kidnappers started the process again. Temporarily removing Urschel's blindfold and standing behind him so he couldn't get a look at them—although he did notice one was sporting a gold ring with a large ruby inlay—they handed him a cheap tablet and a pencil and commanded that he compose the note to Catlett, the backup go-between.

In his first composition attempt, when he was nudged more or less politely into a corner of the room and writing with the pad balanced on his knee, Urschel recalled, "I told Mr. Catlett my personal property was all tied up with the estate and if any money was paid it would probably have to be paid by the estate, and I knew they would likely have to borrow the money, and I didn't know whether the courts would approve of a loan for such a purpose, and if the amount they asked was excessive not to attempt to raise it but let it go and it would be okay with me."

Although Urschel and his business associates and relatives were hardly what could be called destitute, the oil business, like so many other enterprises in the country, had fallen on tough times. Still, Urschel's note definitely did not convey the tone the irritated kidnappers wanted, so they angrily ripped it up, not noting that this diversion gave him time to glance quickly out a broken window and spot some shingles missing from an eave. Urschel said the conversation went something like this. "You can't send a letter like that. We don't give a tinker's damn about the condition of your oil company. We want the money. We'll tell you what to write this time. Take this down, word for word," and with that instruction they dictated the message that was eventually delivered to Catlett. They did relent somewhat, permitting Urschel to include the brief note to his wife. They took the messages and left the ranch in great haste. Back without comment several days later, they hung around nervously at loose ends until taking off again on Friday, volunteering the information that they would be back Sunday with "news."

During the times when the kidnappers were absent, the man called Boss took over as the main guard, assisted from time to time by Armon, who played the violin for Urschel a couple of evenings as the Shannons and Urschel slowly developed a somewhat cordial, if understandably strained, relationship. Urschel was fond of hunting with dogs and said he carried on some discussions with Boss about their mutual enjoyment of tracking deer and game birds. An avid angler as well, Urschel exchanged occasional fishing stories with Boss, both of them no doubt exaggerating about their catches, as fishermen will do. Those were about the only subjects approaching common interest, considering the vastly dissimilar backgrounds, interests, and motives of the two men, one of them being forced to endure interminable days of intense darkness, of never seeing the sun or little else. No reading material, obviously, and no radio since there was no electricity. Even a stark prison cell, he fantasized under his blindfold, would have a bunk to sleep on, a window for light, probably a book or two, an electric fan, maybe even a radio. It was a marvel that even though totally "blind" he was able to maintain his sanity and keep his wits about him, never having any idea how long the dark ordeal would continue. Or if it would end.

In the meantime, the boys didn't return on Sunday as promised.

Shannon feared something might have happened to them, as did Urschel; that they might have stumbled into a shootout with the law and maybe have been killed or captured. This led Boss to tell Urschel sympathetically, "If they don't get in, I'll see that you get home if I have to take you in my own car." Urschel said he replied, "Man, you'll never regret it if you do that." But it was not to happen. The story? On Sunday, the kidnappers had run into another downpour (continuing their streak of bad luck with the elements), forcing them to pull over and wait it out. Then, they couldn't get the wet engine to start and had to while away an hour until it dried out.

Not being informed that the boys had telephoned Boss Shannon to explain their delay, and still manacled and still with his eyes taped shut, Urschel would be left to agonize through the weekend with his own thoughts, forlornly wondering what might be transpiring in the outside world. Edgy, with no clue at all—having discounted the strained "down in Oklahoma or Texas" comments as the false leads they were—he must have wondered again: *Just where in the world am I? Is there anything else I could be doing in the way of leaving more incriminating evidence in this God-forsaken hot and thirsty place? Did my letters home even get delivered? How must Berenice be holding up? The children? Can or will the ransom, whatever amount—or conditions—they're demanding, be met? Even if it's paid, will it make a bit of difference? Can these desperate, vicious hoodlums afford to let me live so I can identify them and maybe put them in jail? Not only that, just who are the two gangsters and who are "Boss" and "Potatoes," holding me hostage, all trussed up like this? Finally, Do I have much time left?*

Like his bridge-playing friend Jarrett, Charles Urschel hadn't fallen for the rather forced, clumsily dropped references to "Floyd" either. But he had no clues at all as to whom his captors really were. Yet out of necessity he'd learned a lot of patience from his years on the farm, and that attribute would stand him in very good stead.

6

The (Delayed) Drop

❖ ❖ ❖ ❖ ❖ ❖ ❖ ❖ ❖ ❖ ❖ ❖ ❖ ❖ ❖

Since receiving the instruction letter on Friday morning, the family had precious few hours to prepare for Kirkpatrick's Saturday night journey on the MK&T—the old Missouri, Kansas, and Texas Railway, the "Katy" Line. The ten thousand circulated twenty-dollar bills were still being gathered, and, despite the two explicit warnings and threats, the authorities couldn't have been more involved. Working with the family, they were helping the bank's comptroller and his staff to laboriously record the individual serial number of each one of the bills. Since each number consisted of a combination of the same two Kansas City Federal Reserve Bank's letters ("J" preceding the numbers, "A" at the end) and eight random numbers, that meant eighty thousand nonsequential numbers had to be copied down on individual pieces of paper, then arranged in numerical order to be typed and multigraphed to FBI field offices, banks, post offices, and local law enforcement agencies. The sixty thousand lists that the FBI published ran to eleven oversize pages of fifteen columns each.

As the designated drop man, Kirkpatrick grimly boarded the "Sooner" as commanded at 10 o'clock Saturday night, carrying the prescribed light-colored leather Gladstone grip and a ticket for a Pullman lower berth. But, in calculated disregard for the ground rules, he wasn't alone. As a precautionary backup—because, as Kirkpatrick said, "We were afraid some chiseler would try to hijack us"—Catlett slipped on another coach in the train. Kirkpatrick was carrying the actual ransom, twenty pounds by weight of Federal Reserve notes. Catlett's identical dummy bag, on the other hand, was stuffed with an equal twenty pounds of magazines. As further "insurance," the wary Kirkpatrick was packing a concealed loaded Colt automatic.

Making use of the sleeper berth he'd paid for, as directed in the ransom notes, was the furthest thing from Kirkpatrick's mind that long night. Instead, during the nearly ten-hour trip, he and Catlett positioned themselves on small uncomfortable wooden stools in the vestibule, since there was no observation car. Through the darkness and the heavy smoke, soot, and an occasional hot cinder from the locomotive, they strained to see the first signal fire. The tedious, 340-mile stop-and-go trip faded into a blur of the dim fleeting lights of Oklahoma towns—Luther, Cushing, Cleveland, Osage, Hominy, Pershing, Bartlesville—and then on through southeastern Kansas, past Coffeyville, Angola, Mound Valley, Parsons, in all a total of fifty-one small towns and wide-spot whistle stops. Nervously chain-smoking, Kirkpatrick made more heat than the pair of signal fires he and Catlett were anticipating. What signal fires? Neither of the two that were promised appeared. But there was no way they could have missed them, the two men were certain.

Kirkpatrick must have wondered: We're almost to Kansas City. Has something gone wrong? Was this whole exercise some sort of sick joke at our expense? Or had Catlett, who ducked back inside the coach at every stop, been spotted somehow when he boarded? Could one or more of the gang (the size of which was unknown but feared to be large) have been on the train the whole time, waiting for the opportunity to grab the money, shove the two drop men overboard, and make a run for it? Or were the couriers going to be hit when they arrived in Kansas City, a place noted for its jazz clubs but not so favorably as the wide-open "center stage of the Crime Corridor" run by Tom ("Boss") Pendergast? Worse, could it be that Charlie had already been killed, as Kirkpatrick and Catlett silently feared they, too, might be before or after the ransom was handed over?

They didn't know it, but as it turned out, all their questions and fears were groundless. The fire instructions were a clever smokescreen. Unbeknownst to them, one of the kidnappers had boarded the train a few stops back up the line, at Arcadia, Oklahoma, and spied the pair of couriers, one more than specifically instructed. His motoring coconspirator was easily able to stay ahead of the frequently stopping train, and he picked up his train-riding partner several towns farther along. Fearing that the unrecognized Catlett might be a government agent, they drove on to Kansas City to ready their real plan for getting the money. Insofar as Kirkpatrick and Catlett were concerned, the absence of the signal fires became the possible "hitch in the plans . . . not your fault" that the kidnappers had provided for in their instructions. Of course, the sleepless and emotionally drained Kirkpatrick and Catlett didn't know all this when they detrained about 8:15 Sunday morning at the massive Kansas City Union Station, just forty-three days earlier the scene of the bloody massacre.

All too conversant with the lurid details of that bloodbath and fearful now that they themselves might be the targets of opportunistic hijackers or robbers coveting the $200,000, Kirkpatrick and Catlett hustled through the busy depot to the taxi stand in the plaza parking lot, where purported machine-gun bullet nicks in the nearby eastern entrance from the massacre are pointed out to tourists to this day. With Kirkpatrick firmly gripping the Colt in his belt, the two men nervously but without incident rode into the downtown business district to the city's finest hotel, the elegant Muehlebach.

Checking in and cautiously following directions to the letter, Kirkpatrick took a room in the name of "E. E. Kinkaid, Little Rock, Arkansas" (Catlett was in another room as "E. E. Catwell of Little Rock"), sincerely hoping the whole journey wasn't going to turn out to be some sort of cruel hoax. Kirkpatrick's weapon always within arm's reach, the two men aimlessly played cards with little interest, dozing fitfully while waiting for the next move in the game. Both of them jumped involuntarily when the phone rang at 10:10 A.M., making known the arrival of a postal telegram at the front desk. It was from Tulsa, for "Mr. Kinkaid": "Owing to unavoidable incident unable to keep appointment. Will phone you about six. C. H. Moore."

Eight more hours, an eternity, to have to sit or pace about helplessly! Kirkpatrick couldn't help letting his mind wander, no doubt thinking: *Have we overplayed our hand by having Catlett come with me? Is Charlie even still alive? Are we just being played for stupid fools, being set up to be mugged and robbed? Murdered?* His and Catlett's nerves stretched to the breaking point; the wait was excruciating.

At last, suddenly, the follow-up call came. It was 5:30. A husky voice said, "This is Moore. Are you ready to close the deal on that farm?" Grasping for any kind of advantage, Kirkpatrick reconstructed how their conversation went. "I told him I was in the bath, and had ordered my dinner. He said he would like it very much if I would hurry, but if I had ordered the dinner to go ahead and eat it. He said he was in a hurry and would like to complete the deal. I told him I was in a hurry, too, and if he would tell me when, I could call home and tell the folks and give them some relief. And he said within twelve hours I could tell them that everything would be all right. So I told him I would meet him in thirty minutes, ten minutes after six. I told the man, 'I have a friend here with me. Would it be all right to bring him along?' 'Nothing doing,' the man replied. 'We knew all about that "friend." We knew that on the train. Come by yourself and come unarmed and be damned sure that there are no federals covering you.' "

The plan swung into operation. This time, Kirkpatrick went by himself, exactly as ordered. But in defiance of the instructions, he was still armed as he rode a taxicab to the designated midtown location. With the bag containing the ransom money in hand, after paying off the driver he lit a cigarette with a shaky hand and cautiously started walking along the sidewalk, as directed, to await the contact. He glanced apprehensively across the street toward the thirty or so windows in the nine-story LaSalle Hotel he was passing, wondering whether some sniper might be peeking out, aiming, ready to ambush him, gun him down. Those thoughts were suddenly interrupted when a tall, dapper-looking man, fedora brim pulled low over his forehead, stepped out from behind a parked auto and passed by him, then swung around. Kirkpatrick remembered the conversation almost word for word.

"I'll take that grip. Keep on walking. Don't turn around."

"How do I know you're the right party?" Kirkpatrick asked without daring to sneak a glance.

"Hell, you ought to know by now I'm the right party."

"What assurance do I have that Mr. Urschel won't be harmed? When may we expect him home?"

"Don't argue with me. Give me the goddamned bag. The boys are waiting for me. Give me the grip. The boys are over there watching me. I'll see you in twenty minutes at the hotel."

At that, Kirkpatrick slowly turned around to get a good look at his adversary, a moment to take in everything he could about the criminal. Finally, he spoke again, slowly: "Not until you give me some definite assurance to give to Mrs. Urschel."

After what Kirkpatrick felt was an eternity came the reply, couched in terms of the newspaper ad. "All right. The title deed to the farm will be delivered within twelve hours. You can count on that. Give me the grip. The boys are over there watching me."

It was roughly 6:30 P.M. when Kirkpatrick reluctantly let the bag containing the largest ransom in history drop to the sidewalk and forced himself to walk away evenly, but rapidly, in the interest of self-preservation. He wondered whether somebody in the hotel or an apparent accomplice he'd spied in a nearby car cradling what appeared to be a shotgun or a submachine gun might be inclined to pump a round or two into his back. Instead, with great relief, he heard the door slam and the car squeal away. The driver had had the weapon at the ready should Kirkpatrick foolishly have tried anything while his accomplice was retrieving the bag.

Shaken and emotionally drained, Kirkpatrick was barely able to light another cigarette before looking for a cab. Back at the Muehlebach, he filled in Catlett as he was placing a call to Oklahoma City. "They got the money," he told Berenice Urschel. "The man—and I got a good look at him—assured me that Charlie will be home no later than twelve hours from now. No, I don't know where he is. That's all the man told me."

Kirkpatrick had steadfastly maintained an outwardly stolid and confident demeanor for the sake of Berenice and the other family members. Twenty years after the fact, however, he revealed the tension that had been gripping him. He wrote the following in *Geese Flying South: A Collection of Poems*, a one-of-a-kind handcrafted book with a wooden cover:

> I had left a letter to my wife to be delivered to her on Tuesday, if I
> had not returned. In it I told her I would most likely never return.
> I was carrying a fortune to deliver to gangsters in a city under the
> unspeakable Pendergast administration. I had learned from the
> underworld that the top price for murder in Kansas City at that
> time was $500.00. I dreaded the thought of being murdered by
> gangland without a chance to fight back. The long grueling hours
> were torture. At 4:00 in the morning I came to a decision. I made up
> my mind I would not worry. I would put my trust in God to take a
> hand in my behalf.

7

The Hunt

❖ ❖ ❖ ❖ ❖ ❖ ❖ ❖ ❖ ❖ ❖ ❖ ❖ ❖ ❖

The strain of the drawn-out payoff and the face-to-face confrontation with his friend's kidnapper finally over, it was back on the train for the weary Kirkpatrick. He arrived at the Urschel residence Monday morning expecting a jubilant homecoming greeting from his friend since it now was a good two hours past the promised deadline for his return. But one look at the horde of reporters still on their "death watch," and he knew he was sadly mistaken. Berenice, whose stricken expression told it all before she said it, met him at the door, saying, "Charlie's not here."

There had been no sign, no word, of Charles. The emotional anxiety was at its highest level yet. Spirits and morale were at their lowest. Despite her resolve, Berenice in particular was finally becoming more and more despondent, trying hard not to consider the unthinkable: Could the kidnappers have panicked and murdered Charlie despite all everyone had done? Had the whole scenario—gathering the money, recording the numbers, the police staying out of sight, the payoff itself, all of it—been just a macabre game? Should the family be steeling itself for more ransom notes, further demands for additional money, more threats on Charlie's life? Perhaps they could be doing more, trying as a family to live up to the declaration by the oil editor of the *Daily Oklahoman:* "There isn't an employee of the company today who wouldn't take a machine gun or a pen knife and walk into the kidnappers' hideout to rescue him."

Kirkpatrick, bravely putting on an outwardly calm face, counseled patience. "The kidnappers probably want to wait until after dark and, besides, they may have held Charlie a long way away. He'll probably show up after dark."

Still, every jarring ring of the telephone seemed to foretell doom, no call bringing any news. The mood in the house grew darker as the minutes and hours ticked by agonizingly and night came.

What had happened to delay Urschel's promised homecoming was that the kidnappers had first pulled over on a desolate side road somewhere along the way to count the money, all neatly wrapped and tied in ten packs of exactly $20,000 each. Satisfied, and sneaking at respectable speeds over a succession of unfamiliar back roads to avoid any contact with the law, they took until almost two o'clock Monday afternoon to negotiate the five hundred miles from Kansas City to Paradise. Finally arriving at the farm, they joined up with the lead kidnapper's wife and, before anything else, proceeded to examine the bills meticulously—front and back, held up to the light—to assure themselves they weren't marked. The money didn't seem to be, but the three of them had some apprehension that, despite the short time frame they had deliberately set, it just might have been possible for the family or the law to have recorded some or all of the serial numbers. In any event, they gleefully counted the money a second time—yes, every dollar was there—and then they proceeded to divvy it up.

After the leader took a "deduction" of $11,500 for what he termed were "expenses"—the big-ticket items being the motorcar they had left behind at the relative's farm on the trip from Oklahoma City and another they'd abandoned near the Katy tracks the night of the drop that didn't come to pass—the two men took $94,250 each in equal half shares. In the giddy mood of the moment, the men agreed to flip a coin for the ransom suitcase as a souvenir.

Now was the moment for the big decision: Since he wasn't of any use to them anymore, how should they dispose of their hostage? Life or death? The woman, stridently and at length, held out for extermination by any means; obviously a dead Urschel wouldn't be able to identify them. "It's the only way. If not, he'll talk and we'll all get caught."

But her husband wisely argued against that. "We'll spoil it for everybody if we kill him, and we'll have no friends anywhere."

Stoutly backed by his comrade, he stood up to his wife this one time, pointing out that murdering Urschel would just intensify the hunt for the three of them and probably lead to the electric chair. "We'll be signing our own death warrants if we kill him."

"It was a stormy session," Hoover elaborated further five years afterward in *Persons in Hiding*. "The gangsters desired to turn their victim loose in accordance with their ransom promises. They reminded [her] of this fact, though they need not have done so. . . . At last the pleadings of the others won over [her] insistence that the victim be murdered instead of returned to his family. It was exceedingly fortunate that [she] had no knowledge that even at that moment the Federal Bureau of Investigation had started on her trail."

The gratifying outcome for Urschel—more in the dark than ever by now and beginning to reconcile himself for the worst—was that one of his kidnappers informed him, "You can cut off your whiskers." His freedom, his life, had been successfully ransomed! He was going to live. *They're taking me home!* Standing behind Urschel as they'd done centuries ago (it seemed) when forcing him to compose the ransom notes, they temporarily slipped off his blindfold and furnished him with an old straight razor, some shaving cream, a brush, and a basin of water to scrape away his nine-day growth of beard in preparation for the return trip, all the while staying where their victim couldn't get a glimpse of them in the mirror they provided.

Overwhelmed at this unanticipated sudden turn of events, but still plotting his revenge, Urschel used the moment as one final opportunity to deposit some additional fingerprints—on the razor handle, the basin, and the small cracked and cloudy hand mirror he was permitted to use by laying it on the bench.

Thus, at 11:30 P.M. on Monday, the last night of July, like an apparition, Urschel strolled into his house—through the back door. The place exploded with elation, sheer emotion, and copious tears.

Berenice almost fainted.

It had been a terrible nine days and a particularly long and stressful final twenty-nine hours—seventeen more than the promised twelve—since the ransom payoff on the Kansas City sidewalk. Now, in the excitement and outpouring of relief, it would be almost an hour, until 12:30 in the morning to be exact, before someone thought to suggest phoning the *Daily Oklahoman*'s city desk to let the good news out.

"Mr. Urschel is home. That is all we have to say tonight." So saying, Seeligson broke the connection and left the phone off the hook for the night.

The questions flew at Urschel. How had he gotten home, the family and officers were all asking him at once, and why the back door approach? First, though, what was the whole story? What all had happened to him? How was he treated? Mistreated? Where had he been held? What did the kidnappers say and do to him? Who were they? Where were they?

Patiently, though terribly weary, he related that after he was allowed to shave, his still anonymous captors produced a brand new short-sleeve sport shirt and an ill-fitting straw hat for him to wear on the return ride. Urschel hadn't particularly cared whether he shaved or not, but the boys told him they weren't taking him on the road with his whiskers on.

Urschel later recalled that Boss had come into the shack, "shook my hand warmly, and told me he hoped I wouldn't have any further trouble."

Then he was propped up in the backseat in his new shirt and hat and with dark glasses intended to conceal the blindfold for his second lengthy trip. It was another deliberately roundabout journey, consuming roughly eight hours, despite the fact that the direct route from Paradise to Oklahoma City is less than two hundred miles.

Charles Urschel's captivity came to an end at last on the northern outskirts of Norman, the state university town some twenty miles south of home. Given back his watch and a ten-dollar bill for taxi fare, he was free at last, but only after being severely threatened one more time that if he ever revealed any details at all, "they would kill me and my entire family. They made this promise to me. They said that if I would tell them I could get home without disclosing my identity they would not tie me up. Otherwise they would chain me to a tree in the woods and I would be found the next morning. It had rained. It was then raining, and I told them I felt sure I could get home."

With that, they raced away. After standing and listening for a few moments to be certain they were gone, Urschel carefully peeled off the bandages holding his blindfold in place. It hurt terribly, but he could see! He could get his bearings. Trudging through the drizzle on legs weakened from nine days of disuse and strain, Urschel had what seemed like forever to consider the connection between that parting warning and what one of his kidnappers had told him in one of their conversations at the ranch: "If we thought you would ever see anything here or ever tell anything when you go back, we would kill you now. That really is the safest way. But if we take your word and release you after the ransom money is paid, and you betray us by giving the federals any information, we'll choose our own method of punishing you." And, one last threat when they let him out: "Make no calls other than the one for the cab."

Finally reentering civilization—as represented by a combination filling station and popular college student roadside barbecue stand called Classen's, with flashing neon "Bar-B-Q" and "Beer" signs—the unrecognized Urschel rested on a counter stool after his damp hike. One of only a handful of customers in the "pig stand" that late in the evening because it was summer vacation at the university, he drank coffee and made idle conversation about the weather with the owner while waiting for the taxi the proprietor's cousin had called for him. During the ride, Urschel chatted amiably about automobiles and the weather with the cabbie, who wouldn't learn of his famous fare's identity until reading the next day's news. Requesting that the driver make a brief stop at a druggist's shop, Urschel went in and got change for the ten dollars and rode on to his house, where he paid the driver three dollars—two-fifty for the fare, fifty cents for the tip.

Urschel would quip about the officer guarding his front door. "A man I never saw before answered the door and refused to let me in. I got a big laugh out of being refused admission to my own home. I went to the back door and family began to show up and everything was rosy." Unaware of the ransom payoff and hardly expecting that the victim would simply ride up to his front door in a taxi in the middle of the night dressed in a sport shirt and straw hat, the newsmen camped out across the road were very likely napping or playing cards. They missed the big moment entirely.

As for the ransom, Urschel maintained that he didn't learn for a week after his release what the amount had been; inquiring about it had been the furthest thing from his mind.

❖　❖　❖

Although Urschel arrived soaked from the rain, bone-weary, the skin around his eyes blistered from the ever-present bandages, and close to mental and physical exhaustion, no time could be wasted in turning Hoover's eager forces loose on the chase. So, pacing up and down briskly to ward off sleepiness, he spent half an hour filling them in as best he could in his condition.

"They told me that if I told anything they would get me and torture me, would kill and maim members of my family. That they were more powerful than the federal government." Gus Jones, noting that the victim was "very nervous and in kind of a bad physical condition," finally acquiesced to Berenice's demands and permitted Urschel to turn in for the first prolonged sleep he'd had—in a real bed— in ten days. He estimated he hadn't slept more than eight to ten hours total the whole time he was gone, but on the occasions when he did doze off, he would "wake up with horrible dreams."

Somehow Urschel was up early the next morning, ready to "star" in two extraordinary sessions. The first was an 8:00 A.M. meeting with fourteen newspapermen and photographers on the very sunporch where the bridge game had been so rudely interrupted.

Relaxed, he was nattily attired in shirtsleeves, blue tie, tan slacks, and black-and-white oxfords. But belying his apparent nonchalance were large red splotches that marked where his blindfold had been taped. Not intending to disclose anything that would be helpful to the kidnappers or in any way hinder the manhunt for them, Urschel carefully portioned out only a small ration of selected minor facts, obfuscated others in a ploy aimed at bolstering his kidnappers' confidence ("I have not a shred of information which would aid officers; I saw the light of day only twice"), and casually joked about his abduction. "They didn't like the newspaper pictures," he told the photographers. "They said I was a better-looking man than the pictures."

At that point, Berenice, who had earlier embraced her husband warmly and repeatedly for the photographers, joked, "They said to him, 'If you look like those pictures maybe Mrs. Urschel paid us to kidnap you.'"

With his teenage son Charles Jr. seated beside him, his arm tightly around his father the whole time, Urschel gave the group carefully crafted statements he hoped the kidnappers would read—and swallow. "I don't know a single thing we could tell the officers, since I was handcuffed and my eyes taped from the moment I left until they let me out. I think the house they held me in was probably a backwoods bungalow. It seemed to be of three rooms. The two men who took me seemed to alternate in guarding me. They talked very little, although they were friendly, and I never heard them call each other by name." Well, he was asked, did they harm you? Were they decent to you?

"We got along fine. They told me, 'We don't want to make this any more difficult than we have to. If you fight, we will have to mistreat you. If you don't, we'll get along.' " This statement ended the uniquely non-news conference, one with a subliminal secondary purpose. It was hoped that these and other deliberately misleading statements and false clues that family spokesmen had fed to the press would cause the kidnappers to lower their guard, become overconfident, make mistakes.

After this early morning meeting with the press, Urschel moved on to a six-hour debriefing the likes of which none of the officers had ever been part of or heard tell about. Urschel proved to be a mental sponge for detail, having absorbed practically everything he had heard, smelled, felt, seen, and deduced. "From the first," Urschel told them in his calm, understated manner, "I made plans that I hoped would lead toward identifying the place where I was held." He indicated that he'd repeatedly exhorted himself: *Stay in control, Keep my equilibrium. Don't succumb to depression or desperation, get to feeling sorry for myself, but do whatever I can to get the guards in conversation. Above all, keep my wits about me. Remember e-v-e-r-y-t-h-i-n-g!*

He did just as he'd resolved, even talking the guards into letting him stumble about a little after a few days without those painful skin-scraping handcuffs. "I told them I simply had to get a little exercise. But as I walked around I would touch the furniture and leave fingerprints."

He recounted what little he could about the trip to Paradise—the power plant he recognized before being blindfolded, the muffled conversation at the filling station about the crop and weather situation, the sliding off the wet road, the stop to ask directions—and then the return trip to Norman. And much, much more in between.

One senior FBI agent present would marvel that "despite the fact he was very nervous and in kind of a bad physical condition . . . I learned every move that had been made from the moment he left his house, the condition of the weather, the kind of roads, when it rained, the hour it rained, the day it rained, and everything he heard or that was said in his presence." Agent Gus Jones told Urschel that "if there were more like you, the kidnapper would soon be out of business." Still another wrote him afterward, "I would under no circumstance wish you any harm, but I cannot help [but] wish that all our kidnap victims were you. Our work would be easy." Another put in his report, "He is a man of brilliant mind and cool-headed." Even Hoover's personal publicist felt compelled to add high praise. "If even ten percent of those who are stolen each year had the acumen, the fearlessness, and power of observation of Charles F. Urschel, the racket would die quickly," wrote Courtney Ryley Cooper in 1935 in one of his own books, *Ten Thousand Public Enemies*.

This understandable outpouring of admiration was actually understated. After describing what he could about the trip from Oklahoma City following his friend Jarrett's release, Urschel recounted explicit details of his first, brief places of confinement: initially a large outbuilding with a tin roof (obvious because of the rain beating on it) and the big house Boss and Ora Shannon occupied.

Upon his arrival Urschel was kept until after dark in what—because of his experience around farm equipment and automobiles—he correctly surmised was a garage. He recognized the sounds outside of horses, cattle, several dogs, chickens, guineas, and a lot of quail. He was made to sit on a large, high wooden box containing what he could feel were some golf bags. *Do these low-lifes, these bandits, these thugs, pretend to be gentlemen by playing golf?* If there were any other possible pieces of information he could pick up, he didn't get the chance. It was time to move on. Still blindfolded, he was led outside and through a narrow, squeaking gate onto a boardwalk of some kind. He began silently counting off the number of paces from the garage and the number of steps up into the house itself. Inside, from his uncomfortable perch on an iron cot, he overheard some faint conversations in an adjoining room. At a small plain table with no tablecloth, he ravenously devoured his first "meal," a plain ham sandwich. Plus a cup of coffee, no saucer, but, he noted, served in a china cup. Breakfast the next day—fruit, a bacon and egg sandwich, and coffee—was delivered to his bedroom on a wooden tray. That first afternoon, he was prodded gently into a different auto for a short ride to Armon's hovel for the rest of his imprisonment.

One potentially helpful bit of information that Urschel grasped the first morning of his confinement was the sound of a plane headed westward. Late in the afternoon the same plane or an identical twin two-motor aircraft flew over in the opposite direction, he theorized from the pulsating throb of the propellers. When those flights were repeated at what seemed approximately the same times the second day, Urschel figured this might possibly provide a small, isolated clue to his whereabouts. With little else to do, he made it a priority to ascertain as accurately as possible when each of the planes flew by, noting that they did so with regularity. Never giving the slightest indication of being even remotely aware of the solitary aircraft, he began by mentally counting off several minutes after each flight, second by second—*one thousand one . . . one thousand two . . . one thousand three . . . one thousand . . .* up into the hundreds—then apparently rather apologetically asking the unsuspecting guards what time it was. Subtracting the minutes he'd ticked off on his makeshift mental clock gave Urschel the approximate time the flyovers occurred. On other days he subtly altered his technique, finding out the time beforehand and counting off the seconds and minutes until the plane made its accustomed appearance. By the end of a week, he had the plane's schedule pinpointed almost to the second: the morning plane went over at 9:45, the afternoon return flight at 5:45. He verified this every day and filed it away in his ever-growing memory bank on the theory that while it might not be helpful at all, it just might be a useful long shot in helping to find this dreadful place—if he ever got away.

The only key information the kidnappers succeeded in keeping from Urschel was their identities and his exact whereabouts. Those small victories on their part wouldn't count for much, however. Because even though Urschel was always blindfolded, like many people with severe vision impairment, he "saw"—and remembered—more than the average sighted person generally does. He told the officers he was absolutely certain he could identify all the principals by the intonations of their voices and by their different speech mannerisms. One in particular, he said, because of his soft twangy voice and hearty laugh. Once (while pretending not to, of course) Urschel overheard someone breach security and voice the name of the rural delivery letter carrier (it sounded to Urschel like "Worth Harris"), and that became another item for the memory file.

Finally, from answers he got to his carefully well-timed but seemingly nonchalant and innocuous questions, from conversations he either took part in or overheard, and from "observations" he had made as he shuffled about in the constant darkness and wilting heat, Urschel pieced together a remarkably precise list of characteristics about Armon's place and its environs.

His list included the crude shack and its contents, a banging screen door, the three small rooms and their dimensions, two small porches, several shingles missing from a corner of the roof over the dilapidated front porch, the direction of the bare floorboards, the single step up to the front door, a potbellied wood cook stove in the tiny kitchen area, a blue high chair with his many scratches on it, an old-fashioned organ, a hole in the door where a knob had once been, the iron bedstead he had also scratched, a missing front window pane filled with a piece of cardboard, the mirror with a crack in the upper left corner that he used when he shaved, a round-top trunk, a five-foot-long wood bench, the steel chain with which he was shackled, and the shack itself, "infested," as he put it, with rats.

The immediate surroundings included a well west of the house with a squeaky pulley and rusty pail, the dipper or cup with a handle broken off and the pungent mineral taste of the water, a corn patch in front, two small chicken coops also in front, and a ramshackle barn next to the shack.

He also remembered stock and other animals, four milk cows and a couple of calves, three hogs, two pigs in a pen behind the shack, a frequently bawling whiteface bull in a pen to the southeast, one mule, a pet dog, and a small flock of chickens.

Recognizing the animals by sound and smell had been easy for Urschel, an oversight on the kidnappers' part. They didn't know he'd grown up on a farm raising corn, winter wheat, beans, and livestock. Physical chores had filled out his frame—still a trim six-foot-one 190-pounder of rugged build—and had taught him self-reliance and patience. Furthering his strong self-discipline was the time he'd spent in the army. For a seasoned farmhand like Urschel, having almost nothing else to do for nine days but dwell in the dark and count minutes and hours, it was easy to identify each and every animal. There weren't that many on the premises to begin with, and Armon had helped by innocently verifying the head counts.

Never ceasing his strategy of attempting blanket recall, Urschel felt and identified things inside the shack when going through his blind man's bluff of deliberately stumbling and bumbling about with arms outstretched tentatively. When he banged into things or simply wanted information, he probably dropped carefully spaced questions and received straightforward automatic responses from the unsuspecting guards. "What's this (stove, trunk, wood bench, and so on)?" "Ow, that hurt, what did I run into?" "Where did this come from?" "Why is the dog barking this time?" "What are you going to do about the rats under the floorboards?" "I'm kind of hungry, isn't it about time to eat?" (getting the response, "No, not yet, it ain't even close to _____ o'clock").

As unobtrusively as possible, while carrying these inquiries off without suspicion or detection, Urschel also was depositing fingerprints profusely throughout the place, even outdoors in what passed as the privy and at the well, plus leaving fingernail scratch marks on the sparse furniture in the shack. With the engaging, friendly conversational manner his friends back home knew so well, he was able as the days dragged on to pry more and more information out of the guards. One FBI interviewer wrote in his summary, "In casual conversation with one of his guards, he [Urschel] heard about a young girl in the community who was a public prostitute, with bookkeeping proclivities as to her business with the male sex."

In addition to finding out that Boss shared his interest in hunting and fishing, with true friendly interest Urschel elicited the fact that Boss made his living primarily from raising corn, cotton, some hogs, and beef cattle, fifty head at the moment. A few days before Urschel had arrived at Armon's, a neighbor had been inquiring about a runaway hog. Armon had found the animal and promised to deliver it. But now, while watching over Urschel, he and his father kept a wary eye out to head off the neighbor should he decide to pay a visit to reclaim the hog. The Shannons, fearful and cautious, certainly didn't want him stumbling across their famous blindfolded ward.

Assuming Urschel was released, would any of these random recollections he was amassing be of use at all to the law? More than J. Edgar Hoover could have dreamed. Combining the elements of Urschel's invaluable ready-made checklist with the various distances he had measured off in and around the shack and the big house, it was an easy matter for Agent Jones to sketch a detailed map of Armon's dwelling and immediate surroundings so precise in scale that officers on the scene later would know at once it was the right place.

This large catalogue of useful details might well have been enough in and of itself, yet there was still another element, the most important one,

one that would prove to be the ultimate clue in finding the Shannons and getting the FBI off to a running start. Urschel had calculated from day one the times that the lone airplane passed overhead every morning and every afternoon. With commercial aviation, all aviation, still in its infancy, it was the only plane of any kind he heard.

After a week of counting off the flights came an act of God that would turn out to be a major break.

On Sunday morning, the day of the steady rain, Urschel realized something was out of the ordinary. It was nearly 10:00 o'clock. What had happened to the 9:45 plane? Very puzzling. Where do you suppose it is? What could have happened? Had the storm grounded it, kept it from making its usual morning pass over his prison? Even in his own unhappy state of confinement, he hoped there hadn't been an accident. Maybe it had simply been canceled due to the weather. Or rerouted. The FBI interrogators eagerly pounced on Urschel's revelation of this unexpected no-show, perhaps remembering the telltale clue of the usually noisy hound that didn't bark in the Sherlock Holmes memoir *Silver Blaze*. That one missing plane flight—coupled with the helpful information the filling station attendant had unknowingly supplied about the drought having wiped out all but the broomcorn—was to be the key for locating the hideout and hopefully trapping the criminals and conspirators at the scene.

Fine, but how to find it?

At the FBI's request, airline officials and U.S. Weather Bureau meteorologists zeroed in on the broad area within a six-hundred-mile radius of Oklahoma City, based roughly on the length of time of Urschel's return trip back to Norman. That was yet another of Urschel's valuable leads. Although still obviously totally in the dark as to where he'd been held and the route home they were taking, he had easily recognized the long, rattling Purcell-Lexington Bridge spanning the Canadian River south of Norman that they had crossed just minutes before putting him out in the rain. The police and FBI were getting warmer. Painstakingly, they pored over huge maps and scrutinized the sketchy timetables of the nine pioneer commercial airlines that had scheduled routes in the vast search area covering all or parts of Oklahoma, Texas, Kansas, Missouri, Colorado, and New Mexico, looking for normal flight patterns that hadn't been followed that one Sunday morning.

At the same time, the meteorologists worked on their own charts from two other angles, looking for and eventually finding the locale where the summer's severe shortage of rainfall had devastated everything but broomcorn and where there also had been strong winds followed by rain on the day in question.

The FBI and police finally turned up the daily report sheet that an American Airways pilot had routinely filed showing that the stormy weather on Sunday, July 30, had forced him to delay takeoff of the regular Dallas/Fort Worth/Wichita Falls/Amarillo morning passenger flight for twenty minutes. Eventually airborne, he had made a wide detour off course, away from Paradise, to spare the passengers the turbulence. And again as Urschel had correctly perceived, it was a two-motor aircraft, a Pilgrim. That information, combined with the corroborating weather and crop data, enabled the FBI to determine approximate coordinates for a general search area. Now the problem became how to locate Boss's farmhouse and Armon's shack in that vast expanse of north-central Texas.

8

The Kidnappers

❖　❖　❖　❖　❖　❖　❖　❖　❖　❖　❖　❖　❖　❖　❖

By now the identity of at least one of the kidnappers was fairly well established, thanks first to Walter Jarrett's tentative mug shot identification and then to some other unexpected and helpful clues. As a result, the FBI and other authorities were all but certain who the two main perpetrators were: George ("Machine Gun") Kelly and his wife and partner in crime, Kathryn (aka Kate or Kit). Pending the outcome of rescue efforts, and in keeping with the attorney general's advice and the standard FBI policy of controlling publicity (and doing nothing contrary to the wishes of kidnap victims' families), the FBI and the local police didn't immediately share this information with the press.

George Kelly, who'd been referred to breathlessly by a local officer as "one of the most vicious and dangerous criminals in America," would shortly be branded by one overly dramatic and embarrassingly inaccurate newspaper reporter as "a former convict and known killer . . . a ruthless slayer." A former convict he was, yes. But vicious and a killer? Neither. Kathryn Kelly, meantime, would earn begrudging recognition from none other than J. Edgar Hoover himself. In *Persons in Hiding*, a book bearing his name as the author (but widely known to have been ghostwritten by his publicist, Courtney Ryley Cooper), he referred to her as "a woman of superior intelligence" and "one of the most coldly deliberate criminals of my experience."

The boy who would become the criminal Machine Gun Kelly came into the world supposedly on July 17, 1900, as George Francis Barnes Jr., the son of respectable middle-class parents who were temporarily residing in

Chicago. (Some other records, including his FBI and prison files, indicate earlier purported birth years, and while in the penitentiary at Leavenworth in 1930, he told the federal census enumerator he was thirty-two and that his occupation was "baker," apparently reflecting his duties at the time.) Nothing in his early formative years in Memphis, where his parents moved when he was two, would give any indication of his future career in crime. George and his older sister Inez had a not especially strict Catholic upbringing. He attended public schools, caddied at a country club, and had a newspaper route to pick up spending money to supplement his allowance. The Barnes family was by no means poor, nor what could be called well-to-do. George Sr. had held several jobs in his career— railroad engineer, insurance agent, proprietor of a dry goods store—that kept the family reasonably well cared for, so Mrs. Barnes (Elizabeth) did not have an outside job, seeing instead to bringing up the two children.

Growing up in this rather placid environment, George adored his mother but had an ever-increasing intense dislike, bordering on outright hatred, of his father. In perhaps the first hint of the boy's antisocial behavior to come, when George discovered his father was having an affair, he employed blackmail. He confronted his father, threatening to disclose the tryst to Mrs. Barnes unless given a substantial increase in his allowance and unlimited use of the family car. Panicked, his father hastily caved. But rather than endearing him to his fifteen-year-old son, the cover-up actually exacerbated George's contempt for him. It was, in no uncertain terms, a mutual loathing. Another turning point in George's life, a severe blow, followed with the death of his mother while he was a high school student of sixteen. Somewhere in his teen years he discovered that with his father's car at his disposal he could slip out of state—to nearby Arkansas or Mississippi, since Tennessee had its own prohibition law before the federal one went into effect—and acquire alcohol to sell to his classmates for a tidy profit. With this newfound source of income, he became the school fashion plate and a ladies' man, even getting reprimanded at least once by the principal for necking in a stairwell.

Restless and bored with book learning (which in reality he was rather good at, even with little effort), he dropped out of high school prematurely but then managed to be accepted as a conditional college freshman, purportedly majoring in agriculture. Quitting college after little more than a single semester, doubtless due at least in part to the fifty-five demerits he was hit with for various rules violations, he eloped at the age of nineteen with seventeen-year-old society belle Geneva Ramsey. Her father considered George a ne'er-do-well and had forbidden her to see him. In what might have been an omen of the future, their car broke down on the way to the justice of the peace, and the couple had to hitch a ride across the border to Clarksdale, Mississippi, for the ceremony.

Although anything but pleased with this turn of events, Geneva's loving father reluctantly set up his new son-in-law with a job as a clerk in his contracting business. It didn't take long for the truly charming and easygoing George to win over Mr. Ramsey, whom he greatly admired, by working hard and doing far better than expected on the new job. He was a good and caring husband as well, and the couple would have two sons, George Jr. ("Sonny") and Bruce; another child was stillborn. But then Geneva's father was killed in a tragic industrial accident. This second untimely death of a loved one almost devastated George (who would pathetically tell Bruce years later, "If your Granddad Ramsey had been my father, my life would have been entirely different"). Absent Ramsey's leadership, the business soon folded. Out of work and financed by his widowed mother-in-law, George tried his hand with little success at some shaky endeavors in Memphis—operating a garage and a used car lot, even running a forty-acre goat farm. The only trouble with that agricultural effort was that despite George's enthusiastic hustling and promotional efforts, how many people in Tennessee were ready to drink goat's milk or eat goat cheese? Not enough, as it turned out.

Frustrated by these failures, he turned first for a short time to what he found to be a stiflingly humdrum life of trying to peddle insurance as a traveling salesman. Next it was driving a cab—but supplementing his fares by returning to the practice of surreptitiously running a little liquor on the side in defiance of the Volstead Act (Prohibition). Somehow, smooth talker that he was, he was able to keep this little illegality, this dual personality of his, barely concealed from Geneva and her mother for about a year; they wondered between themselves how he could make so much money driving a hack. It didn't take long for the marriage to start to fall apart because of his long unexplained absences secretly doing liquor runs and his increasingly frequent heavy drinking bouts when he was home. The tangled situation came to a head with a phone call late one night. He asked his surprised wife to please take a train to Jackson, Tennessee, eighty miles away, and bring enough cash to bail him out on a "phony" bootlegging charge. Tearfully, she did so, but that was just about the last straw. She took the boys and moved out soon after. In despair, George apparently attempted suicide by overdosing on drugs but recovered after emergency room treatment.

After that, and now alone, instead of even continuing to pretend to be legitimate, George decided to take what appeared to be minimal risks and turn, full-time, to the promised easy rewards of crime. Prohibition, although on the way out, still offered him the instant opportunity. He became known around Memphis as the "Society Bootlegger," selling liquor that was smuggled across the border from Canada to speakeasies and pharmacists. However, big-time strong-arm competitors and several more arrests made it imperative for him to beat a hasty retreat out of town, all the way to New Mexico, as it turned out. Some months thereafter—it was now June 1, 1926—Geneva was granted her divorce, remembering later that "he was running in bad company" and that "I had to advertise notice to get a divorce because I didn't know where to reach him." It had been six years since their ill-fated elopement.

Dropping the name Barnes to try to forget the father he detested and now calling himself George R. Kelly (the "R" standing for Geneva Ramsey's father's name and Kelly his mother's maiden name), he was arrested in short order in his new domicile for a Prohibition violation, fined $350, and dispatched to the state prison in Santa Fe for a couple of months in 1927. Relocation to the Kansas City area, and a brief second marriage (to a Bess Williamson of Wichita, Kansas, who reportedly couldn't put up with his long absences while on his bootleg runs) followed.

So did yet another arrest, this one resulting in an $850 fine and a sentence to the dreaded federal penitentiary at Leavenworth, the "Big House," for "possession of liquor in Indian Country" (attempting to sell liquor on an Oklahoma reservation). The ensuing three-year term for that ill-conceived plan introduced him to some notorious big-time cons: murderers Wilbur ("Mad Dog") Underhill and Verne Miller, safecracker Morris ("Red") Rudensky, bank robber Charlie Harmon, and bank/train robbers Frank ("Jelly") Nash, Francis ("Jimmy") Keating, and Tommy Holden. Kelly easily ingratiated himself with them and won their appreciation by forging counterfeit trusty passes that some of them (but not Kelly) used for a 1930 jailbreak. More important, he got a first-class education, an insight, about many tricks of the criminal trade from these veteran experts.

For a change, Kelly proved to be an attentive and adept pupil. Upon his release for good behavior shortly after the jailbreak (his forgery handiwork unknown by the warden), he quickly put to good use the lessons he'd learned. He joined and sometimes even led various roving hit-and-run holdup gangs plucking money from banks in small towns over a range of at least ten states. His weapon of choice was a .38-caliber revolver, which he favored as a persuasive method of obtaining cooperation, but never to kill or even wound (the machine gun and the nickname would come later). As a matter of fact, a teller at a Mississippi bank Kelly and others heisted described Kelly to police as "the kind of guy, that, if you looked at him, you would never have thought he was a bank robber."

Freely spending his takes from these holdups, Kelly turned again into a clotheshorse and paid cash for a string of expensive custom-made luxury Cadillacs and Buicks. Exuding charm and pseudo-respectability, he impressed listeners by saying he was in the "banking business."

As for Kathryn Kelly, she was christened Cleo Mae Brooks when born in 1904 in Saltillo, up the road from Tupelo in northeast Mississippi. Her parents were James Emory Brooks and Ora (nee Coleman) Brooks; Ora divorced Brooks and became the wife of Boss Shannon in 1927.

Changing her name from Cleo to Kathryn, which she considered more stylish, she dropped out of school after the eighth grade, was married at fourteen or fifteen to a nondescript fellow by the name of Lonnie Frye and had his child. Divorced and remarried to an Allie Brewer while still a teenager, she lived in rural Oklahoma where her parents had relocated. She then divorced and married still again before hitching up with Kelly, who would become husband number four. Her bootlegger third husband "officially" killed himself, but under extremely mysterious circumstances after one of his frequent vocal and alcoholic disagreements with Kathryn. Found dead of a gunshot wound, alongside his body with the weapon was a precisely typed, error-free note: "I can not live with her or without her. Hence I am departing this life." Even his "signature," Charlie Thorne, was typed. Although the deceased had little book learning, no known typing ability, and probably wouldn't have had a clue what "hence" meant, a coroner's jury in Coleman County, Texas, ruled his shooting a suicide.

Combining the small estate Thorne had left her with the proceeds from minor unlawful activities on her own (using the alias of Dolores Whitney, she was convicted only once, for robbery, but the verdict was reversed on appeal and she served no time), Kathryn was able to maintain a freewheeling lifestyle of fashionable clothes and frequent nightlife. Freewheeling is probably far too tame a description. Hoover would quote a man who went out with Kathryn a few times as saying: "She took me to more speakeasies, more bootleg dives, more holes in the wall than I thought there were in all Texas. She knows more bums than the Police Department. She can drink liquor like water. And she's got some of the toughest women friends I ever laid eyes on."

The paths of the flamboyant, strikingly comely brunette and the tall and handsome George seemed almost destined to converge. It happened one night in a Fort Worth speakeasy where George was meeting with his new rum-running partner who happened, until that moment, to be Kathryn's beau. This encounter led to a torrid whirlwind fling for Kathryn and George and the forming of a conspiratorial liaison, one that was inter-rupted only by George's spell in Leavenworth. When he got out, in Sep-tember 1930, the two were married forthwith by a Methodist minister in Minneapolis. From that point on, the stories of these partners in crime conflict in some instances, even to their roles in the Urschel case. The gen-erally accepted version—even reported in a sympathetic book Kelly's older son would privately publish years later after a number of visits with his father in prison and lengthy correspondence with Kathryn—is that she was without question the dominating impetus, the plotter, the insti-gator, the brains behind the entire Urschel scheme, as Hoover also always asserted. She would vehemently deny to her grave, however, having had anything more than an unwanted, forced, but entirely passive role in the crime, notwithstanding a mass of convincing factual and circumstantial evidence to the contrary.

Within just the first months of their marriage, the free-spending Kathryn became increasingly dissatisfied with the paltry proceeds George was earning from his hits on small-town banks. Many of the banks were run-ning short of cash themselves (those that survived the Depression, that is; 11,000 of the 25,000 banks in the country in 1928 had failed by 1933). She wanted bigger and better things—fancier roadsters, more stylish jew-elry and clothes, furs, picture shows, dancing, constant nightlife. Study-ing and absorbing the news headlines, she noted that the law hadn't been able to solve the Lindbergh case and that substantial ransoms were being collected for these new "citizen" kidnappings. This new direction in crime was a great get-rich-quick opportunity. But the first amateurish plunge George made into these unfamiliar deep waters (whether with or without Kathryn's aid is unknown) should have sent a strong message to stay with bank stickups.

Hooking up with a small-time car thief, bank robber, and bail jumper by the name of Edward ("Burlington Eddie") Doll, the newly tough-talking ex-con George zeroed in on the son of a bank president in South Bend, Indiana. As unsuspecting victim-to-be Howard Woolverton and his wife were motoring around the town one January evening in 1932, they were overtaken and captured by the gun-wielding Kelly and Doll. Keeping her husband, they let Mrs. Woolverton loose with a note demanding $50,000 ransom for his release. Impatiently awaiting this new pile of easy money, they kept Woolverton imprisoned in a basement for three days until he was finally able to convince them that no funds were available for ransom because his family had suffered severe economic loss in the Depression. Confronted with what amounted to a figurative dry hole, Kelly and Doll reluctantly let him go—but only after extracting his written "promise" to pay the $50,000 in full when he could, or else. The gullible pair managed to avoid being arrested for this escapade by quickly fleeing the state. Naturally, Woolverton and his family ignored this unusual and ridiculous IOU. But they also nervously reported receiving periodic threatening letters and menacing telephone calls demanding payment "or be prepared to suffer dire reprisals" of an unspecified nature.

Kathryn, who appeared outwardly unfazed by that misadventure, began devising a more grandiose plan. As a start, she invested $250 at a pawnshop in February 1933 for what was to become George's trademark submachine gun, even if he would never by any account fire it in anger. She demanded that her reluctant husband delay starting his customary evening drinking bouts and instead target practice for hours on end at the Paradise ranch, her mother and stepfather's property. He did so, and in fact supposedly became a rather proficient marksman with his new "chopper" (or "Chicago typewriter," as the big city mobsters called it).

During her late-evening social jaunts in and around Forth Worth, Kathryn spread the story that George—who she'd taken to admiringly calling "The Big Guy"—was so expert with his new weapon that he could pop walnuts off the top of a fence at thirty feet. There is no question that Kathryn did purchase the weapon from a Fort Worth pawnshop. But although George's purported shooting skills with it were repeated and embellished as fact over the years, this claim should probably be viewed with more than a little skepticism. First, George wasn't at all keen on firearms and, second, pecan orchards were and are dominant in the area. Whatever the case, the vivacious Kathryn took to carrying handfuls of spent machine gun cartridge cases when she cruised her various social haunts, passing the brass shells out as souvenirs with the pronouncement that the fearsome "Machine Gun" Kelly had fired the bullets in the course of pulling off one of his latest jobs. Thus it was Kathryn who created and promoted the name by which George would forever be known. The FBI itself cleverly played up the frightening nickname while seeking Kelly after the kidnapping, subliminally painting Hoover and his agents as heroic and courageous in their pursuit of this dangerous, heavily armed, trigger-happy, sharpshooting public enemy. The FBI's wanted poster would warn ominously that Kelly was an "expert machine gunner," while at the same time some of the bureau's press releases labeled him "a desperate character."

Slow learners, obviously, after the Indiana debacle, the Kellys began lurching toward what would be their second kidnap failure. This one never got off the ground because Kathryn actually talked about the plot to a couple of Fort Worth police detectives she hopefully but erroneously believed were on the take. Her brainstorm this time was to snatch the son of a noted Texas oilman. Probably having imbibed too much, as she and George were known to do with some regularity, Kathryn sidled up to the plainclothesmen at a party and not too subtly hinted they could share in the payoff if they would see that she and George weren't apprehended. Hastily, they begged off with the excuse it was too close to home and thus too risky for them. Well then, would they agree instead to stand at the ready to seek Kelly's extradition to Texas if he should happen to be picked up in another state? Leaving her to believe they might possibly go along with that idea, the detectives couldn't get away from the party fast enough and immediately filed a report on the conversation. The intended kidnap victim was placed under deliberately overt police protection so the befogged and puzzled Kellys had to abandon the whole plan—but not the general idea of a big-time kidnapping.

Poring over newspapers later for other possibilities, Kathryn must have experienced a quickened pulse when she spied the information about Tom Slick's huge estate. And the fact that one wealthy trustee of the millions and Slick's widow, herself another of the "council of three," were now husband and wife and living not so far away in Oklahoma.

❖   ❖   ❖

Then, two days after Urschel's abduction, Kathryn blundered into the next of the Kelly errors. Fueling the Fort Worth detectives' suspicions even further by insinuating herself into the picture, she inadvisably sought them out again to inquire rather awkwardly what they knew about any leads in the case. She claimed she'd been "back east" visiting friends in St. Louis and was inquiring merely out of idle curiosity. One of the detectives became suspicious, though, when he spotted on her car seat an Oklahoma newspaper headlining the kidnapping. And he noted that her car's tire sidewalls were caked with the red soil common to the farmland in that area. He passed on his observations and suspicions to his superiors, who in turn quickly relayed them to the FBI.

Coincidentally, because Kathryn had made the clumsy, alcoholic attempt to suborn the pair of Fort Worth detectives into helping with the Kellys' earlier botched kidnap scheme, alert officers did a little discreet checking. They learned she was the wife of the convicted felon Kelly and that her mother, the aforementioned Ora, had not long ago married the owner of a small spread in Wise County.

Wise County, a sprawling expanse of 922 square miles some forty miles south of the Oklahoma border, was inhabited by a sparse population of only 20,000. Using binoculars and the map Agent Jones had drawn from information Urschel supplied, federal officers crisscrossed the terrain numerous times in a low-flying open biplane donated by friendly competitor Phillips Petroleum Company of Bartlesville, Oklahoma. They also retraced the American Airways' routes until they got a good picture of the lay of the land that would assist the ground reconnaissance effort other agents were carrying out.

One agent visited several Paradise farmers under the guise of being a helpful banker offering to refinance mortgages before casually working his way to Armon's place. Jones's line drawing map in the agent's pocket was accurate almost to the inch. It might as well have been a photograph taken from the air. Feigning thirst, but actually anxious to start checking out other details from Urschel's memory, the agent took note, with growing excitement, of the squeaky pulley. He picked up the cup with no handle and sampled the water, found it tasted heavily of minerals. He observed the corn patch, the four cows, the bull, the mule, the barn,

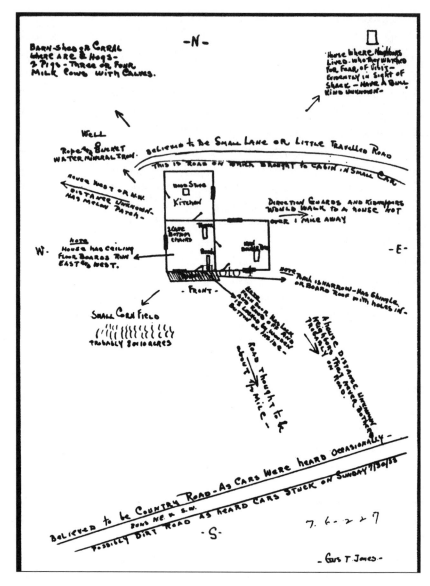

FBI Agent Gus T. Jones constructed this accurate map of Armon Shannon's house and grounds from Urschel's description.

everything precisely as Urschel had spelled out. The L-shaped shack consisted of the three small rooms, shingles were missing from the porch roof, the high chair and bedstead were there. Again, everything tallied, as did Urschel's descriptions of all the Shannons themselves, their voices, their manner of speech, Armon's unusual nickname. Plus, as the agent recorded in his written report, "It was ascertained by cautious inquiry that a sixteen-year-old girl prostitute lived nearby."

The agent couldn't disengage himself and race to the nearest telephone pay station fast enough to call in to confirm that the hideout had been found. Back in Washington, Hoover happily barked the order to move in on the ranch as soon as possible, secretly but with all necessary force. But to take the fugitives alive if at all possible. He didn't want the kidnappers or anyone else who might be loitering in the area to become overly alarmed about those unusual biplane flights and that citified stranger showing up out of the blue. He wanted them alive to put on trial. Now Hoover finally had the gang in the crosshairs. Or so he confidently (but erroneously) thought.

9

The Roundup

❖　❖　❖　❖　❖　❖　❖　❖　❖　❖　❖　❖　❖　❖　❖

A unique multijurisdictional squad of federal and Texas lawmen consti-
tuted the heavily armed and wary posse that packed into several automobiles in Fort Worth to head for Paradise. There were thirteen men in
all. The fearless and angry Urschel himself, adamantly brushing aside
pleas to stay to the rear for his safety's sake, was in the first vehicle, armed
with a double-barreled shotgun he well knew how to use.

"I wish they'd tell us what to expect when we get to wherever we're
going," a young Fort Worth burglary detective by the name of Charles
Carmichael muttered to nobody in particular. The civilian in the front seat,
the man cradling the shotgun, replied matter-of-factly, "I thought you
knew. I'm Charles Urschel, the man Machine Gun Kelly kidnapped. We're
going after him." Grimly quiet after that, the group drove slowly to within
a mile of the Paradise ranch. It was early Saturday, the twelfth of August,
and still dark as they smoked and stomped around impatiently. As dawn
broke, they separated into four groups and quietly moved in on the big
house from every direction. First off they stumbled upon a huge unsus-
pected bonus prize: Harvey Bailey, the nation's premier bank robber, the
"King of the Heist Men," as he was often called. He'd been a most-wanted
fugitive ever since he and eleven fellow inmates, using an American
Legion exhibition baseball game as a diversion, had taken the warden and
several guards hostage during a Memorial Day escape from the Kansas
State Penitentiary in Lansing, where he was serving ten to fifty years for
his most recent armed bank job. The unlucky Bailey was in no way involved with the Urschel crime; he had slipped away to the Shannon place

simply to lie low for a spell while recuperating from an ugly, slow-to-heal calf wound he'd suffered in an exchange of gunfire after the breakout. He did know Kelly, however, having borrowed his famous machine gun to use as a threat in at least one of his bank holdups.

Unfortunately for Bailey, at the time of the Paradise raid he was carrying a bankroll amounting to $1,211, including $680 in Urschel ransom bills that Kelly and his partner had solicitously given him to pay for a doctor. But he was in no shape physically to follow their advice and flee the ranch before the law got to looking around for the Urschel kidnappers. The posse literally almost stumbled across Bailey, sleeping on a cot outside the house, an arsenal of loaded weapons within arm's length and a pistol under his pillow. After they woke him with a shotgun at his nose—"Move an inch, and you're a dead man"—he calmly surveyed the heavy array of firepower leveled at him. Very deliberately he raised his hands, saying simply, "I know when I'm beat." Bailey was a truly major catch. In addition to twenty-nine known bank robberies on his record, eleven years earlier he'd been charged with pulling off a spectacular holdup of a government armored truck parked in front of the U.S. Mint in Denver. His arrest in Paradise was a definite coup, one Hoover would claim as part of the roundup of Urschel perpetrators. Disappointingly, though, the Kellys were nowhere to be seen.

Urschel had never set eyes on Bailey until the morning of the raid and thus said nothing then or ever to link him to the kidnapping in any way. But Urschel did positively identify the panicky Boss and Ora Shannon, who were also placed under arrest. Bailey and Boss were handcuffed to a convenient fence post. Ora, meanwhile, was described by one of the raiding party as "jumping about, running around from room to room. Finally I told her, 'You have got to sit down here and stay put or somebody is liable to shoot you.' Finally she sat down."

Although no reporters accompanied the party on its highly secret raid, a newspaper account the next day said Urschel "courteously lifted his hat and thanked Mrs. Shannon for the fried chicken she prepared for him while ransom negotiations were going on." (Urschel said later that while in Paradise it had been his only decent meal: fried chicken, mashed potatoes with gravy, biscuits, a lettuce and tomato salad, and a piece of cake, "a very nice meal.")

During the raid, meanwhile, Ora and Boss were vehemently denying any knowledge of the crime or of any sort of forced confinement at the ranch, Urschel or whomever. This stranger, this accuser, whoever he might be, was mistaken, just plain dead wrong, in fingering them, in alleging that they had anything to do with a kidnapping. They stuck to this story despite the fact that the "stranger" was methodically and accurately identifying for the officers all the landmarks and animals he had noted while being held. And the agents overheard him tell the Shannons, "I'm sorry, but that well water of yours was the worst mineral water I've ever tasted."

Leaving a couple of guards to watch over the three prisoners, the rest of the posse and Urschel moved on to Armon's place, less than a mile distant, hoping they wouldn't meet any resistance from Armon or the Kellys. They needn't have worried. The surprise continued to be complete, Armon and his wife surrendering without a whimper. Still no Kellys, though. But after identifying Armon, aka "Potatoes," Urschel marched purposefully toward the shack, followed by the officers.

In its next edition, five days later, under a unique eight-column, three-line banner headline breathlessly proclaiming

FEDERAL OFFICERS RAID SHANNON HOME
Nation-Wide Hunt for Gangland Chief Ends in Wise
Kidnappers Hide Millionaire Victim Near Paradise

the weekly *Wise County Messenger* stated, as part of the front-page coverage of its biggest and most sensational local story ever, "Urschel entered the shack. Smiling and obviously pleased, he examined the roughly papered walls. He went to the pump and examined the dipper. The handle was broken off exactly as he had told federal investigators. He counted the livestock in the barnyard. There were exactly the right number of cows, hogs, and chickens. About twenty-five other details were checked up, and Urschel said, 'I am positive this is where I was held captive. I can't be mistaken.' " He found the chain that had been attached to his handcuffs. Every item on his checklist was verified. He pointed out the scratches he'd made on the furniture, and the FBI lifted some of the mass of latent fingerprints he had planted—his "signature"—completing all the evidence needed. A two-column subhead told the second part of the story:

Harvey Bailey, Bad Desperado
Is Captured As He Sleeps on Cot

Unlike the elder Shannons, Armon was ready to tell what little he knew, even though Ora hollered at him, "Keep your mouth shut. Don't tell them a damned thing." Armon went on, however, to relate with little urging that a pair of armed kidnappers had forced him to keep their prisoner in his dwelling as well as to help his father stand watch over him. When Urschel had first been brought to the shack, Armon told the officers, "His eyes were covered with white tape. I took a mattress and put it down on the floor and they told the man he could sleep there." *They? They knew there was at least a second kidnapper, but who was he?* the officers wondered silently. In a matter of minutes, Armon divulged what was to be the second big, unexpected, welcome jackpot of the morning: "They brought Mr. Urschel here. I know him. What he says is true. They made me do it, Kelly and Bates."

So the law now knew the identity of another of the kidnappers, someone named Bates. The third and only other member, as it turned out, of what had been wrongly assumed all along to be a sizable kidnap "gang," the Kellys' lone accomplice was a petty criminal by the name of Albert Bates. Bureau publicists quickly labeled him "a hardened criminal with a lengthy criminal record." Other than that, little is known about Bates the person (aka J. B. King or George L. Davis). Like Kelly a product of the times, Bates was an otherwise uninteresting and rather nondescript crook who had served time dating back to 1916 for such offenses as petty theft, burglary, bank robbery, safecracking, and carrying a concealed weapon. His record also showed at least two successful prison breaks, one in Utah and another in Colorado, plus a drunk driving charge. He was also suspected of, but never charged with, murdering a pair of his burglary accomplices. Thirty-nine at the time of the Urschel crime, he had an intriguing footnote to his earlier rap sheet: "Silver plate in wounded shoulder." He and Kelly were a pair that one observer would later describe as "noted gunmen and general malefactors."

Armed with this important new piece of information, plus the unexpected capture of Bailey—described by a contemporary *Daily Oklahoman* reporter as a "brainy, cool, ruthless killer when his path is blocked . . . known as the Southwest's most dangerous gunman"—the roundup that included the Shannons, some of their kin, and Kelly's famous submachine gun could be termed a partial success. Yet it was far from a satisfying one. An intensive three-hour search of the buildings and grounds by Urschel and the lawmen failed to turn up any of the ransom bills other than the few Bailey had in his pockets. And also, of course, neither of the two principal suspects in the nationwide hunt, George and Kathryn Kelly, nor the newly identified third and final member of the gang, Albert Bates, were on the premises. Plus, aside from a closet full of elegant women's clothes—no doubt Kathryn's—no other useful clues about the kidnappers were to be found.

A small cadre of officers remained behind on stakeout, hoping to nab Kelly and any other members of the gang if they returned. To help pass the time and do something useful, one of the agents shed his coat and tie, donned a pair of Boss Shannon's bib overalls, and milked the cows. But a three-day wait by the officers turned out to be in vain. They didn't know it, of course, but none of the three fugitives would ever set foot on the Shannon place, nor in Wise County, again.

Compared with the sensational day-by-day national press coverage of the case, how the small-town *Messenger* played its local big story in later editions offers an interesting look into weekly journalism of the day. Just a week after the historic triple banner headline, there was but a two-paragraph follow-up to report that the fugitives were still missing. The week after that, the main story on page one was about a local Presbyterian church encampment. Down near the bottom of the page was this report, with no headline, quoted here in its entirety: "Machine Kelly [sic] has been reported here and there in the county during the week. One report had Mr. and Mrs. Kelly came [sic] to Decatur [the county seat] and dined at one of our cafes."

10

The Trail and Trial (No. 1)

❖ ❖ ❖ ❖ ❖ ❖ ❖ ❖ ❖ ❖ ❖ ❖ ❖ ❖ ❖

Six hundred miles away, Albert Bates saw his freedom come to an igno-minious end the same afternoon as the day of the raid in Paradise. Apprehended by local police while sitting in a classy late-model Buick Victoria coupé outside a rooming house where he'd holed up in Denver, he was picked up for questioning totally unrelated to the kidnapping: occupying an apparently stolen automobile.

But with thirty-three of the Urschel ransom twenties included in his bankroll, which at $775 was suspiciously large for the times, Bates knew he'd better do something and fast. He confessed, a little too eagerly in the opinion of the suspicious Denver police, to a bank job in Texas for which he said he would be willing to go back and stand trial. It was an unsuccessful attempt at the familiar "vanishing trick"—trying to escape from a severe charge by admitting to a lesser earlier crime in another jurisdiction in hopes of being extradited back. Meanwhile, thanks to the cooperation of a prison trusty ("Tell her her husband's in jail; she'll pay you," Bates was said to have told him), the Urschel kidnapper managed to smuggle a frantic note to his purported wife. Whiling away her time while guarding some of the money, she read the note: "There is nothing you can do for me. Move."

This "Mrs. Bates," actually Clara Feldman by name, urgently dispatched a Western Union wire to one of Kathryn's two supposed detective confed-erates in Fort Worth. Clara pleaded with them to try to extradite Bates back to Texas on any kind of pretense, anything to get him out of Denver quickly. This turned out to be the worst stratagem she could have employed.

The Fort Worth police turned her wire over to the local FBI officer-in-charge, who immediately notified his counterpart in Denver. Agents there sped to the city jail and appropriated Bates as the bureau's own federal prisoner, the clutch of Urschel twenties in his pocket providing damning prima facie evidence of his role in the kidnapping. Bates got out of Denver after all a few days later, but in handcuffs and with five heavily armed federal agents escorting him on a private flight to Oklahoma City.

Waiting at the airport were the Urschels, who without hesitation identified the handcuffed prisoner as one of the pair of sunporch intruders. "That's him, all right," Berenice said. "I'm so glad to see him like that. He didn't have on those gold-rimmed spectacles that night, but he is the one." The newspaper reporter on the scene provided this further account of what happened next:

> Then Mr. Urschel stepped up and greeted Bates: "Hello, Albert." Bates regarded him coolly, then said politely, "I don't believe I know you." Then a strange thing happened. The accused kidnapper and his millionaire victim grinned sheepishly, then both laughed. They both seemed embarrassed. If Bates really was one of the kidnappers, their situations at that moment were exactly reversed. This time the guns were on Bates; when last they met, the guns were on Urschel.

Bates stayed mum about the ransom, not revealing that he'd entrusted the bulk of his share to Clara Feldman. She wisely hadn't waited around to see the result of her telegram to Fort Worth, hastily fleeing Denver and hiding a large part of the loot near Laramie, Wyoming. Only $46,000 of Bates's share of the ransom was ever recovered, most of it by then having found its way to another hiding spot, this one in Oregon, where Feldman led the FBI to it in exchange for parole from the sentence she'd received many months later in an Oklahoma City courtroom for her minor role as a conspirator receiving stolen money.

The day after the Paradise roundup was very nearly Kathryn and George's last day of freedom as well. Two U.S. Customs agents were randomly flagging down vehicles on the Laredo Highway twenty miles south of San Antonio, searching for contraband being smuggled in from Mexico. Blithely unaware they were the subjects of a yet unpublicized nationwide all-points bulletin, George and Kathryn were among those halted, but the agents waved them on through after their car and baggage checked out clean. The Kellys were in the dark because the cooperative press had all acceded to Hoover's request for a two-day national news blackout about the Paradise raid and the arrests of Bates, Bailey, and the Shannon family, all of whom were being held incommunicado. As a newsman explained after the two days, "It was in the hope that Kelly would fall into their trap that federal agents patrolled the roads of the Paradise area Sunday night and prevailed upon Monday morning's newspapers not to publish the facts of Bailey's arrest." The only concern George and Kathryn had came when they had learned of the arrest of several Minneapolis money launderers to whom they had sold some of the ransom bills.

But on Tuesday, August 14, front-page headlines and radio newscasts throughout the country blared details of the arrests of Bates, Bailey, and the others in the Paradise raid. They carried the even more sensational news that the principal gangster wanted for the kidnapping was George ("Machine Gun") Kelly, now the new Public Enemy No. 1 in the press. Hoover dramatically built up the case, stating later, "Thousands of our citizens shivered in fear of a kidnapper whose name had much to do with the terror he engendered: he was called Machine-Gun Kelly." In a departure from its typical factual, straightforward reporting, the *New York Times* chimed in, "Kelly and his gang of Southwestern desperados are regarded as the most dangerous ever encountered." The writer was presumably repeating a hyped-up FBI description by using the words "gang" and "regarded." The FBI wanted poster, widely circulated throughout the Great Plains, showed the customary front and profile head shots of Kelly, his ten fingerprints and this succinct information:

Age, 35 years
Height, 5 feet, 9 inches
Weight, 177 pounds
Build, medium muscular
Eyes, blue or gray
Hair, dark brown
Complexion, medium ruddy
Expert machine gunner
Remarks: Sometimes wears octagon shaped rimless glasses

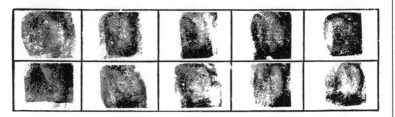

IDENTIFICATION ORDER No.1203
August 14, 1933

DIVISION OF INVESTIGATION
U. S. DEPARTMENT OF JUSTICE
WASHINGTON, D. C.

Fingerprint Classification

23 27 W 0
─────────────
7 W OI 14

WANTED

GEORGE R. KELLY, aliases GEORGE KELLY, R. G. SHANNON.

KIDNAPING

DESCRIPTION

Age, 35 years
Height, 5 feet, 9½ inches
Weight, 177 pounds
Build, medium muscular
Eyes, blue or gray
Hair, dark brown
Complexion, medium ruddy
Expert machine gunner

Remarks: Sometimes wears
octagon shaped rimless
glasses.

Geo. Kelly

CRIMINAL RECORD

As George kelly, No. 1968, received
State Prison, Santa Fe, New Mexico,
March 14, 1927; crime, violation
National Prohibition Act.
As George Kelly, No. 5298, arrested
Police Department, Tulsa, Oklahoma,
July 24, 1927; charge, state vagrancy.
As George Kelly, No. 2332, arrested
Sheriff's Office, Tulsa, Oklahoma,
January 12, 1928; charge, National
Prohibition Act.
As George Kelley, No. 2962,
received United States Penitentiary,
Leavenworth, Kansas, February 11, 1928,
from Tulsa, Oklahoma; crime, Possession
of liquor (Indian Cy); sentence 3 years.

George R. Kelly is wanted for the kidnaping of Charles F. Urschel at Oklahoma City, Oklahoma, on July 22, 1933.

Law enforcement agencies kindly transmit any additional information or criminal record to nearest office, Division of Investigation, U. S. Department of Justice.

If apprehended, please notify the Director, Division of Investigation, U. S. Department of Justice, Washington, D. C., or the Special Agent in Charge of the office of the Division of Investigation listed on the back hereof, which is nearest your city.

(over)   Issued by: J. EDGAR HOOVER, Director.

The FBI's wanted poster for George R. Kelly, "aliases George Kelly, R. G. Shannon."

There was a companion poster, as well, on Kathryn (noted as using the Dolores Whitney alias when arrested in Fort Worth in 1929), but with terribly unflattering, almost unrecognizable photographs:

Age, 28 years (looks older)
Height, 5 feet, 9 inches
Weight, 141 pounds (probably heavier now)
Build, medium
Hair, black
Eyes, brown
Complexion, ruddy
Remarks: Wears expensive jewelery [*sic*]

Surprised and shocked upon learning that they had been identified and were most wanteds, the panicked Kellys began a headlong flight to nowhere that would eventually take them through at least sixteen states—Arkansas, Colorado, Illinois, Indiana, Iowa, Kansas, Kentucky, Minnesota, Missouri, New York, Ohio, Oklahoma, Pennsylvania, Tennessee, Texas, and Wisconsin—even into Mexico. They would cover what the FBI estimated was 20,000 miles.

Kathryn was alternately maudlin and furious to the point of rage upon learning that her mother had been taken into custody and was being held on $50,000 bond. She was also somewhat unnerved to read Urschel's statement: "Everything the federal government can do to put an end to kidnappings in the United States is an imperative necessity." Over the next couple of days, Kathryn managed to submerge her anger and calculatedly worked out a manipulative scheme whereby George would agree if they were caught to take the fall alone and to accept full blame for the crime, in hopes she might get off or at least get a lighter sentence. Besides, while George had been seen and heard and could without doubt be positively identified by several probable witnesses, Kathryn had played no role in the crime visible to Urschel or others. Meanwhile, she read that the government had obtained grand jury indictments and was going to proceed to prosecute the entire Paradise crowd plus Bates, assorted minor players, and even the uninvolved Bailey in one big showcase trial.

Hoover would later pen in *Persons in Hiding* his version of what occurred next. "In a frenzied effort to abort conviction [of Boss and Ora Shannon], Kathryn, through her dominance, caused Machine-gun Kelly to affix his fingerprints to letters threatening the judge, the witnesses, and all others who might take part in the conviction, even to an Assistant Attorney General of the United States. While the attack was made from this angle, Kathryn indited soulful missives to the Urschel family, proclaiming the innocence of herself and her family, and blaming everything on that terrible person who had led her astray, George (Machine-gun) Kelly."

In one of those letters, the first of several extraordinary communiqués from one or other of the Kellys, Kathryn informed the special assistant whom the attorney general had sent from Washington to Oklahoma to help prosecute the case:

The entire Urschel family and friends and all of you will be exterminated soon. There is no way I can prevent it. I will gladly put George

Kelly on the spot for you if you will save my mother, who is innocent of any wrongdoing. If you do not comply with this request, there is no way in which I can prevent the most awful tragedy. If you refuse my offer I shall commit some minor offense and be placed in jail so that you will know that I have no connection with the terrible slaughter that will take place in Oklahoma City within the next few days.

As part of her flawed strategy to avoid capture, Kathryn thought it prudent that she and George move about separately for a few days to throw off the searchers, who presumably would be looking for a couple. So, motoring along by herself one afternoon in a '31 Model A Ford pickup, she had an inspiration when she happened upon a couple of hitchhiking out-of-work Depression refugees and their twelve-year-old daughter. Ironically, it was Labor Day, and the destitute Luther and Flossie Marie Arnold and daughter Geraldine, who had the grand sum of six dollars among them, gratefully accepted a ride plus "Mrs. Montgomery's" kind offer of food, some new clothes, and lodging that night at an auto tourist camp. With these expenditures as a buy-off, Kathryn felt she could now risk a big gamble and drop the Mrs. Montgomery ruse. Revealing that she and her absent husband were wanted for the kidnapping, she offered to pay Arnold for a little unusual errand. His mission: make contact with an attorney of her acquaintance to ascertain the possibility of "trading" George and his share of the ransom in exchange for dropping the counts against herself and her mother.

Desperate for money ("I would do anything to feed three hungry people," he said in his defense), Arnold accepted her fifty dollars. He traveled to Fort Worth by Trailways bus and made the connection, only to report back that the prosecutor wouldn't consider the offer absent a guarantee that Kelly would return the $200,000 in full.

Why didn't the government buy the deal? "We refused it on the ground it was against public morals," the prosecutor said. "The federal government is not bargaining with anybody for the surrender of Kelly on that basis. We take the position that Kelly will be captured and that it is only a matter of time." Next, Arnold was sent on another mission, this time a successful one, to retain the services of an Oklahoma lawyer to defend Kathryn's mother and stepfather.

At this point, trying to catch up with the fugitives became even tougher. The Kellys switched automobiles half a dozen times and disguised themselves to some degree. First George dyed his dark hair red and then a yellowish blond, while Kathryn donned a red wig, and both of them affected uncharacteristic faded, worn clothing. Both separately and together, they hid out briefly in Omaha, Chicago, Minneapolis–St. Paul, Cleveland, Detroit, Indianapolis, Des Moines, San Antonio, St. Louis, Reno, Biloxi, and who knows where else, the law always just a step or two behind as sightings or ransom bills were reported. Commenting on the scope of the manhunt for the Kellys, Attorney General Cummings estimated that the government's "investigation of the Urschel kidnapping case extended over an area of nearly 700,000 square miles." And the government expended far more than $200,000—exceeding the ransom itself—to chase down, bring to trial, and convict the Kellys.

There was no discernible pattern to their zigzag flight, leading one government agent to complain, "If there was any logic in these movements we would have caught the Kellys several days ago." Generally, they registered at tourist camps or small out-of-the-way hotels posing as "Mr. and Mrs. Robert Shannon." They used the same names to purchase the automobiles along the way. More and more, though, George was suffering a severe case of nerves. Believing someone was shadowing him, he would make the two of them flee only an hour or two after checking in.

With the reluctant acquiescence of the child's parents, Kathryn "borrowed" Geraldine, ostensibly for a short pleasure trip, but in actuality to serve for two weeks as cover, a decoy, for her and George on the theory that the targets of the dragnet were two adults, not a domestic-looking couple with a child. However, they made yet another strategic mistake by letting Geraldine overhear some of their conversations.

The three of them came to ground, at last, in George's old hometown of Memphis. There they recruited a new player, George's former brother-in-law, to attempt to retrieve the bulk of the ransom. George had buried it at the farm of some other kin near Coleman, Texas, out in the desolate prairie a hundred and forty miles southwest of Fort Worth. This naive dupe—a twenty-five-year-old lawyer who should have known better and who would be disbarred and serve time for complicity for such a fool's errand—took Geraldine along to help locate the money and then to return her home to her parents in Oklahoma.

The farm's owner, an uncle of Kathryn's who (correctly) had what he later said was a "suspicion" he was under FBI surveillance like other nearby relatives, refused to disclose the burial site to these two strangers.

So George's frustrated brother-in-law took Geraldine to the nearest station and put her on a train for Oklahoma City to join her parents. He dispatched two telegrams, the first one to Kelly:

> Had several tough breaks. Ran into several rain storms. Caused brake trouble. Deal fell through. Tried to get later appointment. But prospect was afraid. Impossible to change his mind. Didn't want to bring home a sad tale. Can go on if advisable. Wire instructions here.

The second wire went to Geraldine's parents, informing them when her train was scheduled to arrive. Arnold was in Oklahoma City under "protective custody" because he'd been arrested and jailed briefly on a charge of "bringing women across the state line for an immoral purpose." It seems Arnold had picked up two women and foolishly bragged that he was an important person on the Kellys' payroll. "He was arrested by the city officers," the government's prosecutor would recall. "I knew what he was arrested for, and if I desired to employ the means of talking to him, although he was technically guilty, I didn't have to prosecute him if I didn't choose to." Translation: the Arnolds would be cooperative witnesses for the government.

It was September 25 when the girl stepped off the train at the Oklahoma City depot into the arms of her relieved father—and those of the FBI. This reuniting would lead to the big break, the one Hoover had been waiting for. As his luck would have it, the FBI director got a great deal more than he expected or could have hoped. With recall nearly as remarkable as Urschel's, Geraldine guilelessly related details about the Kellys' flight, their conversations, the contacts they'd made, the ransom burial site. But far more important, she provided a solid lead as to where they were probably hiding in Memphis. Hoover eagerly welcomed this unexpected information, which would lead to finally dropping the net on the embarrassingly elusive fugitives.

Unrelated to the manhunt for the Kellys, but almost to the hour that Kathryn was enticing the Arnolds into her pickup on Labor Day, Harvey Bailey again made sensational headlines of his own. He broke out of the supposedly escape-proof Dallas County skyscraper jail, sawing his way through the bars of his tenth-floor cell, overpowering a guard, and fleeing in a stolen car with the guard in tow as a hostage. In a matter of only four hours, however, he was recaptured after a police chase when one of the wheels of his car collapsed as he careened into a curb. The chase ended in Ardmore, Oklahoma, a mere ninety miles from the jail. His vehicle hopelessly out of commission, Bailey meekly surrendered without a struggle, never to make an escape attempt again. Yet while his brief freedom from jail had no effect on the Kelly manhunt, it added to fears that Bailey might have confederates on the outside ready to move against Urschel and his family or to try to free Kelly. The police reacted by stepping up their protection. Tom Slick Jr. reportedly began carrying a gun.

This apprehensiveness resulted, as well, in intensified guarding of Bailey and Bates when they were later confined in the Oklahoma City jail, in adjoining second-floor cells, awaiting trial. An officer with a shotgun was stationed directly across from their cells around the clock, a large pushbutton within arm's reach to summon help instantly if needed. The two prisoners were handcuffed, each with a steel bar between his hands preventing a touching of hands, and with shackles chained to the floor. Their cells were meticulously searched daily. Outside the building, from across the street, three machine guns were trained on the jail door, and huge lights could flood the entire area at any time.

The lawyer Arnold had found and retained on Kathryn's behalf again presented Kelly's offer to surrender if charges against Kathryn and Ora Shannon were dropped or reduced. Still no deal. But Joseph B. Keenan, newly appointed as the special assistant in charge of the Criminal Division of the Department of Justice in Washington, wrote to the Oklahoma U.S. district attorney, Herbert K. Hyde, asking, "If we could obtain the return of Kelly and the ransom money without any commitment as to what shall happen to Kelly, I am hoping that Judge Vaught could see his way clear to being very lenient to Mrs. Shannon and Mrs. Kelly, even to the point of absolute release if Kelly and the money could be obtained and if we had a free hand to deal with Kelly, Bates and Bailey as the facts justify."

This tentative suggestion, apparently made without conferring with either the attorney general or Hoover, came to naught. There would be no bargaining, no negotiating. In the meantime, Bailey's attorney pleaded strenuously to have his client's trial moved to another city, preferably out of the state. "The newspapers have published inflammatory, untrue, false, highly colored, and exaggerated articles, making it impossible for Mr. Bailey to get a fair trial in the western federal district of Oklahoma."

This request was received without favor by the judge, who was in no mood to tolerate any delays in seeing that justice would be served. "I was in another state [New Mexico, on vacation] in August. There was just about as much in the newspapers there as anywhere else. It is a matter of such great public interest and importance that the press of the United States has carried a great deal on the case. Newspapers have speculated on the case and the witnesses. I can see no advantage to the defendant in a change of venue."

From this point on, the drama would undergo a marked shift in focus, from the hunt for the gangsters to their prosecution. The numerous perpetrators, whether directly or only peripherally involved, were the first criminal defendants indicted and tried under the so-called Lindbergh Kidnapping Law.

The largest, most historic criminal trial of any kind in Southwest history for decades to come got under way the morning of September 18 in the courtroom of U.S. District Judge Edgar S. Vaught. Well respected, affable, a noted fisherman, a popular and humorous after-dinner speaker, and a Methodist Sunday school teacher and substitute pastor in private life, Vaught was a veteran jurist who ran a tight courtroom with a stern demeanor. The two Kellys were the only truants missing from the defense table that day. Nevertheless, tension was high. Everyone else was in place except Bates and Bailey.

A reporter on the scene described what happened next:

Everyone is awaiting them. Eyes are trained on the door. The cameras swing toward the doors at the right. The doors open. There stand Harvey Bailey and Albert Bates. They are handcuffed together. Behind them are a half-dozen clean-cut young men. They are graduate law students. They are something else—Department of Justice agents. Under their coats are guns.

Bailey creates a sensation. Heretofore he has been seen only in disreputable overalls or dirty underwear. Now he has suddenly blossomed forth as a fashion plate. He wears a double-breasted gray suit. A black tie is loosely knotted at his soft collar. His shock of black hair, beginning to gray, is newly cut. Most radical change of all, he is very clean. Bates doesn't wear a coat. The bailiff doesn't reprimand him. But it's against the rules.

On the following day, with the jury having been selected (under terms of a new federal law providing for two alternates so there would be no mistrial should a regular juror become ill or die), came a terrifying hand-written letter, airmailed from Chicago (and verified later as bearing George's smeared, inky prints). With Urschel standing by, officers carefully slit the envelope open and read what was inside:

Ignorant Charles:

Just a few lines to let you know that I am getting my plans made to destroy your so-called mansion, and you and your family immediately after this trial. And you fellow, I guess you've begun to realize your serious mistake. Are you ignorant enough to think the Government can guard you forever. I gave you credit for more sense than that, and figured you thought too much of your family to jeopardize them as you have, but if you don't look out for them, why should we. I dislike hurting the innocent, but I told you exactly what would happen and you can bet $200,000 more everything I said will be true. You are living on borrowed time now. You know that the Shannon family are victims of circumstances the same as you was. You don't seem to mind prosecuting the innocent, neither will I have any conscious qualms over brutally murdering your family. The Shannons have put the heat on, but I don't desire to see them prosecuted as they are innocent and I have a much better method of settling with them. As far as the guilty being punished you would probably have lived the rest of your life in peace had you tried only the guilty, but if the Shannons are convicted look out, and God help you for he is the only one that will be able to do you any good. In the event of my arrest I've already formed an outfit to take care of and destroy you and yours the same as if I was there. I am spending your money to have you and your family killed—nice eh? You are bucking people who have cash—planes, bombs and unlimited connections both here and abroad. I have friends in Oklahoma City that know every move and every plan you make, and you are still too dumb to figure out the finger man there.

If my brain was no larger than yours, the Government would have had me long ago, as it is I am drinking good beer and will yet see you and your family like I should have left you at first—stone dead.

I don't worry about Bates and Bailey. They will be out for the ceremonies—your slaughter.

Now I say it is up to you; if the Shannons are convicted, you can get another rich wife in hell, because that will be the only place you can use one. Adios, smart one.

Your worst enemy,

Geo. R. Kelly

I will put my fingerprints below so you can't say some crank wrote this.

Give Keenan my regards and tell him maybe he would like to meet the owner of the above.

See you in hell.

An "outfit"? An assassin or gang of assassins in or near Oklahoma City with the goal of decimating Urschel and his family? With "unlimited connections"? With planes? Bombs? Considering Kelly's rap sheet and the various underworld characters with whom he'd been imprisoned or carried out jobs, these threats had to be taken seriously, so security was reinforced even more. Urschel and his family responded quickly with a terse, no-nonsense public statement:

> We are eager for this letter to be published so the people of the United States will know it is no fabrication from the air and will know the sort of people we have defied and are opposed to. We still have faith in the ultimate success of the federal government in its struggle with crime, and are gambling the safety of every member of our group on that success. We have thrown our lot with Law and the Government and are in this fight to the finish. The Urschel family does not waste one moment in giving gangland its answer.

Emphasizing his point, Urschel firmly planted himself prominently in a front row of the courtroom on the first day of jury selection. One light moment occurred with the dismissal of an undertaker from the panel when Judge Vaught dryly commented, "We're not ready for that yet." Sitting in the same chair throughout the trial, within feet of the defendants, Urschel conferred frequently with the government prosecution team, Kirkpatrick, and family members.

An angry Special Assistant Keenan also took note of the Kelly letter. "We appreciate fully the patriotic response of Mr. Urschel in casting aside personal considerations. It is encouraging to the government in its drive to wipe out gangster depredations. The federal government will respond by giving Mr. Urschel and his family full protection. Neither Mr. Urschel nor anyone else will be left to further attacks of the underworld."

The judge and the prosecuting attorney were also recipients of threatening diatribes from one or other of the Kellys. Playing her own high-stakes defensive game, Kathryn mailed Urschel a note proclaiming her own innocence and that of Boss and Ora: "The entire blame for this horrible mess is squarely on the shoulders of Machine Gun Kelly." Hyde, the Oklahoma trial attorney, received an alarming unsigned letter: "You will be destroyed. The Shannons and Kathryn Kelly must be freed. It will save you and others a lot of trouble if you heed this warning. You do not realize whom you are bucking. We intend to destroy you along with others if you convict these people."

Next, Kelly fired off a vituperative, rambling handwritten letter (again airmailed and postmarked from Chicago and addressed "For Editor") to the *Daily Oklahoman,* which reproduced it in its entirety on page one on September 20:

Dear Sirs—
You will please publish the enclosed in your paper as I want the Shannons to be sure to read it. Yours truly, G. Kelly.

Gentlemen:
I desire the public to know that the Shannon family are innocent victims in the Charles F. Urschel case the same as Urschel was.

I understand that they are now government witnesses also defendants, and I don't want them convicted, for I desire to settle with them in my own way and with no assistance from the government.

Mr. Urschel and the government prosecution know that the Shannons had no part or no intentions of aiding in the matter and were forced to do so the same as Urschel was forced to leave his home.

Why didn't Urschel call the law to Norman when he was released, instead of riding a cab peacefully into the city and waiting a given time to call them? Fear, gentlemen, fear, the same fear that dominated the Shannons.

I hate and despise the government for their crooked dealings and do not wish them to convict people as innocent of that crime and guilty of one thing—talking to me. I can take care of my end and will the way I want to. You might state for Mr. Keenan's benefit that he has never come anywhere near catching me, although I have even been in Oklahoma City four nights and up town each day.

We will see how the trial progresses and can adjust our end accordingly. I am putting my prints on this so you will know it is genuine.

Yours truly,

Geo. R. Kelly

With his much-admired courage and remarkable memory now publicly on display from the witness stand, Charles Urschel was the undisputed star of the proceedings against Bates and the three Shannons. Seven forlorn minor characters, unknown to Urschel, were in the dock as well, apprehended trying to pass the ransom money they'd bought. As for them, District Attorney Hyde had stated, "If investigations disclose that anyone consciously concealed a portion of the ransom money they are guilty of a part in this conspiracy . . . and would be prosecuted." Bailey, who had played no part whatsoever in any aspect of the kidnapping, rounded out the group of twelve defendants. To the government's way of thinking, the more conspirators who could be sent away the better, no matter how tenuous their connection to the kidnapping. Besides, Bailey had indeed had a wad of the ransom bills in his pockets when he was captured; according to Hyde, that well qualified him as "part of the conspiracy."

Security in and around the courthouse was airtight in light of the mailed threats, particularly Kathryn's prediction of a "terrible slaughter" and the dangerous underworld contacts Kelly, Bates, and Bailey were assumed to have. Hanging over everything was the question haunting everyone: where were the Kellys and what were they up to?

"We can expect anything. Gangland is desperate," Hyde said, while Justice Department Special Assistant Keenan sneered at Kelly as little more than a "brutal, boasting moral derelict, just another rat who has had a lot of luck."

The courthouse and the area for blocks around resembled a war zone; every available officer was on duty, openly flaunting submachine guns, sawed-off shotguns, and revolvers. All elevators were blocked off two levels below the ninth-floor courtroom so everyone—men (including those holding press credentials), after being thoroughly patted down, and women when the contents of their pocketbooks had been inspected—had to walk up two flights of stairs past a phalanx of more heavily armed deputies. Admittance to the courtroom itself was by pass only, and it had to be signed personally by the U.S. marshal. It was before air conditioning, but in those more formal times, coat and tie were de rigueur despite the ninety-degree heat; in fact, men would have considered anything else improper and socially incorrect in a court of law. An exception was made for the jurors, though, most of whom happily removed their coats.

A sizable number of the spectators making up the audience—which included standees, another apparent first for a federal trial—were women from the city's upper level of society. Many brought lunch so they wouldn't risk losing their places by leaving. What was everyone wearing? It might have been a fashion show, according to writers on hand. One day Berenice Urschel wore a black dress, "crepe, with long sleeves and trimmed with galyak at the cuffs and neckline." Her sister, Ramona Seeligson from North Carolina, had on a "frock of satin, fashioned with full elbow-length sleeves, with white collar and cuffs." Defendant Ora Shannon showed up the first day "neatly dressed in a blue serge suit and white straw sailor." Everyone was sweltering, though. "An important accessory to almost every frock was a newspaper, plus palm leaf fan or other article that might be moved to stir the surrounding air."

First, to set the stage, Berenice and the Jarretts testified briefly about the interrupted bridge game. In a moment of light relief, Berenice drew laughter throughout the room and even from the judge and Bates himself when she pointed out the abductor. "There's one of the men who came in our house, and he certainly wasn't invited."

Now it was Charles Urschel's turn. Seemingly oblivious to the oppressive temperature, the "Ignorant Charles" letter, and the other personal threats, Urschel (in his customary dark business suit) remained remarkably cool and self-composed on the stand. He enhanced his reputation as a "walking, talking memory machine," as author Myron J. Quimby aptly described him in *The Devil's Emissaries*. With no hesitation, Urschel left the witness chair and strode over to within two feet of Bates. Pointing directly at the unflinching defendant, he condemned Bates as one of the two armed invaders of his sunporch. He later positively identified the Shannons:

"Were you guarded all the time?" the prosecutor asked. "Can you point him out?"

"Yes, sir. The young man with the light blue tie and purple suit." This time Urschel pointed out Armon.

Later, another question to the witness: "After Friday, who guarded you?"

"Boss Shannon."

"What did he say about Mr. Bates and Mr. Kelly?"

"That they were both very bad men, that they were desperate, and that they were very 'hot' and would never be taken alive. He said they would shoot it out if they met any officers."

Urschel identified for the spellbound jurors and the three hundred or so perspiring spectators Kelly's machine gun ("Government's Exhibit No. 9"), the chain, and the dipper with the broken-off handle. Despite heated cross-examination, he displayed no anger or scorn as he proceeded matter-of-factly through his testimony. The ransom correspondence to his family was entered into the record, as were photographs of Armon's shack, inside and out. And he positively identified George Kelly from a photo ("Government's Exhibit No. 8"): "He is the other man."

"Did Kelly talk about you or your family?"

"He told me he knew all about our family; knew all about the children; knew about the cars they drove; that he had been by the house and had seen a trailer set up in our back yard which the boys used in going on a camping trip the week before. I made the statement or asked him whether he didn't consider they were lucky that they found that door unlocked, and he said they probably were, that it would not have made any difference; that they were coming for me that night and would have taken me even if I had been in bed. He also said he knew what room in the house I slept in. He talked a good deal about automobiles. He seemed to know a lot about cars, especially the mechanics of cars. He preferred Chevrolets and Cadillacs."

As the trial continued—it would stretch out over the better part of twelve days—related events were happening outside the confines of the steamy courtroom.

First was a suspected attempt to kidnap or possibly kill the head county jailer or his wife and children. A mysterious Packard automobile that witnesses said was occupied by five suspicious-looking men and a woman pulled up in front of the jailer's house, idled for a few minutes, then raced off, only to circle the block very slowly four or five times. From then on the jailer, his family, and their house were heavily guarded. The auto and its occupants disappeared without a trace.

About the same time, a highly respected citizen rode in like a one-man posse out of the past to post rewards for information leading to the capture and conviction of Kelly and Kathryn—wanted dead or alive, just as in the not-so-distant Wild West days. This highly regarded former lawman, Charles Francis Colcord, had been Oklahoma City's first chief of police forty-three years earlier. Colcord was deeply offended by the kidnapping of his good friend Urschel, and others, telling a *Daily Oklahoman* interviewer:

> An outraged citizenship feels that something should be done to assist our federal and state governments in stamping out crime in this country, and particularly kidnapping. After conferences with many citizens from all walks of life, I am offering a reward of $10,000 in cash for the delivery of George Francis "Machine Gun" Kelly, charged with the kidnapping of Charles F. Urschel, to the sheriff of Oklahoma County or to any agent or officer of the U.S. Department of Justice; and a reward of $5,000 in cash for the delivery of Kathryn Kelly, wife of George Francis Kelly, charged as a conspirator in the kidnapping of Charles F. Urschel, to the sheriff of Oklahoma County, or to any agent or officer of the U.S. Department of Justice. If, in the making of the captures or arrests, either of said parties should be killed, the respective reward will be paid.

❖ ❖ ❖

Then, at last, came the most-awaited development of all, the big breakthrough the nation (and most especially Hoover) had been nervously awaiting:

Memphis, Tenn., Sept. 26 (International News Service)—George "Machine Gun" Kelly, America's no. 1 desperado, sought for a series of abductions, bank holdups and massacres that have terrorized the nation, fell into the clutches of the law today.

The man who had sent the organized forces of law of the 48 states and the federal government on the greatest manhunt in history, taunting his pursuers with scornful, threatening letters, surrendered meekly to Department of Justice agents who trapped him in a Memphis hideout.

The Kellys' flight was finally grounded after fifty-six remarkable days on the lam with every reward-seeking person in the country in search of them. The tip-off was supplied by Geraldine Arnold, the girl who had traveled with them. She mentioned that "Tich" was the unusual nickname of an acquaintance of Kelly's who gave them shelter in Memphis. Police puzzled over this for awhile, until one Memphis officer turned to the telephone directory. There he found a listing for a John Tichenor, a motor car dealer. On the premise that this might possibly be their man, police quickly put his house under round-the-clock surveillance.

In a couple of days of observation, they determined that a couple who seemed to be the fugitive Kellys were inside the Tichenor bungalow, almost in a sort of self-imposed exile. So a squad of lawmen executed a dawn raid September 26 and got the drop on Kelly, entering through an unlocked front door. Surprised at being awakened at 6:45 A.M. by the eight-man raiding party and finding a sawed-off shotgun embedded firmly in his navel by a nervous young Memphis police sergeant, a hungover Kelly, clad only in his underwear, surrendered meekly and with no fuss, mumbling, "I've been waiting all night for you." To which the officer replied, "Well, here we are."

Surrounded by empty beer and gin bottles and ashtrays overflowing with cigarette stubs, Kelly even put the cuffs on himself, reported the sergeant, who boasted to reporters, "Kelly was never nearer death than he was at that time. If he had raised one finger I would have blown him in two. When I shoved my gun into his stomach, he dropped his .45 as meekly as a lamb." A quick search of the premises and Kelly's automobile turned up no ransom bills or anything of value except a loaded Colt .45 automatic. Were George's and Kathryn's Miranda rights to remain silent until obtaining an attorney read to them? That legal doctrine was thirty-three years in the future. A search warrant to storm into the house in Memphis? What warrant? Kelly was Public Enemy No. 1; forget the protective niceties that are today's legal standards. And besides, they indicated they would accept extradition to Oklahoma and would plead guilty.

That version of Kelly's capture wasn't the one the expectant, eager public heard, though. In pure hyperbole, the FBI publicity mill put out as factual a much more dramatic version: that Kelly had cowered, groveled even, before the arresting FBI/Justice agents (Memphis police were not even mentioned, nor was the fact that the FBI had no power to make arrests) and had desperately whimpered, "Don't shoot, G-Men! Don't shoot!"

It made no difference that the several local policemen who were present verified the sergeant's account. Hoover had a national publicity machine that, in those days, was trusted implicitly by an overwhelming majority of the press and the public. And for the rest of his life, Hoover would repeat the "Don't shoot, G-Men" canard as truth. Furthermore, it is to this day still contained in an official bureau public handout about Machine Gun Kelly: "First criminal to call FBI agents 'G-Men.' The term, which had applied to all federal investigators, became synonymous with FBI agents." Hoover would later brag, correctly, that because of the capture of Kelly, "along the grapevine of the powerful empire of crime passed whispered words of warning about the G-Men."

Kelly would later smirk about supposedly originating "G-Men" and comment that if it made Hoover feel tough and heroic, so be it. A straight-faced Hoover would say of the "G-Man" myth a decade later, "These words became the subject matter of many headlines as they typify the cowardice of this boastful Kelly."

It might be noted that at the time of Kelly's booking in Memphis, a Justice Department official told the press Kelly had confessed to him, "You got me on the Urschel kidnapping but not on the Chicago robbery or the Kansas City Union Station job." So why, the puzzled chief of police asked Kelly, had he returned to Memphis, to Shelby County? "Oh, any old port in a storm, you know. It's my old home town and it's natural for me to stop off for awhile."

Rudely awakened in an adjoining bedroom by the raiding party, a blowsy Kathryn displayed her customary hostility and moxie by giving the arresting officers a predictably hard time, loudly raging and lashing

George Kelly in jail after his arrest in Memphis, Tennessee. (Copyright September 27, 1933, the Oklahoma Publishing Company)

out at them. She refused for a time even to change into street clothes so she could be transferred to police headquarters for fingerprinting and booking along with George. But eventually the officers got her and George to the station and assigned to holding cells.

Kathryn wanted out, desperately. She first thought up the idea of feigning an attack of appendicitis. When that didn't work, she vainly attempted to bribe one of the deputy sheriffs, telling him she would make it worth his while to the tune of fifteen thousand dollars to let her out. With all the officers and press milling around, the man was no fool, and there was no deal. Then, as another, longer-range tactic, she got the chief's permission to let reporters interview her. This provided the first inkling of the defense strategy she would put forward. "I was going back tomorrow and give myself up. Kelly told me he would kill me if I did, but I was going anyway. . . . I feel responsible, not for the kidnapping, because I'm absolutely innocent of any part in that, but it's all my fault that my parents are in this because I married him in the first place. I'm glad of one thing, though—that we're both arrested, for I'm not guilty and can prove it. Afterward I'll be rid of him and that bunch. I don't want to say anything about that guy Kelly, but he got me into this terrible mess and I don't want to have anything more to do with him."

Hoover had a typical rejoinder to that, stating five years later in his *Persons in Hiding*, "Even with the arrest, Kathryn Kelly did not cease to be a cunning, shrewd criminal-actress. She wept. She protested her innocence. She decried the hoodlum who 'had brought this disgrace upon her family.' She raved, cried, begged, sneered at, and jibed at her captors. It was all a terrible mistake, she said."

Hoover went on: She was "of good carriage, and pleasing mannerism. She was excellently and expensively dressed, especially when driving about in her sixteen-cylinder automobile, with silver fox furs floating from her smooth shoulders. . . . Here was a woman who could conceive a kidnapping, and force it through to a conclusion largely through her domination over her husband, who, in spite of his terrorizing name, could only bow before her tirades and do as she bade him."

In another interview shortly before going on trial, the "criminal-actress" told a reporter, "Kidnapping is the dirtiest business in the world. I'd die if someone kidnapped that kid of mine," referring to her fourteen-year-old daughter Pauline.

On learning of the Kellys' capture, the greatly relieved Urschel—still surrounded by heavy protective police guard, as were all members of his family as well as those of the Slicks, Hyde, Vaught, and the county jailer—shuttered the company offices and told his employees with gratitude they were free to attend the trial or just relax on their own for a few days.

❖ ❖ ❖

A manacled George Kelly is escorted to a plane in Memphis for his return flight to Oklahoma City to face trial. (Copyright August 31, 1933, the Oklahoma Publishing Company)

The day after the arrests in Memphis, FBI agents, acting on still more information that Geraldine had supplied, descended on the Texas farm where the Kellys had concealed most of their half of the ransom. Kathryn's cousin Cass Earl Coleman, cooperating in hopes of avoiding arrest himself, led the agents to the spot in the cotton patch where he'd stood by as George had buried "something." As Coleman would reveal in court:

> Well, they drove in my gate and Kathryn got out and come to the porch and told me Kelly wanted to see me, and I walked out to where he was and he opened the door of his car and was taking out some bundles, and he laid them down and shut his car and picked them up and told me to come on, and we walked down to the barn, some seventy-five yards, and he told me then what he had—a bunch of hot money and wanted to get shed of it—and I had to figure for

a place to put it and see that it wasn't found. And he told me if I let it be found that I would be killed, so I went down to a well in the field and told him there was a place I figured was all right.

In less than ten minutes the FBI dug up (and took an hour to count) $73,250, all in the ransom twenties except for one unexplained ten-dollar bill. The cash had been stuffed in a two-gallon thermos jug and an old molasses can.

About the same time, George and Kathryn were being flown under heavy guard to Oklahoma City. There Kelly shuffled awkwardly down the portable stairway in handcuffs and leg irons to be met by more officers, the Urschels themselves, a small group of curiosity seekers, and a reporter, who told what was said.

"Hello, gang. Nice trip," Kelly quipped, puffing on his usual Lucky Strike.

"That's the man," was all an unsmiling Urschel needed to say. Berenice, peering out of the car window, confirmed it. "That face will haunt me as long as I live." As George and Kathryn were being hustled as quickly as possible toward one of ten autos in a heavily armed motorcade that would whisk them to the county jail, Kelly was heard to complain, "I can't walk fast in these things."

Back in the Oklahoma City courtroom, meantime, Urschel's straightforward, unemotional testimony and his placid, responsive demeanor under often hostile cross-examination were just about all that were needed to seal the fate of Bates and the Shannons. Bates, having no credible defense to offer since he'd been identified by the bridge-playing Urschels and Jarretts, didn't even bother to waste the court's time by taking the stand in his own behalf.

The case against the constantly tobacco-chewing Bailey, though, was impressionistic at best because the only evidence against him was the dab of "gift" ransom money found in his pocket. He, too, declined to testify, having several very plausible reasons for not doing so. One was a death sentence hanging over his head in Kansas for kidnapping the warden in the Memorial Day jailbreak and the other was Hoover incorrectly (and apparently deliberately) naming him as one of the Union Station

Charles Urschel takes the stand as jurors (foreground) listen. (Copyright September 20, 1933, the Oklahoma Publishing Company)

Massacre murderers. Bailey also would allege years later to a biographer that one of Hoover's special assistants had privately approached him before the trial to say, "Guilty or not, we have orders to put you away."

So, accepting their fates, the relaxed Bailey and Bates actually seemed to rather enjoy the proceedings and the attention. With their armed guards always alertly hovering close by, the two defendants posed during recesses for photographs with spectators, signing autographs and chatting it up with them. "Be sure you get a good picture, ma'am," the smiling Bailey would politely tell the ladies. During some recesses, prosecutor Hyde even bummed an occasional cigarette and packet of paper matches from Bates and lit up for both of them as they spoke quietly out of earshot of the spectators and newsmen.

The first defendant to admit a role in the kidnapping, naive but terrified, was young Armon Shannon (wearing a suit that George had purchased for him). The young man related to the court that Kelly had promised some days before the crime to pay him $1,500 for some undisclosed task, "if I would do as he told me."

Q: Did you know or suspect what was to be done?
A: No, sir.
Q: What followed?
A: Bates and Kelly and Mr. Urschel came to our home.
Q: How did Mr. Urschel appear?
A: He was blindfolded. I thought maybe he had been shot or something.
Q: Why did you guard Mr. Urschel?
A: Kelly said if I didn't, he would shoot me with a machine gun.

The two elder Shannons, by this time, had stopped futilely denying their involvement. Changing course, they stoutly maintained that they had been coerced under threat of physical harm, even death, to harbor and help guard Urschel. Ora's version was that the family "was forced into this thing with machine guns, the same as Mr. Urschel." Her voice cracking on the stand, she broke into tears. "I was afraid of George Kelly." Boss said he was shocked and outraged when he realized who the blindfolded man was. "After going to bed, my wife and I talked about it and I told her I was going to kill them. She pleaded with me not to do it. She said, 'You're going to get us all killed.' "

Telling the court and jury that Kelly and Bates threatened instant death if he didn't cooperate, Boss said he feared that "if I told off on them they would come back and I would not be alive, my boy Armon would not be alive, and maybe Mr. Urschel would not be alive today. The reason I didn't phone no officers or the sheriff was for the simple reason I had a boy over there at this place, and if I phoned the officers, or if they had come over there, there would have been a battle and perhaps my boy would have been killed, or perhaps Mr. Urschel would have been killed."

But in the opinion of Judge Vaught, discrediting this line of defense, "The excuses offered by Robert G. Shannon and Armon Shannon as to their reason for holding and guarding the said Urschel do not constitute a defense at law. . . . A threat of future injury is not enough. The evidence shows that the Shannons knew there was a kidnapped man at their home. If they knew he was kidnapped and they guarded him, then they would be just as guilty as if they had kidnapped him, transported him, and collected the ransom. Fear of individual punishment is no excuse for a violation of the law."

Earlier, the judge had explicitly expressed his strong feelings about the case and the new federal kidnapping law inspired by the Lindbergh case: "If there is any way to put teeth in this act, this court is going to do it. . . . This is absolutely a revolutionary measure. Congress passed it for one reason alone—to try to stop kidnapping. A kidnapper is more than a murderer and is so recognized over the country. No more vicious character in this country exists than one who kidnaps a man and holds him for ransom."

Now it was the turn of the U.S. prosecutor from Washington, Keenan. Turning the proceeding into a morality play—a test of strength between the beleaguered public and gangsterdom—he tore into the defendants. The issue was whether "we are to have a government of law and order or abdicate in favor of machine gun gangsters":

> If this government cannot protect its citizens, then we had better frankly turn it over to the Kellys and the Bateses, the Baileys and the others of the underworld and pay tribute to them through taxes. Kidnapping has become a modern art. The plotters lay their vicious plans, bold strong-armed men carry out the abduction, hirelings stand guard, and later, when ransom has been paid, the money-changers arrange for its dissemination through underworld channels. In this case the government has shown you the whole picture of how this heinous scheme was conceived and carried out.
>
> Through four states of the Union these criminals plied their trade and defied the government. A single state could not control such swift operations. The federal government was forced to step in and take a hand. Now that government has been defied by these gangsters and we have caught them red-handed, we are convinced that they are all guilty of this conspiracy and demand that a verdict of guilty be returned.

Hyde followed Keenan, concluding his own ringing statement by exhorting the jury to convict every one of the defendants to the fullest extent of the law. The kidnappers had put "this fine citizen through the tortures of hell. I beg of you, in the name of my government, to return a verdict of guilty against these defendants. This is one of the most important cases ever tried. Precedents are being set that will guide the courts and the bar in all future trials that grow out of this determined effort of your government to stamp out this most damnable of crimes—kidnapping."

Bates, no stranger to courtrooms, leaned over to the perspiring Hyde when he resumed his seat and spoke in a stage whisper just loud enough for reporters at the press table to overhear, "Congratulations, Mr. Hyde, that's the best I ever heard." Looking each other squarely in the eye, they grinned, then shook hands.

After these statements and all the testimony they had heard, the jurors, who had been sequestered every night without benefit of newspapers or radio, were served a final supper of chicken-fried steak and mashed potatoes with gravy. Then they took but a single ballot to find Bates, Bailey, the three Shannons, and a couple of the money launderers guilty as charged—sealed verdicts that would be revealed in court first thing in the morning.

Incredibly, Bates and Bailey held an impromptu thirty-minute "press conference" in the U.S. marshal's office that evening with half a dozen reporters. Nothing newsworthy came out of it, the two of them agreeing, as Bailey put it, that "the government's on one side of the fence, we are on the other." He did add cryptically, "I had an absolutely fair trial except for three witnesses. I won't name the witnesses."

Before Judge Vaught pronounced sentence the next morning, the newly arrested George and Kathryn were dramatically escorted into the highly charged courtroom for the first time. Anticipating the guilty pleas that the two had indicated they would enter, the judge intended to sentence them at the same time as the others. However, they stunned everyone when each said to Vaught, when asked how they pleaded, "Not guilty." Now there would have to be another whole trial. To most observers, it was a totally needless waste of time. Was there anyone who seriously believed they weren't guilty? Visibly displeased, the agitated Vaught made them wait as he handed down his sentences to Bates, Bailey, Boss, Ora, and Armon. The judge's harsh glare and cold words, spoken with benefit of only a few notes, are preserved on a flickering, scratchy film:

"Guilty as charged." Standing to hear Judge Vaught pronounce sentence at the end of their trial are (from left) Ora Shannon, Robert (Boss) Shannon, Armon Shannon, Harvey Bailey, and Albert Bates. (Copyright October 1, 1933, the Oklahoma Publishing Company)

The defendants will please stand. Now in this case the jury has returned a verdict of guilty. The court is of the opinion that this verdict is fully sustained by the evidence. And while it is not a pleasant duty for a court, even in the face of a verdict of guilty, to impose a sentence to deprive one of his liberty, yet there are times when duty requires that one assume the full responsibility of his office. There are some things that I might call to your attention this morning. Something is more at stake in the trial of this case than the mere punishment . . . [here stopping in midsentence to glare over his glasses and sternly admonish someone in the courtroom not to light up a cigarette] . . . something is more at stake than the mere punishment for the crime that has been committed in this case. The question before the American people today is whether or not crime will be recognized as an occupation or a profession. Or whether the people will enforce the laws of the nation as they are written. So far as this court is concerned, it is its purpose to try to enforce the laws as they are written.

Therefore, the judgment of this court is that Albert L. Bates be sentenced to the federal penitentiary for the term of his natural life. It is the judgment of this court that Harvey J. Bailey be sentenced to the federal penitentiary for the term of his natural life. It's the judgment of this court that R. G. Shannon be sentenced to the federal penitentiary for the term of his natural life. It is the judgment of this court that Ora L. Shannon be sentenced to the federal penitentiary for the term of her natural life. It's the judgment of this court that Armon Shannon be sentenced to the federal penitentiary for a period of ten years, but that sentence will be suspended during good behavior and you will be paroled . . . if your conduct is what it should be and you violate no laws, either state or federal, this parole will be ended.

Ever loquacious in front of a microphone or with the press, Hyde was ready with a comment afterward: "This verdict means the government is on top of the fight against kidnapping and we are ready to shoot the works." Coprosecutor Keenan was equally stern: "We are going right on down the line until we get every criminal and gangster in the United States. The new law has provided a powerful weapon and we are prepared and eager to use it to the finish."

As reporters and spectators watched, the Urschels and Ramona Seeligson sought out the jurors in a corridor, shook the hands of as many of them as possible, and thanked them for the verdicts. "I am so glad I can't keep from crying," Mrs. Seeligson said. Urschel commented, "I am sorry punishment was necessary, but I believe the jury did its duty as it saw fit." This was on Saturday, the last day of September.

For the luckless Bailey, it was a crime of which (for once) he was totally innocent. But for being in the wrong place in the wrong company at the wrong time, he drew his longest sentence ever. Armon, thanks to his twenty-one years, his early and continuing cooperation, and the unanimous recommendation of leniency by the jury and the prosecution, got off with the ten-year suspended sentence, allowing him to return to Paradise to his wife and two children, one of them a week-old son he hadn't yet seen.

Boss was granted sixty days' grace to put his affairs in order and to get acquainted with his new grandson. The U.S. Circuit Court of Appeals denied a hasty plea for reversal, and Boss was ordered to report to Leavenworth on January 13, 1934, to begin his lifetime of incarceration.

The front pages weren't the only sections of the local papers watching the case. In an article headlined "Kidnapping Menace to Be Theme of Sunday Sermons in Several City Churches," it was reported that the title of the message at the First Baptist Church would be "Who Is Responsible for Our Kidnappings?" It was also announced that "a unique prayer service for the spiritual benefit of the kidnap defendants will take the place of the morning sermon at Calvary Baptist Tabernacle Sunday morning."

Several days after the verdicts, and the church services, Urschel would receive a terse letter:

> Perhaps I should have at an earlier date advised you of my gratification because of your wholehearted cooperation with this Division in its conduct of the investigation of the kidnapping of which you were the victim. The convictions on Saturday, I am sure, bear ample testimony of the wisdom of the advice given by this Department to the families and friends of persons who have been kidnapped, and I am quite sure that if the government enjoyed the same measure of cooperation which you have afforded it from all others who are visited by this despicable crime, kidnapping would no longer be popular in the underworld.
>
> I thank you sincerely for your cooperation and extend to you my congratulations upon the successful presentation of this case, to which you contributed in no little degree.
>
> With expressions of my kindest personal regards, I am
> J. Edgar Hoover
> Director

These were some very carefully worded, almost begrudging thanks. Why was the letter even written? The answer is contained in a memo to Hoover from the Oklahoma City agent-in-charge. "I think a personal letter from the Director to Mr. Charles F. Urschel, the victim in this case, commending him for his wholehearted and fearless cooperation would be in place." The agent prodded further, "Also a similar letter to Mr. E. E. Kirkpatrick . . . commending him for his splendid and fearless cooperation would be appreciated." Thus a similar Hoover note went to Kirkpatrick dated the same day: "I want to take this occasion to thank you sincerely for the full measure of cooperation which you have rendered to the Division of Investigation in its inquiry covering the kidnapping of Mr. Charles F. Urschel. It has been the cordial, effective assistance rendered by Mr. Urschel, himself, his immediate family and friends, which has permitted a successful investigation."

No mention of the principal clue, which had somehow found its way into the press, that helped the FBI get the case off the ground—Urschel's timing of the planes and the missing plane, which the government had tried in vain to keep out of the papers. And Urschel was never questioned about it on the stand. Why was that? curious reporters asked Hyde. Perhaps acting on instructions not to share credit with others, the U.S. attorney replied that how the government found the Paradise hideout wasn't important. "The fact we produced the defendants was sufficient. The airplane angle had had widespread publicity and there was no need to continue it by having Urschel testify about it." The "leak" to the press did not come from the authorities. Rather, the teenage son of the *Daily Oklahoman*'s managing editor was a good friend of Betty Slick and passed on to the paper's reporters some of the conversations he overheard in the Urschel house where she was living. "I was secretly proud of the information that he had smuggled to the office," Editor Walter M. Harrison reminisced nearly two decades later in *Me and My Big Mouth*. "In the interest of proper bringing up and so on, I had to pull 'Dub' off of the spying job."

It did get publicity, but only because of the pretrial leak, much to the bureau's chagrin. Not only that, but there was little questioning at all during this or the upcoming trial—that of the Kellys—about most of the numerous other valuable facts Urschel provided that led the authorities to the discovery of the Paradise hideout and the first arrests. Strange indeed.

11

The "Big" Trial

❖ ❖ ❖ ❖ ❖ ❖ ❖ ❖ ❖ ❖ ❖ ❖ ❖ ❖ ❖

IN THE DISTRICT COURT OF THE UNITED STATES
FOR THE WESTERN DISTRICT OF OKLAHOMA
The United States of America, Plaintiff,
vs.
George R. Kelly and Kathryn Kelly, Defendants.
No. 10,478—Criminal
October 9, 1933—2:00 O'Clock P.M.

Unhappily for all concerned, except perhaps for the reporters getting rare bylines for covering the event, there now had to be a second trial. It was convened a mere nine days after the sentencing in the first trial, and Judge Vaught again was on the bench. He had brusquely turned down all pleas for delays or change of venue. With security somewhat looser than before and the courtroom surprisingly only half full, Urschel reprised his role as the star witness. In light of the wholesale convictions in the previous trial and Urschel's emotionless and detailed testimony, the climax was never in doubt. Conviction was obviously a foregone conclusion in the judge's mind and everyone else's. Vaught steadfastly reflected the relentless urgency on the part of the government, the FBI, and Hoover himself to bring the full force of their weight to bear on the kidnapping epidemic through this case. Technically, of course, the fate of the two defendants was in the hands of a newly selected twelve-man panel of jurors—a carpenter, three utility company workers, a filling station operator, a general store owner, a grocer, and five farmers. But the Kellys were obviously foredoomed to serve as the highly publicized—and heavily punished—examples of the law's reach.

As in the first trial, the defense attorneys tried their best with slight variations to slow down the obvious. Over and over they interrupted and complained. "Objected to as incompetent, irrelevant, and immaterial." Over and over Vaught responded, "Overruled." "Exception," the attorneys came back lamely. Nothing was to be allowed to slow the process toward a verdict.

Hoover blatantly prejudged the court case in a seething interview with United News Service, describing the arrest of the Kellys as the "federal government's ultimatum to the underworld that kidnapping is an unsafe business." The article went on to say, in part:

His eyes heavy from loss of sleep, the 38 year old director of the government's man-hunters was at his desk as usual all day cleaning up details of the case. "Kelly's capture means something to the underworld that the average person doesn't understand," Hoover said in an exclusive interview with the United News. "The criminal fears death more than anything else. At heart they are all rats—dirty yellow rats. A gangster will kill you, oh sure, if he has a machine gun and you are absolutely helpless. They like to think they are above the law. But they actually operate most of the time with one eye on the electric chair. The underworld doesn't like to feel that our men or the police can reach in with a moment's notice and pluck their big shots out of bed—and that's just what we have been doing."

Judge Vaught's resolve had been stiffened even more when he received a terrifying anonymous threatening letter the day before he brought down the opening gavel: "If you do not dismiss these people, you and your family will be killed and your house will be blown up." He refused to be intimidated. "Men such as Kelly, who write letters boasting what they are going to do, seldom carry out their threats. As a federal judge, I could hardly be expected to show the white feather to hoodlums."

An angry Keenan, himself the target of similar threats, weighed in with a retort of his own: "We are ready to meet the challenge of these gangsters and outlaws fearlessly and with their own weapons. The government intends to stamp out these outrages if it takes the United States Army to do it, but that will not be necessary. This statement is made in deadly earnest and with no desire to be melodramatic."

Kelly's attempt, from jail, to send a message requesting an unidentified confederate to "get" Hyde through his son—"Snatch the child of this prosecutor to calm him down"—was thwarted when the police intercepted it. From that point on, the four-year-old and his mother spent the rest of the trial at an undisclosed location under the watchful eye of law enforcement officers.

On the surface, this second trial appeared to be following the unwritten code of the underworld in those days of chivalrous men shielding their women from blame and punishment, George manfully and passively attempting to take the fall alone. Appearances were not, however, what they seemed. Neither the government nor the press seemed to know of the understanding Kathryn and Kelly had apparently reached, which was why George sat by so totally mute. He did come to life during a recess on the opening day, giving Urschel the familiar throat-slashing gesture with a forefinger and telling him in a loud voice, "This is for you. You'll get yours." Conditioned by now to these threats, Urschel wordlessly and icily stared Kelly down as a number of spectators gaped.

About the only other animation George displayed during the trial was when he and Kathryn were being escorted toward an elevator to be taken to court the first day. Kathryn, attempting to kiss her father, was roughly shoved away by a guard. She stumbled but turned and gave the agent a solid slap. Although handcuffed, George gallantly rushed forward and raised his arms threateningly. Another agent was too quick for him, cracking George lustily two or three times on the head with the butt of his six-shooter hard enough to draw blood. Stunned, the bandaged George sat placidly through the morning's testimony with egg-size knots on his temple and back of his head and with traces of blood caked in his hair. He denied that he'd planned to attack the agent, just wanted to "tell him not to hit my wife again."

Kathryn didn't hold back in telling bystanders her version. "I stopped to kiss my father and the agent hit me in the back. When George told him not to hit me again he began beating George with his pistol. Sure I slapped him, and I'd like to do it again." Other than those uncharacteristic outbursts, George maintained a glum silence throughout the proceedings, smoking in the courtroom (it was a more permissive era, at least in that regard) and vigorously chewing gum. He offered not a word in his own defense, while Kathryn and even his own attorney proceeded to try to lay the entire blame for the crime on him and the already convicted Bates.

George Kelly pats one of the wounds he suffered when an officer outside the courtroom struck him with a pistol. (Copyright October 10, 1933, the Oklahoma Publishing Company)

Charles Urschel (in dark suit) sits in the courtroom. The man in the suit with the pencil in his pocket is E. E. Kirkpatrick, Urschel's friend who dropped the ransom money. (Copyright September 27, 1933, the Oklahoma Publishing Company)

In neither trial was Urschel asked whether, during the automobile trips and his entire captivity, he'd ever heard, seen, or picked up any reference to anyone named Kathryn. For that matter, other than the filling station attendant discussing the crop situation and the woman hollering about the kidnapped man being on her property, he'd heard no woman's voice the whole nine days. The Urschels and the Jarretts had seen Kelly at the scene of the crime, the men were with them in the getaway car, and Urschel had heard his voice at length, which was why Kelly saw no purpose in trying to establish any kind of alibi. Besides, it was obvious the government was predisposed to convict him. The testimony by bridge-player Mrs. Jarrett early the first day must have all but made up his mind:

HYDE: You positively identify this man as one of the men, do you?
A: Yes, sir.
HYDE: Let the record show that she pointed to Mr. George Kelly.
VAUGHT: Which one is it over there you pointed to?
A: Would you like for me to walk over there and show him to you?
HYDE: Yes.
A: I will be glad to do that. (Hereupon the witness leaves the witness stand and points to defendant Kelly.)

KELLY: I appreciate that.

A: I'm not supposed to respond to him. Whether he appreciates it or not, I am glad to do it.

HYDE: That is all.

No longer Kathryn's pawns and with Luther Arnold having a potential government charge hanging over his head, the three Arnolds cooperated wholeheartedly with the prosecution and ripped gaping holes in Kathryn's anticipated line of defense. First came Geraldine, who took the stand wearing a red woolen dress (ironically one that Kathryn had bought for her). Poised and precocious beyond her twelve years, the girl went through an examination of what Kathryn and George had talked about while she was with them. For a while, they were holed up in Chicago:

Q: While you were in the apartment house in Chicago did anyone write any letters?

A: Yes, sir.

Q: What did George Kelly have to do with those letters?

A: He wrote some of them and Kathryn wrote some of them, and I seen him put his fingerprints on one of them.

Q: What did he and Kathryn talk about when they were writing those letters?

A: Well, sir, mainly what they talked about was killing somebody.

Q: Whom did he say they were going to kill? What did Kathryn say about it?

A: Well, she said that—I don't believe I remember what she said about it.

Q: Whom did he say he was going to kill?

A: Judge Vaught, Keenan, Urschel, and Hyde.

Q: Was Kathryn there when he said that?

A: Yes, sir.

Next on the stand was Geraldine's father, also incidentally wearing clothes Kathryn had purchased for him:

Q: Did you hear any conversations between George and his wife about the Urschel kidnapping matter?

A: No, I never heard any details of it at all, any more than I heard

George remark that "If I had that to do over again, I would stick his head in a barrel of lime," or something like that. He said they should have took him out in Arizona and buried him, killed him and buried him.

Q: Who said that?

A: George.

Q: What did Kathryn say when he said that?

A: She said, "That is what we ought to have done." (Then a quick bit of cross-examination.)

Q: The government has agreed to dismiss your own case if you would be a witness in this case, haven't they?

A: Well, he said it wouldn't be weighed heavily. He didn't say it would be dropped entirely.

Mrs. Arnold, up next, was asked whether Kathryn had said anything about the Urschel kidnapping in her presence. Yes, "she said she ought to kill the son of a bitch, is what she said she ought to do to him."

Q: When this statement was made, that she ought to kill him, did she mention anybody's name?

A: Only one. She mentioned calling up Mr. Urschel.

Q: What did she say?

A: She said she would like to kill the son of a bitch herself, referring to Mr. Urschel.

Q: Did she use Mr. Urschel's name?

A: Yes, sir.

Q: Who was present at that time?

A: Her husband, Mr. Kelly.

The FBI agent who had been in charge of initially questioning the Kellys in Memphis offered an interesting twist on purported discussions about Urschel's possible fate. The agent testified that Kelly told him he'd met in Chicago with one Verne Miller, who was wanted for several murders and for allegedly being one of the killers at the Union Station Massacre:

Q: Did he tell you about any agreement he made with Verne Miller?

A: Yes, he said he and Verne Miller had agreed that one or the other would kill Mr. Urschel.

George and Kathryn Kelly in court with their attorney, James Mathers. (Copyright October 10, 1933, the Oklahoma Publishing Company)

Q: Anyone else besides Mr. Urschel who was kidnapped?
A: Mr. Jarrett.

Next to take the stand was the special agent in the FBI's Oklahoma City office, Ralph Colvin, from whom Hyde drew additional recollections of conversations with Kathryn Kelly, further incriminating her:

Q: What was said by her with reference to the safety of Mr. Urschel?
A: She told me she understood that Mr. Urschel had filed suit to seize from her certain jewelry that had been found, I believe, in a safe deposit box in Fort Worth, and she wanted me to ask Mr. Urschel to come and see her. She said she couldn't afford to lose that jewelry because it was all she had left to provide for her daughter, Pauline, and she thought Mr. Urschel was a heartless man to try to do that. And she went on to remark that if he won the suit, it would

not do him much good because he wouldn't have long to live anyway, and that was about the extent of the conversation along that line. She said this jewelry was not the proceeds of this kidnapping, that she had bought that long before.

Q: But she did say that Mr. Urschel did not have long to live?

A: Yes.

Q: How did she say she knew that to be the fact?

A: She said she knew some of George's associates would get him.

After the agent stepped down, more damning evidence continued to come in against Kathryn. Eighteen-year-old Gay Coleman proved a devastatingly hostile witness against his cousin. Like Kathryn, he was a grandchild of Mary L. ("Ma") Coleman, the elderly bedridden woman whose farm the noisy kidnappers had stopped at with Urschel en route to Paradise. Gay Coleman related how George had casually mentioned during the midday dinner in early July, "There's more'n apt to be a kidnapping in Oklahoma City soon." And that Kathryn had immediately chimed in to brag, "We're going to be in the big money before long."

Another witness who cast a cloud over Kathryn's defense was her stepsister, twelve-year-old Ruth Shannon. She recounted how Kathryn had appeared unannounced early Sunday—the day Urschel was in transit from Oklahoma City to Paradise—and bustled her along with Armon's young wife and Kathryn's daughter Pauline to Kathryn's Fort Worth home, where they all stayed for ten days. Kathryn had brushed off the timing and the length of their "vacation" as a mere coincidence, saying the junket was nothing more than an opportunity for the four of them to do a little leisurely window shopping, take in a few moving-picture shows, have some good times in the big city, and visit with Kathryn's ailing father who was staying in the house.

The clincher was supplied by the elderly Ma Coleman, whose doctor dramatically pushed her into the courtroom in a wheelchair. In a weak and weary voice she corroborated the dinner conversation about the upcoming kidnap and told about the noisy appearance Kelly and Bates had made on the fateful night on their way to Paradise with the blindfolded hostage being transferred from one car to the other at her farm.

The identity of the potential Oklahoma City bank president kidnap target, one Frank P. Johnson of the First National Bank and Trust Company, also came out at the trial. Contacted for his reaction, he told a reporter,

"I don't wish Charles any hard luck, but I'm glad it was he instead of me." Coincidentally, Urschel was a director of the bank.

During a recess, Kathryn stunned her attorney by saying she wanted to confer with Judge Vaught and make an offer to plead guilty if he would release her mother. A reporter revealed the essence of the brief confrontation that occurred.

"What does this mean?" the equally stunned Vaught demanded heatedly when they were in his chambers. "This is wholly improper."

Kathryn spat out quickly, "Judge, if I will plead guilty will you dismiss my mother?"

Livid, Vaught sputtered, "Get out. I can't talk to you about the case." And, turning to her hapless lawyer, "What in the world are you thinking? Or were you?"

The court back in session, it was time for what everyone in Oklahoma City, everyone in the nation, had been eagerly awaiting: Kathryn's turn to be heard.

Sweeping elegantly to the stand, she spared no histrionics. It was a display of an extremely creative and selective memory in an attempt to convince everyone—the judge, the jury, the press, the public at large—that she was totally blameless, an unwilling and mere passive naif quavering under George's terrible iron fist. "He always told me not to mess in his business in any way, and I didn't. I had planned to leave Mr. Kelly."

She seemed to take over the witness chair, appropriating it grandly as if it were her throne. She turned it into her stage. One reporter wrote that she wore a "smart black dress and hat, [and was] completely at ease. She sat down, crossed her legs and smiled a winsome half-smile at jurors and attorneys." Another added: "She was smartly attired in a black skirt and a black satin waist, with a black bow at the neck. She wore a small black hat, black pumps and sheer stockings. A murmur of comment went up from the many women in the crowded courtroom."

Dramatically weeping into her handkerchief from time to time, nervously twisting it throughout, Kathryn portrayed herself as the real vic-

Kathryn Kelly on the stand. (Copyright October 11, 1933, the Oklahoma Publishing Company)

tim. She insisted that she had been forced to participate after the fact of the kidnapping and did so only because of her intense love for, then later fear of, George—even though she had just heard her own relatives testify to the contrary. Clinging to this implausible thread, Kathryn insisted that it had been George who conceived and planned the whole scheme. It was George, along with the equally nefarious Bates, who had captured and imprisoned Urschel, collected the ransom, and wanted to murder him. But she, of course, had strenuously and successfully argued them out of it, saving his life. "What did you ask Kelly about the kidnapping?" she was asked.

A: He told me it was none of my business, that they had a man at Armon's house. I told them if they did I'd tell the officers, even if he killed me. I begged him to release him. I said he would get my folks into trouble.

Q: What did he say?

A: He threatened me. He said it was none of my business.

Q: Did he say anything about what he intended to do with the kidnapped man?

A: He said he was going to kill him.

Q: What did you do then?

A: I begged him not to. Asked him to please release him.

With that, her credibility seriously in question, neither the prosecutors nor her attorneys saw any need to go further. She was dismissed from the stand.

Next, the government's case included a puzzling appearance by a local self-styled expert handwriting analyst, who testified that without any doubt in his opinion it had been Kathryn who'd penned the "Ignorant Charles" and other threatening letters.

Not so, not at all, Kathryn had adamantly claimed. Then, shown other writing samples by the defense, the handwriting witness said he would need at least a full day to study them. Surprisingly, the witness then said he would gladly appear on behalf of the Kellys, too. Vaught was startled. "You have no hesitancy in appearing here as a witness for the defendants if they give you an opportunity to examine any handwriting they desire you to?"

"No, sir. I think I have testified for both sides in numerous cases."

"And you would do so in this case?"

"Yes, sir."

The judge, by now impatient with the delaying tactics of the defense, denied this maneuver, saying, "Well, I am not going to continue this case all Fall."

Prosecutor Hyde delivered a flowery summation in his final argument to the jury. "How can you believe that this was the demure, loving, and fearful wife she pretends to be after hearing that she roamed the country like a millionaire's daughter or wife, buying machine guns? This sweet-smelling geranium. Do you think she schemed with George and others under threats? I tell you, she was the arch-conspirator."

Hoover, who was closely following the proceedings from his head-quarters in Washington, characterized Kathryn's entire line of defense as a blatant but clumsy attempt at blame shifting.

Judge Vaught wasn't buying any of her protestations of innocence, either. Before allowing the jurors to retire and begin their deliberations, he instructed them that "the defendant was not wholly truthful" and that she "knew about the kidnapping and knowingly participated. Other testimony from this defendant is utterly convincing to this court that Kathryn Kelly had criminal knowledge of the abduction conspiracy. However, you can ignore my remarks altogether. They are not binding on the jury."

Kathryn's astounded attorney was apoplectic at this admonition, sputtering, "There is no doubt about the verdict after those instructions." Kelly's attorney, who had worked hard to exonerate Kathryn at George's expense, protested that the judge's comments "virtually amounted to an instructed verdict of guilty."

Indeed, the verdicts by the panel, reached in just an hour on the third day of the trial, were as predictable as the judge's ensuing sentences. International News Service correspondent Kilgallen caught the mood in his dramatic dispatch:

A hushed silence, broken only by the faint whir of motion picture cameras, fell over the crowded courtroom as the verdict was read.

Kelly, the man who boasted he can write his name on a wall with machine gun bullets, and his 29-year-old wife who had stuck with him throughout during their hectic married life and criminal career, stood up, side by side.

She was pale, her lips tightly compressed and her long slim fingers closing and unclosing. She wore a black silk dress, with red buttons

George and Kathryn Kelly hear themselves pronounced guilty. (Copyright October 12, 1933, the Oklahoma Publishing Company)

down the front of her waist, and a smart black hat of the latest mode. Kelly, a heavy-set ex-convict, wanted for murder and robbery in several cities, tried to appear nonchalant, but his face was serious as the judge leaned forward. Kelly's dyed hair stood out like a beacon, its yellowish-red hue giving him a grotesque appearance. "Have you anything to say?" asked Judge Vaught in a quiet voice.

"No, sir," said Kathryn in a low, tremulous voice. Kelly said nothing. . . . .

Kathryn's lips trembled as the judge imposed the sentence—the maximum penalty.

Was the trial—were both trials—fair? Except for the case of the uninvolved Bailey, everything points to the affirmative. Clearly, Judge Vaught thought so when he concluded the Kellys' day in court: "The jury has found you guilty and the court fully concurs in its verdict. It is therefore the judgment of this court that you be sentenced to the federal penitentiary for the rest of your natural lives. The court is of the opinion that this verdict is fully sustained by the evidence."

Naturally, Kathryn had a somewhat different point of view, snorting, "My Pekinese dog would have gotten a life sentence in this court." And, in a threatening tone, "They know I've got plenty of friends who will come and get me if I say the word. But if I'm with mother I won't want to escape." Kelly still said nothing, his stolid silence during and after the trial leaving him practically no hope for favorable consideration of any kind of plea on appeal. But out of earshot of the judge, Kelly snarled that the verdict was "no news to me."

Afterward, Berenice Urschel walked up to the bench, clasped Judge Vaught's hands and told him, "We thank you so much for our lives."

After he, too, had warmly shaken the judge's hand, the self-effacing Urschel told the waiting press horde, "The government deserves all the credit in the world in this case. I have no feeling of revenge or triumph, but only the highest regard for the officers who worked on the case and the juries which rendered the verdicts. Now, back to work."

It was back to work, as well, for the government. Several fringe conspirators—other money changers, people who had harbored the Kellys, even Bates's attorney, who stupidly accepted some ransom bills as part of his fee—were tracked down relentlessly, tried, and convicted. The final prison term wasn't handed down until the first day of October 1936.

The box score, by the FBI's precise calculations, was twenty-one people convicted, six of them receiving life sentences and the other fifteen sentenced to jail time aggregating fifty-eight years, two months, and three days.

As the two Kellys were being readied for the rest of their lives in prison, Hoover had to take still another shot at each of them. In letters to the director of the Bureau of Prisons, he wrote:

> I feel that it is not necessary for me to indicate to you the reputation which Kelly has as an underworld character. . . . He has boasted that he could not be held in a penitentiary and that he will escape. He

has expressed regret that he did not kill Mr. Urschel . . . and he threatened Mr. Urschel throughout the trial of this kidnapping case.

With reference to Kathryn Kelly, I am of the firm opinion that she is a very dangerous criminal. . . . Kathryn Kelly purchased the machine gun with which her husband, Kelly, was arrested at the time of the kidnapping. She has been identified as the writer of threatening letters received by Mr. Urschel during the trial.

Hoover had repeatedly made it abundantly clear that he didn't appreciate any lifers being released for "good behavior." So as a bar to their possible future parole—which he termed "one of the major menaces of our country"—the government held over theft charges against Bates and Kelly for "stealing" the pocket money from Urschel and Jarrett the night of the kidnapping.

George Kelly (thirty-three years old at the time of sentencing), Albert Bates (thirty-nine), and Harvey Bailey (forty-four) were immediately incarcerated in the "Big House" at Leavenworth, Kansas, the nation's first federal penitentiary (it opened in 1906). Kelly was accorded the dubious distinction of transport to the fortress in a special prisoner's railcar. "I'll be out of here by Christmas," he was heard to boast. It would turn out to be a hollow threat.

Kathryn Kelly (twenty-nine) and Ora Brooks (forty-five) were jointly assigned and subsequently reassigned over the years to prisons in Michigan, California, and Texas, eventually winding up for good in 1942 at the minimum-security Federal Industrial Institution for Women at Alderson, West Virginia.

Since the Kellys had no way to pay their main attorney, James Mathers, he sued for and was awarded Kathryn's diamond-studded wristwatch and other jewelry, furs, and clothing, plus George's last car, a sixteen-cylinder Cadillac roadster, in lieu of normal legal fees. The latter item brought Mathers into conflict with Urschel, who maintained that the auto was partly paid for with his ransom and therefore should rightfully be his. The machine had cost $6,250, for which Kelly laid out $4,940 in cash as a down payment, then paid the balance with ransom bills. After the legal argument with Urschel, Mathers eventually got to keep the car. He sold various other items—one being the watch, along with a letter Kathryn had written about it—for $3,500.

❖   ❖   ❖

A rare archival newsreel made for motion picture theater audiences—a jerky, grainy view shot from either a high window or the roof of the Oklahoma City courthouse—shows heavily armed guards escorting George and Kathryn through a crowd of onlookers into a paddy wagon after their sentencing. The excited narrator practically shouts, "Thus, Uncle Sam rolled up his sleeves and dealt gangland a swift, decisive blow. They are going for a ride, and with the federal government at the wheel. And here's the end of the road [a background shot of the Leavenworth Penitentiary]—and oblivion—the inevitable destruction of the lure of easy money."

Shortly after entering Leavenworth and apparently wanting to establish a tough-guy image, Kelly found himself written up for "institutional rule violations":

> Disobedience of orders and attacking an other [*sic*] inmate. After being released from his cell for recreation he insisted on entering the orderlies quarters and when told by orderly #12276 not to enter, subject took offense and began to cuss the orderly, but did turn away muttering an oath at the orderly. The orderly again told him not to enter but that if he wished to get something, such as salt or information to call for it during the feeding hours. Subject, Kelly, then turned back and remarked, who are you to tell me what to do you black son of a bitch and made a rush at #12276. Action: Placed in isolation restricted diet and reduced to second grade.

The following September, Kelly, Bates, and Bailey were transferred by special train to Alcatraz when the new California penal facility had been converted from a military disciplinary barracks. Attorney General Cummings crowed that Alcatraz would be a dead-end jail for criminals "with advanced degrees in crime."

It was an excruciating two-day train ride to Alcatraz that Kelly, Bates, Bailey, and exactly one hundred other Leavenworth inmates took in 1934—almost a story in itself. They rode in special cars with windows barred and covered by heavy metal screens and door locks that could be opened only from the outside. The prisoners were very heavily guarded and moved in utmost secrecy along the circuitous route, both for fear of ambush and to avoid press coverage (the latter not always successful). Shoeless, the prisoners were securely shackled to one another, right leg to left leg, left to right, as they faced one another on long bench seats. They were provided paper plates and plastic utensils for eating. Fitfully, they slept, as best they could, sitting up. When anyone had to use the men's room, his shackled "partner" had to go along. One of the guards told a Hoover ghostwriter, "It was watch, watch, watch every minute, night and day, but especially at night. Even when we were relieved by the reserves and went to our berths in the sleeper we didn't dare take off our clothes. Our guns were at our fingertips. We may have dozed, but we didn't sleep. We couldn't sleep."

At the same time, a similar train transported another group of fifty-three prisoners from the federal penitentiary in Atlanta. When the trains reached San Francisco Bay, rather than transferring the prisoners individually to boats, the railcars were barged—escorted by an armed Coast Guard patrol boat and the warden's prison launch—to the island with the felons still manacled inside. Why was Kelly included among the dangerous and hardened first group of inmates exiled to the escape-proof Alcatraz? As explained succinctly in the government's prison transfer form, "Because of the notoriety given in this instant case it would be a shock to the country should he escape. He is considered a dangerous criminal and transfer is recommended with maximum custody." Kelly himself, as he told his son years afterward, was deeply depressed. "How the hell did I ever get myself into this fix? I should've stayed with what I know how to do best—robbing banks."

For all apparent intents and purposes, what still remains one of the most remarkable and intriguing kidnapping dramas in American history was closed, and everyone could, as Urschel said with understandable relief, go "back to work."

The closure of the oilman's nightmare was a tribute to his fearlessness and incredible self-composure, as well as his grim patriotic determination to bring the kidnappers to justice, even in the face of the vicious threats to himself and his family. Hyde, the Oklahoma prosecuting attorney, summed up the consensus of many, saying at the time, "The credit goes most to Mr. Urschel, chiefly because of his courage and his ability to distinguish what was going on under a blindfold." Thirty-three years later, a *Daily Oklahoman* reporter tracked down Hyde, then retired and residing in the Oklahoma State War Veterans' Facility. Still keen of mind when it came to reminiscing about the famous case, the former prosecutor was even more specific and effusive in lauding Urschel's contributions:

> It was a fascinating case because Mr. Urschel made such a wonderful witness, but it was nothing to my credit. Any young lawyer could have tried it as well. Mr. Urschel really won the case. His eyes were taped but he heard an airliner pass over the farm twice daily. He remembered one day it rained and the plane didn't go over. He looked at that house with his mind. He remembered walking in the house and there were several boards on the porch missing. He felt the hot wind blow in; knew windowpanes were missing on the south and west; knew a quilt was hung over the window; that there were no shades. He knew he was chained to an old-fashioned iron bed. He heard guineas screeching near a squeaky windmill and he saw a windmill near the house the one time his blindfold was removed. He knew the water had a high mineral content. All the information he had was enough for the officers. It couldn't be anyplace else but Paradise, Texas. It was an unusual case and a real experience.

Backing that up was longtime top FBI agent Melvin Purvis, the senior federal cop on the scene in 1934 when the murderous John Dillinger was ambushed and killed in Chicago. In addition to his remarks quoted in the preface of this book, Purvis would also write in 1936 in *American Agent:* "I can recall no case of major importance where the victim was of as much assistance as was Mr. Urschel in bringing about the solution. His memory and intelligence were far above the average. He remembered the details of the trip from his home to the hideout, he remembered when it rained, the type of bed on which he had slept. All of this time he had been blindfolded, yet he exercised his mental powers and was able to relate that he heard noises of cows, dogs, chickens, and other noises usually heard in a farmyard." These compliments from J. Edgar Hoover's onetime favorite field agent add considerable weight to the premise that without Urschel's remarkable input, the case might not have been solved, or certainly not solved as quickly and thoroughly as it was. The Shannons and their spread might not have been discovered, or quite possibly the wounded Bailey either, for that matter. The Kellys might well have escaped capture absent Urschel's many clues, although Kathryn's ill-advised conversation with the two Fort Worth detectives did give them what was as good as a road map to the hideout. And, of course, any ransom bills they might have put into circulation would probably have led back to them.

It is also quite likely that Urschel himself was instrumental in saving Hoover's neck politically. The Union Station Massacre remained unsolved, and "Pretty Boy" Floyd and most of the other highly publicized gangsters were still on the loose. But thankfully the main spotlight of public attention had temporarily been shifted away from these frustratingly dead-end cases to the intriguing pursuit of the Kellys and then the two courtroom dramas in Oklahoma. Hoover simply couldn't afford to have this case drag on or let any of the alleged perpetrators wriggle off the hook. Wrapping up the Urschel case with no loose ends dangling was an absolute necessity for Hoover and his relatively unknown FBI. Coming as it did at the height of the kidnapping surge and the Gangster Era, the quick, dramatic resolution of the Urschel case was a stunning public relations and political coup that the beleaguered director needed.

It put his bureau on the map in the consciousness of the public and Congress, stilling some of the personal criticism he had been getting, silencing the doubts whispered about his agency's efficiency. The press throughout the country reflected the public mood, loudly applauding the convictions and helping to promote the now almost-larger-than-life image the FBI director would maintain for many years. A *Daily Oklahoman* reporter would make the point years later that it was "the first decisive victory against the gangland forces then thought to be threatening the very survival of America." A writer for the *Washington Herald*, a friend of Hoover's, concluded in a seven-part series a few months after the convictions that it was "the finest piece of detective work in modern times." Thus Hoover was suddenly Public Hero No. 1, the epitome of the stronger law-and-order posture and performance the public had so recently begun to demand.

Yet for his pivotal role in solving his own case, Charles Urschel received only that diffident, single-page letter of "gratification" from Hoover, done at the prompting of one of the director's field staff. Possibly the director had convinced himself that his forces had solved the case with little need of Urschel's clues. As friendly biographer Sanford J. Ungar wrote some forty years later in *FBI: An Uncensored Look behind the Walls*, "the Bureau assembled *tiny* clues and *fragments* of the victim's own recollections, once he was safely returned, to track down the place where he had been held, a Texas farm owned by Machine Gun Kelly's in-laws" [emphasis added]. And the FBI stated flatly in the twenty-one-page monograph about the case it issued in 1935 that the information Urschel supplied was "meager." This totally unwarranted word was excised, however, from the revised version made available in July 1989 in print form and subsequently on the agency's web page.

On the other hand, Hoover had to have known he'd been lucky, luckier than when he would win on the long-shot horse races he was so fond of betting on. After all, it was Urschel who steered the FBI to, and personally guided the officers through, the Paradise hideout—as an armed member in the front rank of the raiding party (whereas Hoover had never, to that time, carried a weapon or participated in an arrest or a raid). It was Kathryn Kelly who unwisely aroused the suspicions of the two Fort Worth detectives and all but pointed the FBI toward her mother living in Wise County, now as Mrs. Robert Shannon. And it was the unlikely twelve-year-old Geraldine Arnold who supplied the clue leading to the Kellys' Memphis hiding place and guided officers to the Texas farm where the loot was buried.

Hoover's outlook about the case seemed to have mellowed a bit five years later, when his *Persons in Hiding* contained these two paragraphs:

That story is fairly familiar—how Mr. Urschel's photographic mind had pictured almost every move, action and surrounding of the days in which he had been held for ransom. How he had catalogued sounds, voices, distances and principally the fact that a passenger plane had failed to follow its usual route over the hideout house on Sunday morning when a rainstorm had driven it off its course.

Likewise the story of the investigation which followed has been told often—the chasing down of every little clue, the checking of meteorological reports of records of precipitation, the narrowing down of the possible locale through consultation of airplane schedules until at last Special Agents were able to draw a map of the possible region in which Mr. Urschel was held, and through this map, trace the hideout down to the ranch occupied by Kathryn's mother and step-father.

There is no question, as well, that the case demonstrated the efficiency and effectiveness of the newly available federally coordinated and cooperative effort in the attorney general's and Roosevelt's "war on crime." As government prosecutor Keenan said grandiosely, "This is just a skirmish. We are going right on down the line until every predatory criminal and gangster in the United States is exterminated. The new law has proven a powerful weapon and we are eager to use it to the finish." Hyde, at thirty-five the country's youngest U.S. district attorney, went before the newsreel cameras to declare, "This should serve as a notice to those who would violate and set aside our federal laws that no individual or group of individuals is more powerful than the federal government." The attorney general was of the same opinion: "If convictions may be obtained and heavy penalties inflicted a sufficient number of times, kidnapping can be stopped. It will cease to be a popular criminal activity."

Prior to the extension of federal power under the new law, outmanned and underfunded police forces were disadvantaged by state jurisdictions, legal obstructions, and technicalities like extradition requests, hearings, and writs. But now, no longer restrained by artificial political boundaries, the FBI had demonstrated it was able to chase down criminals, effectively using its national (if still small) network of agents. And the new federal authority that required only showing cause to extradite suspects—in this instance from Texas, Minnesota, Colorado, and Tennessee to stand trial in Oklahoma—was a powerful and welcome new legal weapon. Likewise, the new long arm of federal jurisdiction extended to all facets of the crime—the abduction in Oklahoma, the confinement in Texas, the ransom demand postmarked from Missouri, and the $200,000 itself delivered there after a train ride through Oklahoma and Kansas with the payoff. Also the hate letters sent from Illinois and the unsuccessful money laundering in Minnesota were now a federal crime. The case also marked the government's first use of airplanes to transport prisoners; not only the Kellys but also the Shannons took their first flight ever, from Dallas to Oklahoma City, and Bates was airlifted in from Denver to stand trial.

Certainly the harsh sentences meted out so speedily to the kidnappers and the various "conspirators" sent a powerful message to other criminals, a message given even more clout when the death penalty was subsequently added to the kidnapping law. Here, finally, was a federal statute with sharp teeth, and the eager FBI was working cooperatively with state and local police forces to back it up. When the gangsters and their cohorts realized they couldn't use their old ways to elude capture or avoid maximum punishment, kidnapping quickly lost a lot of its allure. There is no question that the Urschel case was the defining moment in the battle against kidnapping. How had Hoover so succinctly put it? It bears repetition: "The capture of Kelly is the government's ultimatum to the underworld that kidnapping is an unsafe business."

What happened to the other gangsters of the 1930s? Charles Arthur ("Pretty Boy") Floyd (thirty-three) died October 22, 1934, in a shootout with FBI agents. Bonnie Parker (twenty-four) and Clyde Barrow (twenty-five) fell in a hail of police gunfire May 23, 1934. Baby Face Nelson (twenty-six; real name Lester J. Gillis) was killed in a gun battle October 27, 1934. Ma Barker, aka Arizona Donnie Kate Clark (sixty-something), was shot to death along with her son Fred (thirty-two) in a lengthy gun battle with FBI agents on January 16, 1935. Adam Richetti (about twenty-nine) was put to death, screaming in terror, in the Missouri State Penitentiary gas chamber on October 7, 1938, the first person to die there and the only person convicted in the Union Station Massacre. The nude and mangled body of Verne Miller (thirty-seven) turned up in a Detroit suburb wrapped in a blanket November 29, 1933, riddled with bullets. Other gangsters shot Roger ("The Terrible") Touhy (sixty-one) to death December 17, 1959, less than a month after he was released from prison for another kidnapping. Alvin ("Creepy") Karpis (seventy-one) was paroled from Alcatraz in 1969 and died peacefully in Spain in 1979. Al Capone, while not one of that group of gangsters, was paroled because of bad health in 1939 and died in Florida in 1947 at the age of forty-eight. Kelly was one of the few Gangster Era big names who survived to live out his life (although in prison) and die a natural death.

Shortly after Kelly's conviction, motion picture audiences throughout the country viewed "The News Parade of 1933" newsreel between the customary double features. The film included a short segment: a shot of the Oklahoma courtroom and then a handcuffed Kelly—dressed in a stylish dark suit, wearing a tie, and with his trademark fedora and silly lopsided grin—being escorted to an airplane in Memphis by eight grim-faced guards with submachine guns. Following the lead-in slate—"OKLAHOMA CITY, OKLA. Hearst Metrotone News"—audiences heard the high-pitched, staccato narrator on the soundtrack: "Uncle Sam Wars on Kidnappers! Abductors of Charles Urschel, oil millionaire, are sentenced for life under the new so-called Lindbergh federal law! Machine Gun Kelly, mastermind of a snatch gang and desperado extraordinary, gets life, too! A telling blow at gangdom's rule!" Many audiences reportedly broke into spontaneous applause.

Another interesting facet of the case as it unfolded, and of the subsequent trial, was the hyperbole and colorful reporting. One newspaper reporter breathlessly called Kelly "one of the most spectacular desperadoes gangland has mothered." Writers of the day—and for years afterward—showered a long list of outrageously lurid but totally erroneous epithets on his head: "Ruthless killer"; "One of the most vicious and dangerous criminals in America"; "Known killer"; "Trigger-happy gunman"; "Expert machine gunner"; "Machine gunner for the underworld of the Western badlands"; "Jack of all criminal trades"; and purportedly the perpetrator of "massacres that have terrorized the nation."

Urschel's kidnapping by this seemingly bloodthirsty desperado would be a windfall that J. Edgar Hoover would eagerly embrace and use—or adroitly exploit, it could be charged. It certainly wasn't Kelly's intent, but his abduction of Urschel handed Hoover the first major publicity springboard for the reputation he carefully crafted: self-styled, national crime-busting czar. Well aware of the value of perception over reality and cleverly employing plausible-sounding propaganda, this dedicated foe of gangland actually built up criminals through memorable monikers and artfully embellished their fearsome reputations.

Enhancing the "credentials" of the gangsters made them appear much more dangerous in the eyes of the public, most of whom accepted Hoover's pronouncements unquestioningly. Thus when the outlaws were eventually captured or gunned down in dramatic shootouts, Hoover and his beleaguered, undermanned agency were seen as that much more heroic—thanks in no small part to the expert publicists he hired and, in some instances, to admiring journalists.

The follow-up to the Union Station Massacre provided another early hint—not known at the time, of course—of Hoover's press agentry. He wrongfully implicated Bailey as one of the assassins, along with three other gangsters in the public eye as "most wanteds"—"Pretty Boy"

Floyd, Adam ("Eddie") Richetti, and Verne Miller. Bailey, as became known, was nowhere in the vicinity. Floyd, also innocent this time, was irate about being included, so much so that he uncharacteristically sent angry letters to several newspapers denying any involvement in the crime. Miller possibly may have been present in Kansas City that morning, but most evidence about the shooting seemed to point instead to professional syndicate hit men holding a contract to ambush and kill the forty-six-year-old Frank ("Jelly") Nash, the escaped bank robber the lawmen were returning to Leavenworth in manacles.

But there was more prestige attached to chasing down dangerous better-known gangsters than faceless hired assassins. Also, while Hoover maintained that the Kansas City victims had been wantonly gunned down in their car by gangsters, a more recent investigation seemed to show that three of the victims were accidentally killed by a panicked officer in the backseat. Seeing the armed gangsters approaching, he was frantically trying to figure out the firing mechanism of a sawed-off shotgun he'd never used before and apparently accidentally fired in the car before the hit men got off their first rounds. Some years later, Kansas City's chief of detectives at the time of the massacre recalled that "the FBI covered up so many facts about the case we never really knew much."

Hoover's "dirty yellow rats" quote in the United News Service interview was another of the colorful examples of how he had perfected to an art form capturing headlines as well as gangsters, a master "spin doctor" long before the term was coined. He was always readily accessible to the press personally or through a spokesman with a handy stream of picturesque quotable epithets for criminals—"vermin," "public rats," "scum," and the like. He had an equally contemptible opinion of advocates of any kind of early prisoner release, calling them "sob sister judges," "criminal coddlers," "shyster lawyers," "convict lovers," "legal vermin," and "swivelchair criminologists."

The widely syndicated columnist Drew Pearson, a Hoover confidant, recalled that the director held the belief that "the best cure for kidnapping was to build up the FBI, not only in actual strength but in the strength of public opinion behind it." That view was shared by Attorney General Cummings, who complained that "the original case frequently is given much publicity but the solution and conviction are not sufficiently emphasized." To that end, the old *Brooklyn Eagle*'s respected Washington correspondent Henry Suydam was hired on as the department's very effective public affairs spokesman for a brief tenure. At the same time, Hoover worked out a cozy arrangement with William F. ("Buffalo Bill") Cody's former press agent, the prolific writer Courtney Ryley Cooper, to churn out books and countless articles under both Hoover's and his own byline extolling the director and his FBI.

The FBI itself, in a brief history of the Gangster Era posted on its Internet home page as recently as 2003, stated candidly: "Noting the widespread interest of the media in this war against crime, Hoover carried the message of FBI work through them to the American people. He became as adept at publicizing his agency's work as he was at administering it." One author of FBI history said, "No government official has ever communicated to a national audience in such volume as J. Edgar Hoover." However, the crusty veteran senator George W. Norris of Nebraska complained in 1940, "Mr. Hoover is doing more injury to honest law enforcement in this country by his publicity-seeking feats than is being done by any other one thing connected with his organization. . . . A detective who advertises his exploits every time he gets an opportunity, who spends the public money to see that they are spread over the pages of the newspapers in flaming headlines, will in the end be a failure in ferreting out crime and bringing guilty persons to justice." This sentiment was echoed years later in *The Bureau—My Thirty Years in Hoover's FBI* by William C. Sullivan, the longtime No. 3 official under Hoover: "The FBI's main thrust was not investigations but public relations and propaganda to glorify Hoover. Everyone who worked in the Bureau, especially those of us in high places around him, bear our share of the blame. Flacking for the FBI was part of every agent's job from his first day." And Frank J. Donner added in *The Age of Surveillance: The Aims and Methods of America's Political Intelligence System* that "no government official has ever communicated to a national audience in such volume as J. Edgar Hoover."

Milking his version of Kelly's apprehension at every opportunity, Hoover even collaborated sub rosa in the origination, production, and promotion of a nationally syndicated daily comic strip, "War on Crime." It made its debut in 1936 with a fairly accurate, well-drawn depiction of the Urschel case. The strip—with the balloons written by *Washington Evening Star* byliner Rex Collier—unabashedly played up the "keen-eyed, broad-shouldered" FBI director himself. Unbeknownst to the public, Hoover required top-level advance approval by the bureau of the artwork and the dialogue in every panel of every episode for the run of the feature. The publicity machine trumpeted that the strip depicted "the stories of G-Men activities," that these were accounts of "real G-men versus real gangsters, no lurid tales of a fictitious underworld, but actual case histories." The retelling of the Urschel case in the strip perpetuated the "Don't shoot, G-Man" myth (with the addition of more words supposedly in Kelly's mouth when captured: "I know when I'm covered"). The Urschel story ran daily except Sundays starting June 1 and concluding on July 11 with the ringing message that "the ringleaders—Bailey, Bates, and the boastful Kelly—have ended their career of crime in dreaded Alcatraz." Unhappily for Hoover's purposes, though, the strip itself survived barely a year and a half, quietly expiring in January 1938, never able to outdraw another new feature in the funnies, "Plainclothes Tracy" (later to be renamed "Dick Tracy").

Meanwhile, a popular evening weekly radio crime series drew Hoover's wrath. "The Green Hornet" made its debut in 1936, opening with the line, "He hunts the biggest of all game, public enemies that even the G-Men cannot reach." Because of Hoover's reported irritation, the sentence very quickly was shortened in subsequent episodes to end with the word "enemies."

Attorney General Cummings had played a leading role in convincing the newly elected president to keep Hoover on in 1933, despite some strenuous opposition in Congress and even among a few of the president's advisers. At first, Cummings stood stoutly behind the director against attacks. "If there is anybody shooting at Hoover they're shooting at me. Hoover has my entire confidence and if anybody thinks they are going to get him out of this office they will have to get me first." But years later, Cummings would call his earlier support "one of the biggest mistakes I ever made," because he felt that Hoover was "difficult to handle, could not be controlled, and had the faculty of attracting too much attention to himself."

Despite the sensational descriptions such as "ruthless killer" and "trigger-happy gunman" that Machine Gun Kelly had been branded with, Urschel hadn't actually been physically harmed during his captivity, nor had any of the death threats against him and the others been carried out. True, Kathryn and George had both *threatened* to kill, if the trial witnesses were to be believed. But since neither the Kellys nor the Bateses had ever by any known account fired on or even mistreated their holdup or kidnap victims in any way, it's questionable whether one of them would have actually pulled the trigger on Urschel. Or shoved his head in that barrel of lime. And the supposed "contract" with the notorious killer Verne Miller seems to have been nothing more than a fabrication of Kelly's. Still, kidnapping was a heinous crime that had to be combated; the Kellys and Bates, plus all the other defendants, had to be made examples of in order to attack the epidemic head-on and to send a message. Perhaps because of that message, "gangland" ignored Kelly. Whatever the reason, the fact remains that apparently nobody even tried to come to Kelly's rescue, as he had so boastfully threatened that they would.

The entire case, from the intrusion on the sunporch to the conviction and sentencing of the Kellys, spanned a mere eighty-one days, as no legal delaying tactics were tolerated in those times. Objections were quickly overruled as frivolous, and appeals were summarily denied, which sent the underworld another bulletin as well: from then on, justice would be rapid and severe. Hoover wrote some years later that "during [1933] the FBI solved every kidnapping case referred to it. Among those were the Cannon, Otterly, Urschel, Boettcher, Luer, McElroy, Hart, Bremer, and Hamm kidnappings, in which ransom demands totaled $782,000."

Hoover would proudly inform a Senate committee in early 1936 that kidnapping had "almost been eliminated" in the United States and that since the Lindbergh Act of 1932, the FBI had handled sixty-two cases and "every one of those cases has been solved." With the repeal of Prohibition near the end of 1933, the incarceration of the Kelly crowd, and the violent deaths of most of the outlaws noted earlier, the Gangster Era had in fact pretty much run its brief but notable course. In effect, Cummings's war on crime (or at least against kidnapping) was over. And rising fast in the public estimation was Hoover's FBI.

So was the intriguing Urschel case closed once and for all, as it seemed? Far from it, as will be seen.

12

Echoes and Reverberations

❖ ❖ ❖ ❖ ❖ ❖ ❖ ❖ ❖ ❖ ❖ ❖ ❖ ❖ ❖

Officially, yes, the Urschel case was history: the abduction, ransom, release, pursuit, capture, convictions, and finally the incarcerations of the culprits. But it refused to fade away. The long-running aftermath, much of it not known to the public, was in many ways more intriguing than what had gone before.

First, though, while the Kellys were still being hunted, was a publicized dustup over just how much of a "right to know" the public had regarding the Urschel/Slick family financial affairs. In a letter to the managing editor of the *Daily Oklahoman*, Berenice's brother-in-law, Arthur Seeligson, bitterly denounced newspapers in general, accusing the press of being "responsible for the kidnapping" in the first place.

The unhappiness that Seeligson, an attorney, had with the press in general and the *Daily Oklahoman* (and its afternoon paper, the *Oklahoma City Times*) in particular centered on three premises—first, coverage of public misstatements he unabashedly admitted he and others in the family had made to mislead the kidnappers in the interest of Urschel's well-being; second, that a column the paper published under Urschel's byline after his release was not in fact authored by the victim and therefore didn't accurately represent his views; and, third, that publishing detailed information about the family's wealth and prominence had actually encouraged the kidnapping in the first place. The column that ignited Seeligson's wrath had appeared on page one of the *Times* the day after Urschel's release.

Complaining that the family had withheld information and that the federal government had "duped" the paper with "half truths and misstatements," the column read in part:

Urschel's safety is important, yes, but behind him stand your child and mine. We, the people, want protection from kidnappers. It cannot be secured by permitting the wealthy to pay the price demanded and then to cover up the tracks made by human jackals whose success will embolden them to crimes yet unconceived. . . .

Since the sorry day that the Lindbergh baby was snatched from his cradle on Sourland mountain, the people of these United States have been shamed repeatedly by desperadoes such as did the Urschel job. Next to the Depression, the stamping out of this disgrace is the highest call to arms in America today. Get the kidnappers!

Walter M. Harrison, as asked, printed in full the concerns that Seeligson spelled out in an apparently hastily written letter to the newspaper's managing editor. After asserting that the ransom payment and other details were "personal," Seeligson continued:

You are correct in stating that during the progress of the negotiations I did not give the true information to the papers. Absolute secrecy was necessary to insure the safe return of Charlie Urschel and that was our first consideration. Past experiences have proven to us the inadvisability of giving you, or your papers, any information of a personal nature.

I feel that the Oklahoma papers, and yours, have been among the worse [sic] offenders, were responsible for the kidnapping of C.F. Urschel more than any other one factor. The sensational stories, misrepresentations and insinuations about the size of the estate that have been printed at various times during the past three years, together with all other personal matters involving the different members of the Slick and Urschel families which you have featured, and headlined at every opportunity, has [sic] so focused attention on both of these families as to make them one of the first targets for those in the kidnapping racket.

❖   ❖   ❖

As for the first-person Urschel narrative in question, it too contained some carefully camouflaged and even deliberately misleading statements couched to give no useful information to the kidnappers still evading capture. Urschel tried to make them believe he wouldn't be able to testify as to their identities and that he had hardly a clue about who they might be or where they had held him. (The full two-column account is included in the Appendix.)

❖ ❖ ❖

The accusation that his newspaper was responsible for the kidnapping was a charge that managing editor Harrison would not take lying down. His initial response took the form of a thoughtful open letter to Seeligson, in which he also detailed how the Urschel byline piece came about:

> Your charge that the newspapers are responsible for the kidnapping is too puerile to merit detailed discussion.
>
> If we have erred in publishing the estimated value of the Slick estate, it is because the estate itself never would place a figure upon it for publication. . . .
>
> As one of the richest families in the Southwest, [the Slicks and Urschels] occupied a position at the peak for which they must pay the annoyances of public attention which come with fame and wealth. . . .
>
> As to Mr. Urschel's signed story, I deny that any advantage was taken of Mr. Urschel. I did virtually all of the questioning of the victim on the morning after his return. Upon my arrival at the office, I reconstructed the narrative in the first person. I called Mrs. Urschel on the telephone and told her I was sending out the manuscript. I asked her to read it with Mr. Urschel and requested them jointly to correct, delete and amend it as they pleased.
>
> Mrs. Urschel said she would gladly see that this was done.
>
> The story was revised by the Urschels, one paragraph omitted, another added and returned to me. It was a fair and true report. Most of it was in Mr. Urschel's own language. The only addition made by me before the story went to the printers was the line, "Copyright, 1933, by the North American Newspaper Alliance and the Oklahoma Publishing Co."
>
> Your interest in this case seems to have been single—the safe re-

turn of Mr. Urschel. Our interest is double—the restoration of the victim, and the capture of the culprits for the protection of society.

A second Harrison column followed in a similar vein:

But the family need not be surprised at anything that is said or printed about the case. Walter Jarrett dissembled about his part in the kidnapping. Urschel himself has not been frank and complete in his stories. Arthur Seeligson thought it was quite all right to make definite misstatements to newspaper people who were attempting to cooperate.

If Urschel would tell all he knows the hideout where he was held prisoner could be located within 24 hours.

Finally, a few days later, Harrison would use his front-page "The Tiny Times" column to bring the colloquy to conclusion:

The capture of the Bailey gang eliminates the most vicious ring of criminals loose in the Southwest. The successful drive of the Department of Justice in this case will throw a scare into gangsters everywhere and reassure the people that our government can go places and do things when it gets its blood up.

In the light of subsequent events, we did the Urschel family an injustice in suggesting that they were not cooperating wholeheartedly with the government. In our joy at the outcome of this crime, we are happy to acknowledge our fault.

William Stanley, assistant to the attorney general, said the Urschel family was the first to respond to the request of the government that Washington be contacted immediately in the event of a kidnapping. Mr. Stanley said the Urschel family had Washington on the long distance telephone a short time after the two gunmen drove away with their victim and that throughout the hunt the associates of the victim gave the government complete cooperation.

Harrison had raised the same—and never publicly answered—question that Kelly had posed in the letter he had sent to the newspaper: Why, upon his release that damp night, hadn't Urschel sought out the first telephone he could find and immediately notified the police while the trail was reasonably hot? Sheriff W. W. Jennings of Cleveland County (Norman) complained about the same thing in an interview with the press:

> If Urschel had called me instead of a taxi when he was turned loose near Norman, the kidnappers wouldn't have had a chance in a hundred to get away. It was raining hard Monday night and only two roads leading away from Norman were passable. We could have closed them in ten minutes. Every other road in the county was hub deep in mud and out of the question for a getaway. But instead of notifying local officers, Urschel rode on to Oklahoma City before he told anybody of his release. His captors were hours away before we had any chance to take up the chase.

In the two trials, the defense attorneys had tried almost desperately to make something of the various misleading and evasive statements that Urschel and his family had parceled out to the press, comparing them to the conflicting statements they offered later under oath in court. This tactic led Judge Vaught to state that Urschel and the others were well within their rights, and in fact actually had done just what they should have, to be sure they gave no hint of assistance to the kidnappers while they were still the subject of the manhunt. As for the copyrighted bylined piece, Urschel testified in answer to a question in court: "Mr. Harrison wrote that narrative and sent it out and I read it over very hurriedly because he was pressed for time. He wanted it right back, and I said it was all right and he printed it. I never copyrighted the statement as shown in the paper."

13

Letters from the "Inside"

❖ ❖ ❖ ❖ ❖ ❖ ❖ ❖ ❖ ❖ ❖ ❖ ❖ ❖ ❖

Seeligson wasn't the only letter writer among those involved with the Urschel case. In an effort to combat the worst curses of prison life—sheer boredom and monotony—both Kelly and Bates would compose some extraordinary correspondence. Unfortunately, only a few examples have come to light, and no copies of any responses they may have received are in the public domain.

Kelly sent the following remarkable letter—typed and edited (censored, actually) by a prison clerk trained to look for secret messages, as was the rule for all outgoing and even incoming mail—to Urschel from Alcatraz on April 11, 1940. Insightful and moving, it suggests Kelly's state of mind— and his intelligence—after the first half-dozen years of his life sentence:

From Geo. R. Kelly #117
Alcatraz Is. Calif.
To Mr. Chas. F. Urschel
Oklahoma City, Okla.
My dear Mr. Urschel:

   I hope I am not pulling a prize blunder (or should I say committing a "faux pas"?) in writing to you. I have two reasons for doing so: first, I wish some information; second, I want to appease my curiosity. In respect to the latter, it all came about this way: Several months ago I had a talk with Mr. J. V. Bennett [director of the U.S. Bureau of Prisons for twenty-seven years]; in the course of our discussion, he mentioned that you had paid him a visit, and asked me if I ever wrote to you. Of course my answer was no. Another of his remarks was: "Mr. Urschel mentioned you and spoke well of you considering the circumstances"—or something to that effect. I have pondered over his remarks quite a bit, and often wondered if for some unknown reason you did wish to hear from me.

Now for the information that I desire. I believe that you are aware that both Mr. Shannon and I own farms in Wise County, Texas. Of course you know where the Shannon farm is located; mine adjoins it on the east. I understand that some oil company has struck oil in that vicinity, and at the present time is buying up leases close to the farm. Have you heard anything about this? As I seldom write anyone other than my wife it is almost impossible for me to get any information on the true conditions there. Situated as you are, you should have no trouble in getting the "low down" on what is going on. I would appreciate any information you might give me regarding the oil prospects in Wise County; especially, the prospects around the farm, which is four miles south of Paradise.

Now before I go further don't think I am merely writing this letter to try to get into your good graces. You can rest assured I will never ask you to do anything towards getting me out. Naturally I realize that your enmity could become a detriment in later years. So, to be truthful, I hope you do not feel too vindictive; although, I hardly think that you are a person of a malevolent disposition. After so many years, I must admit that I am rather ashamed of the grand stand play that I made in the courtroom—of course I am referring to what I said to you that day on leaving the courtroom. I was good and mad at the time. Need I of [sic] remind you of the enthusiasm of the days during my trial. You and your friends shared in it; seemed to revel in it. What produced it? The Department of Justice's love of the dramatic; the public's desire for a good free show; an accumulated spirited vitality which found no employment in the things of every day and so was ready to enjoy to the utmost anything out of the ordinary.

Kelly concluded after another page with the somewhat lighter inquiry:

How is your bridge game? Are you still vulnerable? I don't mean that as a dirty dig but you must admit you lost your bid on the night of July 22, 1933.

Ordinarily I am allowed to write only one page, but as this is a special letter, and as I will have to ask the warden for permission to mail it to you, I believe he will allow the three pages this one time. It is awfully hard for me to write a short letter; I get to rambling and seem unable to stop. I guess I am just long-winded.

I hope you will not consider my writing an impertinence, if you do, just tear this letter up and forget it. Of course, I should enjoy hearing from you anytime. With best wishes, I am

Very truly yours,

Geo. R. Kelly

Reg. No. 117

A month later, after the director of the Bureau of Prisons asked Urschel whether he wanted to receive Kelly's letter, Urschel wrote:

Regarding the matter of my wanting to correspond with Kelly, there are several questions we would all like to have cleared up but I seriously doubt that he would give us the information. One is, the location of the balance of the ransom money which has never been recovered; and another, the identity of the person or persons who suggested me to himself and Bates.

If he has anything in particular on his mind that he wishes to write about I would be very glad to have him do so as I do not believe correspondence of this nature could do any harm. Naturally, after all the family and myself have gone through on Kelly and Bates' account, we are not inclined to want to carry on a friendly correspondence with either of them.

With respect to the question about whether there was oil in Paradise, Kathryn would bring Kelly's son George Barnes up to date in a letter she sent from prison in West Virginia in 1948: "Well, the oil situation back home is still raging and so far no money from it. We haven't leased any land yet but my stepfather [Boss] wrote that a well had blew in just three miles away last week and that things looked very good."

Comparing Kathryn's most ungrammatical "had blew" with George's very literate correspondence (which, however, may well have been the work of the prison rewriter/censor), one wonders what could have led

Hoover to dismiss George so arbitrarily as the author of the ransom notes and threatening letters and to insist that "the actual work had been done by some woman of superior intelligence. That woman was Kathryn Kelly."

In another reflection of his mood in prison, Kelly stated in a letter to his wife Kathryn, "I'd prefer not to have visitors. Although I would give my life to see you free, I would insist that you stay away. It's a rotten way to visit, not pleasant for either party, so I'll be happy with sojourns through letters."

To his son Bruce, Kelly poured out his soul: "I admired your grandfather Ramsey more than any man I've ever known and had he not died, I wouldn't be here on Alcatraz. I was a headstrong kid when I married your mother and he made a man out of me with kindness and understanding. When he died, I slowly sank back into my old ways of reasoning. There was no longer a great man to emulate. I was so proud of that good man, George Ramsey Sr., that I even changed my middle name to Ramsey."

But then, on a more upbeat note, he wrote Bruce, "I'll be out of here someday soon, son. It may be a few more years, but I will be free and I'm going to make up for all the years I've neglected you." It was not to happen. As for his father, Bruce later told an interviewer, "It appears to me that he just married the wrong woman and fell into step with what they were doing."

In 1942, Albert Bates got into the letter-writing act. In the several missives that eventually surfaced, he raised interesting points about the still-missing ransom money and whether the Shannons were truly involved:

From Albert L. Bates, Reg. No. 137 AZ
June 19, 1942
Alcatraz, California
To Mr. Charles F. Urschel
Dear Sir:

I have been informed that Mr. and Mrs. George Kelly and Mrs. Ora Shannon are under the impression that the recent denial of Mrs. Shannon's application for executive clemency was based upon the unrecovered portion of ransom money you paid to Kelly and me.

I, of course, feel terribly sorry for Mrs. Shannon; she is getting well up in years, in poor health, and after all, she took no active part in the crime—other than to carry out her husband's instruction to cook a dinner for you on Sunday while Kelly and I were absent.

Bates went on to explain that he was not interested in communicating with any authorities about the case and had avoided doing so during his prison term:

All I know is what I read in the *World's Almanac* (1935) under date of December 8, 1934, that a total of only $126,000.00 had been recovered, which seemed to me to be an awful discrepancy. I have not corresponded with my wife, or any one else for that matter, so I am totally in the dark.

It is for this reason that I am writing to you; if you care to answer this it is possible that I can account for any shortage in the sum recovered from my share of $93,750.00.

I am sure, Mr. Urschel, that you will understand that I have no personal motive behind this. I expect to serve the rest of my life in this, or some other institution, for my crime. . . . My sole interest is to give you an accurate accounting of the money I received from the venture.

With best wishes I am
Sincerely,
Albert L. Bates
Register No. 137A

While sitting out his time on Alcatraz, Bates consistently warded off unwelcome questioning by Kirkpatrick and FBI agents by telling them the money "is buried so deep you birds will never find it." When Bates was on trial, he had told several people outside the court that "if I ever get out, there is one thing damned sure. No one else will ever enjoy my part of the ransom money. I have it buried in a thermos jug, four feet in the ground, and it'll rot there."

Three months after the preceding letter there was another bit of correspondence from Bates to Urschel:

From Albert L. Bates, Reg. No. 137 AZ
Sept. 29, 1942
Alcatraz, California
Prisoner's Mail Box
October 6, 1942
Bureau of Prisons
To Mr. C. F. Urschel
Dear Mr. Urschel:

Your letter of September 10th was forwarded to me by Mr. James V. Bennett, Director, Bureau of Prisons, and though there is little that I can divulge about this case that isn't known, I can answer your query in reference to the division of the ransom money.

After Kelly and I received the money from Mr. Kirkpatrick in Kansas City we returned directly to the Shannon Ranch, arriving there about 2 p.m., on Monday, July 31, 1933. We retired to the front room of the house and divided the money in privacy. . . .

I received the sum of $94,250.00 for my "end." . . . I gave Bailey $500.00 out of my pocket and Kelly did likewise. I left the farm with $93,750.00. When we released you at Norman, Kelly and I separated. I drove via Chickasha to Amarillo, thence to Denver. My wife was in Portland, Oregon, where I communicated with her, advising her to return to Denver immediately. I put $50,000.00 in a bag with surplus clothes, locked it, and left it with friends to keep until my wife called for it. I left instructions in a letter addressed to her in my postoffice box for her to rent an apartment upon arrival and to leave the address in that box. I had been under a tremendous strain for a week, on the go night and day, so I decided I'd have a little pleasure in Denver. I don't believe I spent over $1,000.00 during the three days I stayed there. . . .

When I was alone in the apartment my wife had rented I put $41,000.00 in the same bag with the $50,000.00. I probably spent about $2,000.00 all told and had $700.00 on me when I was arrested three days after returning to Denver. I told my wife when I left the apartment on the date of my arrest that there was over $90,000.00 in a locked bag in the clothes closet.

I did not authorize her to pay any money to anyone after my arrest with the exception of $200.00 to a trusty by whom I sent a message warning her to leave. She was not apprehended until 16 months after my arrest, and I, of course, do not have the slightest idea how much she spent or was bilked out of. She was never extravagant, but, I suppose, living as she had to for those 16 months she spent more than usual.

This explains about all so far as I know. In my honest opinion the Shannons did not, nor would not, accept any of that money. Kelly may have intended to give them some money later on after he exchanged it for other money. I know they refused time and time again to accept money from any of us. It would be purely a conjecture for me to say why "Boss" Shannon permitted us to take charge whenever we were inclined to do so—he just seemed to be fascinated with Kelly's line.

Respectfully,
Albert L. Bates

That letter, along with the previous one from Urschel, raised questions that have never been publicly answered satisfactorily. According to the last FBI statement on the matter, dated July 1989, only about $140,000 had seemingly been accounted for, which includes the $73,250 dug up in Texas and some $44,000 recovered from Bates's wife, Clara Feldman. She pleaded guilty to a charge of conspiracy and was sentenced in January 1935 to a five-year term, which was suspended because of her cooperation; she got probation instead. The FBI and the Urschel family received many communications for several years offering to disclose where the rest of the money was—in exchange for up to 25 percent of it, which Urschel was willing to pay as a reward or finder's fee. But none apparently proved legitimate. It was early in December 1934 when Clara Feldman was let out of prison for one day to lead Urschel, Kirkpatrick, and some officers to an overgrown site on the bank of the Lewis River outside Portland, Oregon. There they excavated half a dozen fruit jars crammed with ransom bills. With her assistance, more money was unearthed in Washington and California.

Not only did Urschel take a train ride to Leavenworth in 1938 to pump Boss unsuccessfully, but he also retained a former deputy sheriff to try to track down the rest of the missing ransom. What—if any—success he had neither the family nor the government ever disclosed. As for the bills that were recovered, the court gave them to Urschel to make his own arrangement with the Treasury Department for replacement currency.

So, officially, the rest of the loot is still unaccounted for. The FBI said a few of the bills turned up individually from time to time within a couple of years. Perhaps after a period of time others may have been slipped back into circulation when people had forgotten and weren't on the lookout for them. Or, with the inscrutable Bates never having been released from prison, they may even now still be buried somewhere.

Boss Shannon would also be heard from, as he and Armon several times had occasion to speak with Urschel. The ailing Boss was the subject of a 1939 petition for clemency that some three hundred of his Wise County neighbors and friends sent to the president. Neither Urschel nor Judge Vaught officially objected to the request. Roosevelt initially denied the petition without prejudice because Boss hadn't served the ten years generally required to be eligible for parole. But on April 5, 1944, the president acted: "Whereas it has been made to appear to me that the said R. G. Shannon is a fit object of Executive clemency: Now, therefore, be it known, that I, Franklin D. Roosevelt, President of the United States of America, in consideration of the premises, divers other good and sufficient reasons me thereunto moving, do hereby commute the sentence of the said R. G. Shannon to twenty years. In testimony whereof I have hereunto signed my name and caused the seal of the Department of Justice to be affixed."

Seven months later, with all the necessary follow-up papers signed and the bureaucratic arrangements finally in place, a parole board released Boss to the custody of a close friend, Will Cleveland, a farmer from Cottondale, not far from Paradise. This brief teletype bulletin went to the world's news organizations:

LEAVENWORTH, KAN., NOV. 6 (AP)—R. G. (Boss) Shannon, convicted in the kidnapping in 1933 of Charles F. Urschel, Oklahoma City oil man, was released on parole today from federal prison and left immediately for his house in Paradise, Tex. Shannon was sentenced Oct. 7, 1933, to a life term, together with George (Machine Gun) Kelly and five others. His sentence later was reduced to twenty years.

Sometime afterward, the bitter and rather reclusive Boss sat for a couple of interviews. Speaking to a *Daily Oklahoman* reporter in 1947, he reiterated his defense: "Tell you one thing right off. I'm just as innocent as that dog. I did what I did because I couldn't help myself, just as any-body'd a-done in my place. That's just what I told the parole board, too. Kelly and Bates, they're the ones who did the kidnapping. They told us they'd brought a drunk man to the farm. I told 'em to get him away when I saw something was wrong. But it was too late then. We had to do what they told us."

Boss went on to recount a recent chance meeting that he and Urschel had had: "I just happened to see him in a restaurant, and he came over and talked to me. I told him I didn't blame him for what had happened to my family because he treated me nice, under the circumstances. Then I asked him if he had anything against me, and he was quiet for a minute, then he says, 'I think you should have told the officers when you found out something was wrong.' I said to him, 'You, Mr. Urschel, with all your guns'—and he had guns, too, he told me he did—I said, 'why did you let 'em take you away?' 'They would have killed me,' that's what Mr. Urschel answered, and I said, 'That's right, and they'd have done the same to me. Kelly and Bates had me under the same kind of threat as you, and they meant business.'"

Turning morosely to the subject of other family members involved, Boss began with Ora. "I'm still trying to get my wife out," he told the newspaper interviewer. "She's innocent, too, but I'm not having much luck. She couldn't help what she did any more'n I could, but there she is under life sentence and I haven't even seen her but one time, for three hours, in fourteen years. Whatever you do, don't say anything that might keep her from getting out. I need her here. I hear from my wife once a week and Kathryn writes every two or three weeks. It might surprise you, but George writes me about once a month from Alcatraz. At first I thought I'd never answer him, but after all he's in there for life and prob-ably never will get out. I can't hold anything against him." And, as for his pardon, "I never would have got out if it hadn't been for Mr. Roo-sevelt. Now there was a President for you. A fine man and close to the common people. I wrote him letter after letter, and I'll say this much for him. I never wrote one that he didn't answer."

Armon had a complimentary comment about Urschel for the same inter-viewer, calling him a "fine fella" and adding, "He came to see me four or five times while I was under my ten-year suspended sentence." Once, early in 1934, Charles and Berenice Urschel paid a visit to take some photos and to urge Armon to look for and turn in the rest of the ransom. Urschel promised Armon he would be richly rewarded. But Armon was unaware of where the money had gone. Another friendly visitor to Wise County was the compassionate Judge Vaught, who dropped by a few times, once while on a deer hunt with Urschel, to see how the young man was holding up under the terms of his probation. "It's a hard crime," Armon philosophized about kidnapping. "I know nobody would want to bother me because I don't have anything, but I'd a lot rather a man would stick a gun in my ribs and rob me as to take part of my family away."

Boss complained to another reporter in 1950, "It's about time somebody told the truth. Lies, lies, nothing but lies have they told about me and my family." No, Boss Shannon did not try to deny he'd stood guard over Urschel, "but what would you do if a Machine Gun Kelly came to your house and told you that you had to do it?"

Kathryn was another letter writer, a prolific one. Ernest Kirkpatrick, the ransom drop man, paid her a visit in prison and said afterward, "She had written President Roosevelt each Christmas begging a parole for her mother, and she assured me that Mr. Urschel's and my opposition was the only block in her path. I asked her many questions, the answers to which I already knew. She either lied in her replies or evaded an answer. She finally, in tearful pleas, asked me if I would relent about opposing her mother's freedom if she would tell me what I wanted to know. I replied in the negative, arose to go and told her I knew most of the answers to the questions I had asked her and that they were a matter of newspaper stories since she had entered prison." He did not elaborate on either the questions or the answers.

After half a dozen years in prison, Kathryn wrote to George saying she wanted a divorce: "I find that I am completely cured of any craving for un-legitimate luxuries and my sincere hopes and plans for the future are of a sane, balanced mode in living. I'll never change on that viewpoint. I have gone through hell and still am plainly speaking, seeing mother as a daily reminder of my own mistake. The mistake was in my love, and marriage to you." But then, in a subsequent letter of September 11, 1940,

Kathryn told George that "if you will really be happier as things are just forget that I ever mentioned the word divorce." Signed, "Devotedly, your Katrinka."

In 1976, Kathryn sent a scathing letter to George's son in response to his request for some information about his father for his book. It was on August 21 that she wrote: "I have no intention of writing anything concerning your deceased father. I am hurt, amazed, and disgusted with his son who would do such a thing for a little publicity and a few dollars. . . . Your father hated publicity and no matter what he may have done that the world considers wrong he was lovable, good hearted, and never hurt anyone or stooped to a cheap deed. . . . The truth was I was the dumb 'patsy' knowing nothing but trying to keep the man I loved [as we were] being chased."

Ever fantasizing about opening a motorcar sales lot, George continued forlornly to hold out hope for parole. First eligible in 1948, he declined to file the papers, however, believing there might still be too much intense ill-feeling about the kidnapping that would adversely affect his chances not only then but, more important, at any later time. In addition, the Oklahoma City sheriff had a "detainer" on file charging him with armed robbery, and the FBI had requested notification if he sought parole.

Adamantly and personally opposing his release as well was Hoover. Responding to a report of parole efforts by Roman Catholic prison chaplain Father Joseph M. Clark on behalf of Kelly and another Alcatraz lifer, Hoover penned a marginal note: "Watch closely & endeavor to thwart efforts of this priest who should be attending to his own business instead of trying to turn loose on society such mad dogs." Hardly a mad dog, Kelly was rated something of a model prisoner in Alcatraz after a brief attitude problem early on ("Talking at mess table; carrying coveralls out gate; joining in strike; participating in strike and refusing to work; causing confusion by constant talking on gallery"). Later, though, Warden James V. Bennett had this to say about Kelly in his book, *I Chose Prison:*

Good looking, well mannered, suave of speech, he worked in the Industries Office at Alcatraz, tended to business and gave no trouble. In my conversations with him, Kelly did not spare himself. While he affected a nonchalant manner he felt the shame and embarrassment he had heaped on members of his family. Kelly minimized the part played by his wife and her relatives in the Urschel kidnapping and contended that, while he should pay a heavy penalty, their sentences were too severe and they should be given more consideration. He admitted that his wife knew about and shared his ill-gotten money but was not around when he committed a crime.

Each prisoner was allowed to purchase three packs of cigarettes a week—about what Kelly had been accustomed to puffing in a day—but there were tobacco "dispensers" in the cell blocks so inmates could roll and smoke as many of their own as they craved. Over time, the warden eased up a bit on some of his harsh rules. One of Kelly's fellow inhabitants, from the Atlanta contingent, was prisoner No. 85, "Scarface" Al Capone, who, first as a tenor banjo player and then on the mandolin, talked the warden into letting him form a prison band. Kelly became his drummer. As further entertainment, the inmates were allowed to see a grand total of four movies a year, and Kelly served as the projectionist.

A former guard at the prison had recollections about Kelly similar to those of the warden: "As far as I could tell, he was one of the most stable prisoners on the island. Kelly never seemed to downgrade anyone. He wasn't like a lot of them who always blamed someone else. He wasn't bitter about things, and recognized that it was his own fault that he was on Alcatraz." Kelly became an avid Bible reader and even assisted at mass as an "altar boy." He also kicked the cigarette habit, preferring to lie in his cell at night smoking a cigar while he voraciously read books from the library. He did file papers in 1939 unsuccessfully seeking release on the rather novel grounds that because the Lindbergh law prescribed no maximum term for kidnapping, the Oklahoma court had sent him to prison illegally. A June 1951 "United States Penitentiary Special Progress Report" from Leavenworth contains the never-explained medical notation that Kelly had had a "previously unreported gun-shot wound of the right elbow without disability." And it added that he had a high-level IQ of 118. Despite Kelly's refusal to tell various visitors from the FBI anything, his good behavior and declining health earned him a transfer back to Leavenworth that same year. There Kelly worked in the laundry and the hospital and also performed some office work. He died on the evening of his birthday in 1954—twenty-one years after entering prison—shortly before a scheduled preliminary hearing looking to his possible parole.

> LEAVENWORTH, KAN., JULY 17 (AP)—George (Machine Gun) Kelly, so nicknamed because he could write his name on a wall with machine gun bullets, died in prison today.
>
> His death was due to heart disease and came a few hours after he had been stricken. . . .
>
> Kelly was one of the most notorious of the hoodlums who terrorized the Midwest twenty years ago.

The prison records show death was due to a "myocardial infarction." When nobody else did, Boss Shannon nobly stepped forward and arranged transportation to and burial in the Shannon family plot in the small Cottondale Community Cemetery. "He ain't got no friends so have him sent back here to Paradise," Boss told a reporter. "He can be buried in one of my gravesites. It's the best thing to happen to George. He never would have gotten out anyway." Local residents told the author that souvenir hunters soon made off with the first several traditional headstones and then a three-foot-high stand with a plaque that read "G. Barnes Kelly." So today there's just a very simple, undistinguished, ground-level eroding concrete marker bearing the simple inscription (misspelled, some locals say, to protect the grave) for this man whose name is still a legend:

GEORGE B.

KELLEY

1954

An epitaph? Kelly probably put it best himself while on Alcatraz when he told the warden, "My people are good people even if I turned out to be an awful heel."

In a documentary that KTUL-TV in Tulsa produced more than twenty-five years after Kelly's death, the narrator quoted the kidnapper as saying, "The biggest mistake I ever made was leaving Tulsa. I got my start there in 'twenty-eight. I was the king of the rumrunners . . . a very good bootlegger. I had the town, a good clientele. Made a good living. Knew a lot of nice people, had a good time. No, that wasn't enough. I had to go to Fort Worth and into that honkytonk. She was pretty, the prettiest redhead I ever saw. But she couldn't even cook. And you know, I still think it could have been the perfect crime."

Besides the missing ransom money, one other mystery remains. What became of Kelly's famous machine gun (serial no. 4907, a 1921 Colt "A" model with an unusual horizontal finger grip rather than the usual vertical one)? After being a principal government exhibit in the trials, it was turned over to the Fort Worth police and simply vanished, no doubt removed from the evidence room by some insider. A gun expert told the author that, depending on its condition, it would be worth no less than $100,000 and might bring more than that at auction.

14

The Case That Wouldn't End

❖ ❖ ❖ ❖ ❖ ❖ ❖ ❖ ❖ ❖ ❖ ❖ ❖ ❖ ❖

In the summer of 1958, Kathryn and her mother Ora successfully and surprisingly obtained a reopening of the proceeding in the same court in which their trials had been held.

Their feisty new attorney was James J. Laughlin of Washington, D.C. How he became involved is an interesting story in itself. In 1949 he had volunteered to defend American citizen "Axis Sally" (Mildred Sisk Gillars) against treason charges for her World War II overseas radio propaganda broadcasts from Berlin aimed at demoralizing U.S. and Allied troops fighting in Europe. Convicted as expected despite Laughlin's efforts, she was sentenced to serve her time at the women's prison at Alderson, West Virginia. There she became acquainted with Kathryn and Ora and told them about Laughlin. "They wrote me from Alderson Reformatory for Women in West Virginia, asking if I wouldn't represent them," said Laughlin, who first tried to get the pair paroled but finally gave up on that stratagem. "It was the same every time," the attorney continued in a newspaper interview. "Urschel, I am told, was prepared to spend $1,000,000, if necessary, to keep Mrs. Kelly and her mother in prison."

In the new trial, Laughlin pinned down the government early. Asserting that the FBI had knowingly employed false evidence concerning who had really written the threatening letters to the Urschels and the *Daily Oklahoman*, he persuaded the judge to order the government to make public its files on the case. The government refused. Just why did Justice/FBI now claim "privilege" and adamantly but "respectfully" refuse at this late date to turn over pertinent files?

There had been far more than enough in the record to convict Kathryn without even bringing up the matter of the hate letters. Since they were posted after Urschel had been released, what could they possibly have had to do with the actual crime? Kathryn did acknowledge all along that she'd been at least marginally involved in the kidnapping, though she always insisted that she'd been forced to do so against her will. In 1933, Hoover had flatly claimed that the letters had been composed "by some woman of superior intelligence . . . Kathryn Kelly." Kathryn herself had made strenuous denials of authorship, and George had asserted that he alone had been the writer. Also notable was Judge Vaught's refusal in 1933 to grant Kathryn's attorney a continuance for any reason.

The underlying answer about why the government wouldn't reopen the case files was finally revealed in *Hoover's FBI: The Men and the Myths*, a 1970 book by William Turner, a former FBI agent whom Hoover loathed and characterized as a "jackal." Hoover was extremely intolerant of any criticism, particularly critical journalism, because he felt it hurt the agency's ability to fight crime and continue to maintain its high level of public approval.

Hoover was reportedly able to keep the Turner book from seeing print for seven years by intimidating potential publishers. One publishing house allegedly turned over Turner's entire proffered manuscript to the bureau, permitting the preparation of a public "rebuttal" even before another publisher eventually brought out the book. Furthermore, as Curt Gentry wrote in *J. Edgar Hoover: The Man and the Secrets*, "Not only was Turner subjected to a vicious campaign of personal vilification and harassment, his editor would be labeled a pornographer, the FBI resurrecting a 1965 indictment of allegedly publishing obscene books, neglecting to mention, when it spread the tale, that the charges had been dismissed."

In his 1970 book, the dismissed agent Hoover so despised made public a photocopy of a suppressed 1933 internal memorandum by the bureau's own highly regarded handwriting expert. It cast a heavy cloud of doubt over the testimony of the local "expert" in Oklahoma. What the veteran FBI expert, Charles A. Appel, concluded in his "Laboratory Report"—submitted to his superiors seventeen days before the start of the trial of George and Kathryn—could have been extremely embarrassing if publicly revealed, then or later:

The handwriting on the letters to the *Oklahomian* [sic] and to Urschel is not identical with that of Mrs. Kelly. There are a great many similarities which on casual examination would lead one to think that these handwritings are the same. However, detailed analysis indicated that Mrs. Kelly did not write these letters. The handwriting in the letters is not to any great extent disguised or changed from normal as far as I can tell, and the same is true of the handwriting of Mrs. Kelly.

A comparison of the signatures of George R. Kelly on three fingerprint cards with those on these letters indicates that he may have written these letters. I do not consider the signatures sufficient to definitely state that he did write the letters but they are sufficient to indicate that he might have done so. If additional specimens of George R. Kelly's handwriting are obtained, further comparison may be made.

Nevertheless, the bureau kept Appel, the nation's preeminent handwriting expert, cooped up in his laboratory in Washington and let the locally retained witness blunder along in the Oklahoma City court.

In a subsequent damaging laboratory report, Appel reiterated, "I am still of the opinion that she did not write these letters." That determination was quoted in an oddly worded FBI memo in 1962—four years after the reopened hearing—that added: "From a review of the above results of examination it is obvious that Appel was vacillating as to the results of his examination and, accordingly, there would appear to be no question as to why Appel did not testify at the trial. There is no indication this information was ever furnished the Department or Joseph B. Keenan. . . . Likewise, Oklahoma City files do not indicate the U.S. Attorney's Office was advised in writing of Appel's findings." Another memorandum in the FBI files states, "These letters did not bear directly on the charge of conspiracy to kidnap for which Kathryn Kelly was charged and it is not known why the Government chose to introduce these extraneous threatening letters."

Another equally puzzled agent wrote, "Insofar as the letters are concerned, it should be noted that Kathryn Kelly was charged with conspiracy to commit kidnapping, and there is nothing in the court record to show why the Government introduced these letters in the 1933 trial since they were mailed subsequent to the abduction and release of victim Urschel."

So, seventy years later the overriding question still remains: why were the letters even allowed to become an issue? Why did the government enter them as evidence in the first place, since the letters, no matter who wrote them, had no possible bearing on the kidnapping itself, the pay-off, or the release of Urschel? And especially when higher-ups in the FBI, including Hoover himself, most certainly had to have been aware of expert Appel's pretrial conclusions? (In fact, in 1964 Hoover would sign a letter telling a reporter, "These letters, therefore, had no direct bearing upon the actual kidnap plot for which Kathryn Kelly was tried and convicted. Furthermore, the examination of the notes in question and the testimony at the trial were furnished by a private handwriting examiner who was in no way connected with the FBI.") Thus, the deceased D. C. Patterson became a convenient scapegoat who couldn't defend himself.

At the 1933 trial, Patterson had presented himself and his credentials as a "public accountant and handwriting expert. As a handwriting expert, I began in 1913 and did very little work on that until 1925 when the demand for such services increased, and I have been continually engaged in that since that time." Judge Vaught's refusal to grant Kathryn's counsel a continuance, perhaps requested in part to attempt to locate a handwriting witness of their own, led her new attorney Laughlin to argue in his 1958 motion for reopening, "Therefore this phase of the case would not have gone to the jury virtually uncontradicted. The jury was of course deceived and misled as to this aspect of the case and this was vital and fatal to the affiant."

In response to a Freedom of Information Act request, an FBI staff member provided the author with a xerox copy of an intriguing undated, unsigned, five-page typewritten report on plain white paper headed "Information Regarding Kathryn Kelly and Harvey Bailey in the Urschel Case." With no mention, unsurprisingly, of the in-house FBI expert's memorandum, the report stresses that one of the government's Oklahoma City trial witnesses was a "handwriting examiner" who was *"in no way* connected with the FBI. . . . It is pointed out, however . . . that D. C. Patterson was located in Oklahoma City where the trial took place" [emphasis in the original]. And, it added dryly, "D. C. Patterson is deceased." Then, this blockbuster follows:

> These two letters were mailed after the kidnapping of Charles Urschel had been completed, the ransom paid, and Mr. Urschel released. They had, then, no direct bearing upon the actual kidnap plot. (The two notes demanding $200,000 ransom were typewritten; whereas the two letters mailed in Chicago on September 18, 1933, were hand-written.) . . . Patterson testified that his examination of the two threatening letters which had been mailed to Mr. Urschel and the Oklahoma City newspaper at Chicago on September 18 reflected that both had been written by Kathryn Kelly. As previously noted, neither of these letters was involved in the actual kidnap plot for which Kathryn Kelly stood trial and was convicted.
>
> D. C. Patterson is deceased. Today, the FBI Laboratory handles all handwriting examinations and testimony in cases investigated by the FBI. It is pointed out, however, that the trial of the Urschel kidnappers occurred early in the Fall of 1933, less than one year from the date the FBI Laboratory was founded; that the trial of Kathryn and George Kelly occurred immediately after their arrests; and that D. C. Patterson was located in Oklahoma City where the trial took place.

This remarkable report is nowhere to be found among the 8,748 pages of assorted information in the FBI headquarters public file about the Urschel case.

It wasn't just the handwriting that was at issue. In truth, that facet was touched upon only lightly during the acrimonious 1958 sessions. The primary allegations Laughlin made were "inadequate assistance of counsel, use of testimony known to be false, denial of compulsory service of process, and conduct of the trial in an atmosphere which prevented a fair and impartial trial"—an "atmosphere of a Roman holiday." These contentions drew a sharp retort from the retired Vaught, then eighty-five years old. He angrily asserted in an affidavit that the two women had been "well represented at all stages" and that "the allegation concerning the handwriting expert and his testimony concerning the ransom note is absolutely false. This court allowed pictures and posed pictures when the court was not in session, but during the actual trial nothing occurred that would in the least distract from the solemnity and judicial decorum of the court. . . . There was no indication, and I feel positive, that there was no false testimony presented by the United States." Of course, Vaught was undoubtedly totally unaware of any or all of the exchange of private FBI memoranda, which came to light later, years after the hearing.

Paul W. Cress, the U.S. attorney for the western district of Oklahoma, and George Camp, his able young first assistant U.S. attorney, were also without knowledge of these suppressed FBI communications. The pair were charged with the unenviable task of reconstructing the old case for the government and defending it. In private practice forty-plus years later, Camp recalled the circumstances vividly and with some amusement. There was a new judge in the case, William R. Wallace Sr., who was noted particularly for his widely quoted remark that to be a good judge, one "needs honesty, industry, and courage, and it sometimes helps to know a little law." Wallace made the routine request for a copy of the transcript of the Kellys' original trial in order to familiarize himself about these new allegations. Camp found that one of the earlier FBI memoranda indicated no transcript could be located. No transcript, no record for posterity or for historians, of the biggest kidnapping trial in the nation's history? None could be found in the courthouse, or anywhere else, Camp told the author in an interview and subsequent communications.

This revelation didn't placate an unhappy Wallace at the time, however. How could he rule on the substance of the allegations, the pleas, the various motions, without a word-for-word history of the earlier proceeding in front of him? Absent the ability to examine their previous words, how could witnesses be properly questioned, or accurately reply, about their testimony and understandably dim recollections of twenty-five years earlier? So he testily threatened to jail the hapless Cress and Camp for contempt of court if they didn't produce the old record in three days—the following Monday. The nervous Camp, Cress, and their wives spent the better part of the weekend laboriously composing and typing up habeas corpus petitions for a fellow assistant U.S. attorney at the chief judicial circuit judge's court in New Mexico to have at the ready if indeed they were ordered to jail.

It had also fallen on Camp at the nonjury hearing to explain the underlying reason, the historical reason, why the Department of Justice would produce no documents: "The matters called for . . . are immaterial, incompetent, irrelevant, hearsay, not the best evidence, therefore inadmissible. . . . The best evidence was the witnesses who have testified." Cress said the refusal came on direct orders from the attorney general of the United States himself, William P. Rogers. "They wanted time to consider the many ramifications of the problem," Cress told a reporter. "Longstanding policies of the department are involved here. Many efforts to break down the confidential nature of the FBI files have been made in the past, but I do not feel Judge Wallace has the slightest intention of doing that. It is simply a matter of law with the judge." Perhaps unaware of those comments, Wallace wondered aloud in court whether Cress and Camp were hiding something: "The very fact you gentlemen are objecting so strenuously makes the court think there were reports."

Wallace did back off on his contempt-of-court threat when he was satisfied that no transcript of the Kellys' 1933 trial had ever been typed up. Why was there no record of such a landmark case? For the simple reason that the attorneys for both sides had pursued the appeal proceeding under what was termed an "agreed narrative statement of evidence." The 1933 court reporter, quite elderly by now, informed the court he was unable to locate his old notepads—if they even still existed. After five days of wading through forty years of records in the courthouse, searchers came across the court reporter's faded handwritten transcriptions of the trial. Courthouse reporters were called on to transcribe them quickly. But there was a major problem: the curlicues were in the old-style Pitman shorthand system. All the current reporters and secretaries were at a loss, having been trained instead in the later, simpler Gregg system or were in the process of converting to operating the newly emerging stenotype machine. None could even make a stab at deciphering the Pitman, which might as well have been in hieroglyphics.

So the aged original reporter agreed to help out and laboriously converted his ancient notes into typewritten form, eventually submitting the transcript to the court in August 1959. It was a strange, abbreviated report of the proceedings, as shown by the first page: "The Court—The government may make its opening statement. (Hereupon opening statements are made by respective counsel, after which the following testimony and evidence was introduced.)" But that, by itself, was it. It then jumped right into the question-and-answer stage. Nothing more. No "opening statements" quoted. No record at all for posterity, just a jump directly to testimony. And, in the author's opinion, there seemed to be gaps throughout the transcript from time to time. These revelations after Kathryn's petition for revisiting her conviction put the government in an awkward predicament, no matter who had been responsible for the legal strategy or the errant testimony twenty-five years earlier.

There was also a sharp difference between the original testimony and the sometimes vague recollections of participants from two and a half decades earlier. (One who testified at length was Hyde, coprosecutor Keenan having died in 1954.) The reopened proceeding, which covered the better part of six days of rambling testimony, was replete with blurred responses from the stand: "I just don't recall"; "Sorry, I can't remember"; "I presume"; "Possibly"; "That may be so"; "As I remember it." Even Kathryn said, "I have tried to forget my trial." Some of the surviving witnesses, after all, were now in their seventies or eighties. One lugged along a huge scrapbook of clippings and photos from the first trial. A retired newspaper photographer produced some of his work in an attempt to refresh memories.

Another witness, appearing for the government this time, had originally been Kathryn's attorney. He had a strange reaction when shown a clipping from 1933 containing several paragraphs of direct quotes attributed to him that he hadn't refuted at the time: "I have no recollection of that, never saw that before in my life." Despite Kathryn's never-wavering testimony to the contrary, her same former attorney—at this point in time the elected county attorney of nearby Coal County—said he couldn't recall having been aware of any conflict over the handwriting testimony. Not only that, but in an unusual disclosure of supposedly confidential attorney-client information—ordered to be revealed by Judge Wallace—Kathryn's 1933 attorney reluctantly testified, "Mrs. Kelly told me who wrote those letters to Judge Vaught, and that her husband made her do it, and she was afraid she would be killed if she didn't."

"He's lying," Kathryn could clearly be heard hissing to her attorney Laughlin. "He's lying."

A sidelight of the hearing was that Urschel and his business colleague Kirkpatrick were both subpoenaed by Kathryn's attorney but spent the six days awaiting the summons to testify that never came. Reportedly registered incognito and on call at a nearby hotel, they were never spotted by reporters.

At the conclusion of the odd hearing, Judge Wallace showed his displeasure with the government's stonewalling and startled everyone by granting the women's petition for a rehearing and releasing them on bond of $10,000 each.

Surprised like everyone else, Kathryn Kelly and Ora Shannon found themselves free after twenty-five years behind bars largely because the government trapped itself in a web of its own spinning. On the evening of June 16, 1958, the two giddy women walked haltingly but triumphantly down the steps of the federal building in Oklahoma City, free citizens, at least until any new hearing. After a few words with the press, the next thing Kathryn did was place a long-distance call to the warden at Alderson: "I'll never be back."

Although tearful, certainly dazed, and a trifle heady at being on the "outside" after so many years, Kathryn was now faced with the stark reality of needing to generate some income for herself and her mother. Were they prepared to face, could they adjust to, the sweeping societal and technological changes that had taken place in the country during their confinement, which included World War II? Of course, Ora told reporters: "We have kept up with the atomic bombs and the sputniks and all of that. We have studied and prepared for this day so we could step right out into the world and take our places." Kathryn seemed less sanguine: "I guess the thing that impressed me most on my first trip out was the fast traffic. I was honestly afraid to cross the streets."

A few days later Kathryn came up with the inspiration that the two of them might go on a coast-to-coast personal appearance tour and tell their side, the "true side," of the story. "That's a long way in the future, though," she confided to a reporter. "Right now I just want to rest and enjoy so many little things. Television, for example, is brand new to me." However, on the wise advice of counsel to leave well enough alone and keep a low profile while the case was still technically open and "pending"

Ora Shannon and Kathryn Kelly return to civilization as free women—for the moment, at least. (Copyright June 17, 1958, the Oklahoma Publishing Company)

(and since Hoover, no doubt, would be looking for any excuse to recommit her and Ora), she abandoned the misguided idea and, along with her mother, settled into a job with a county rest home.

Lending impetus, possibly, to the government's reluctant decision to permit the women to remain at liberty (rather than admitting there had been a cover-up) was an October 1959 memorandum to FBI headquarters from the Oklahoma City agent-in-charge pointing out the potentially embarrassing public relations and political ramifications:

> It should be borne in mind that a transcript of the second trial, which involved only George and Kathryn Kelly, was not available at the time of the hearings on the motion in June, 1958, and it was not then

known exactly what handwriting testimony might have been used against these persons.

Should action be taken at this time to acquaint the U.S. attorney with these circumstances, it is not improbable he might take the position that he was obligated to acknowledge to the court and the defendants at this time that the testimony of the government witness on this particular point of evidence was possibly based on an erroneous conclusion, even though it did not relate to actual ransom notes as alleged by Kathryn Kelly in her motion. . . . To disclose the results of the earlier [handwriting] examination by the Bureau to the U.S. Attorney now could be the basis of some embarrassment to the Bureau, and would probably result in a request from him for a re-examination to resolve any conflict.

Another year passed, and Wallace's original ruling releasing the women was reversed on appeal, a higher court directing that the hearing should be continued "on its merits." After Wallace had a chance to review that decision, he confided to Camp during an automobile trip that he'd based his ruling in anticipation of a new standard of procedures from the U.S. Supreme Court, even though at that point in time he was totally without authority to do so. That new standard still not forthcoming, he told the federal attorney he would schedule a hearing in a matter of days with the intent of remanding the women to prison to serve out the remainder of their life terms. Here fate cruelly intervened. On June 24, 1960, two days after this conversation, the seventy-four-year-old Wallace was killed instantly in a head-on automobile crash near Oklahoma City.

As it turned out, this development left the reopened case forever in limbo, much to the relief, apparently, of all parties involved. Shortly thereafter, Camp left the U.S. attorney's office—it was 1961—to enter private practice. Even though the case had been sent back to Wallace's court for rehearing, Kathryn's conviction was subverted and she remained at liberty. As did Ora, who had also contended that in 1933 their attorney had been under FBI investigation and so intimidated as to be unable to provide adequate representation for them. (Ora probably did little more than prepare the fried chicken supper for which Urschel politely offered his sincere appreciation on the day of the Paradise raid, perhaps also serving the sandwich and coffee his first night at her house plus breakfast in the morning. Nonetheless, in the eyes of the law, those were considered overt actions helping to further the purpose of the kidnapping, thus making her totally involved in the conspiracy. This interpretation served the purposes of Hoover, who seemed determined to trigger the demise of the Gangster Era by sending up anyone and everyone remotely connected with the Urschel kidnapping as an example.)

So, a quarter of a century after the fact, the case against Kathryn and her mother just hung there, suspended, the two sides at an impasse, with the Justice Department seemingly content to let the women remain free on bail. Intriguingly, the two supposed $10,000 appeal bonds were in reality most likely merely property bonds, since court records indicate neither the receipt of any bail money nor any formal request later by anyone that would have been necessary to obtain a "refund" of any cash posted.

Kathryn worked as a $200-a-month bookkeeper at the Oklahoma County Poor Farm, along with Ora, until retiring in 1974. She steadfastly stuck to her protestations of innocence to the end: "There is no bitterness or animosity in my heart toward anyone but the perpetrators of the terrible crime who dragged an honored, honest, respected family down into the depths of blackest despair. My mother has ever been a good, Christian, law-abiding citizen, and my love and marriage to a gangster plunged my family into bitter tragedy through their innocent, hospitable trust and faith in my husband." Tracked down for an interview in 1962, she said: "Why can't they just leave us alone? I'm afraid I'll lose this job if this constant barrage of publicity keeps up." Then, reverting back to her consistent claim of innocence, "I was just a young farm girl when I met Kelly back in 1930. I wasn't used to all the money, cars and jewelry George offered me. Any farm girl would have been swept off her feet, same as I was."

Kelly's son had a different slant, though, saying in his book, "She was a born con artist, never truly accepting responsibility for her role in the Urschel affair." Urschel's friend Kirkpatrick was even less forgiving. Calling her the "Human Tigress," he wrote to Hoover in 1948, "It seems unthinkable that the Parole Board would seriously consider turning loose upon the public again such criminals as Kathryn Kelly and her mother. . . . Vivid in the minds of Mr. Urschel and Mrs. Urschel and their children and of me and my family are the vicious threats penned to us and sometimes finger-printed, promising us atrocious tortures and death in repayment for our efforts to obtain proper punishment for the Kelly gang."

Kathryn died in Tulsa in 1985 at the age of eighty-one. She had never seen George since the day after the trial, when she had kissed him fondly and said, "Be a good boy." "I will," he replied as reporters crowded around.

Time passed. It was now the summer of 1963, and the case that refused to go away was almost resurrected still another time. One Luther Bohannon, who'd been appointed to succeed the deceased Wallace on the bench in Oklahoma City, had been quietly prodding the Justice Department from time to time as to what its intentions were with respect to the two freed prisoners.

Another internal Justice memo ensued, this one from the latest U.S. attorney in Oklahoma City to headquarters: "Judge Bohannon is vexed by the manner in which these cases have been permitted to remain pending, without being disposed of judicially. He has mentioned that Mrs. Kelly and Mrs. Shannon should either be placed on parole or that the hearings called for by the decision of the Court of Appeals should be held. He further stated that the chief judge was 'just sitting on these cases and would continue to do so.' Although Judge Bohannon doesn't approve of the way these cases are being handled, he is very cordial toward this office and has indicated that if the department prefers to leave things just as they are, he will take no action."

The fact that the women posed no threat to society seemed to be acknowledged by a follow-up memo dispatched to Washington a month later: "We are reluctant to press anything on these for fear the chief judge will promptly hold against the government and order new trials. These women served some twenty-five years in prison and from all reports have been getting along satisfactorily since being released on bonds back in June, 1958." Considering Hoover's intense lifelong opposition to parole, he must have been of two conflicting minds about the still-secret memo that would have served only to embarrass him. Obviously his and the department's reluctant preference was not to disclose the events described in the incriminating files. In reality, therefore, the women's convictions were expunged, since Wallace's initial order, never annulled, stated that "the motions of these two just-referred to defendants to vacate and set aside judgment of conviction and for new trial are hereby sustained."

Meanwhile, the screenwriters of the feature movie *Machine-Gun Kelly*, released about the same time in 1958 as Kathryn and Ora were, apparently knew next to nothing about George and Kathryn and absolutely nothing at all about the Urschel kidnapping. Further evidence of the writers' ineptitude is the fact that even the machine gun that the overly quick-to-shoot "Kelly" fired in anger about every other frame was a model that wasn't introduced until the early forties. The film features Charles Bronson—in his first starring role, as Kelly—Susan Cabot, and Morey Amsterdam. Almost as bad factually is another Hollywood production, *Melvin Purvis G-Man*, plugged as "a fact-based account of FBI Chicago Bureau Chief Melvin Purvis' single-minded quest to stop Machine Gun Kelly's reign of terror." Subsequently retitled for television as *The Legend of Machine Gun Kelly*, it starred Dale Robertson. A small bit of permissible literary license for dramatic effect in screen or stage productions is one thing, but if Kelly had been alive, he should have sued the producers and screenwriters of both pictures for defamation of character by grossly slandering and libeling him as a trigger-happy, bombastic, murdering madman.

The pulp crime magazines of the 1930s—such as *True Detective Mysteries, Master Detective*, and *Startling Detective Adventures*—were actually somewhat more accurate in their accounts of the kidnapping case, although they didn't spare the adjectives and more-than-occasional dramatic exaggeration.

Kathryn, by every account except her constant denials, was in on the kidnap plot from the outset and was most likely the instigator, the brains, the actual mastermind behind it. Further, she fled with George and devised the scheme to use Geraldine as cover. So why the Justice Department and the FBI got hung up on the ridiculously minor and totally irrelevant issue of penmanship in one of its most historic and highly praised cases can seem to be explained away only by Hoover's intense zeal to seize and maintain the upper hand quickly in his personal crusade against kidnapping, his "war against crime." Or perhaps was it also another early glimpse into the dark side of the ambitious Hoover, a side probed by few during his reign but at length and in depth by many since?

Or maybe because he seemed to take the case against the Kellys so personally? As one Hoover biographer claimed (without corroboration anywhere else that this author could find), the director was infuriated at supposedly receiving letters from George taunting him and his agents as incompetent "sissy college boys" and by the fact that Kelly had even made one or more threatening calls to Hoover's mother.

Since the public was understandably more preoccupied with the present rather than a dim long-ago era better forgotten, the director rode out this ministorm that was only slightly publicized outside Oklahoma. When the two women were released, the *New York Times*, the national newspaper of record, gave the story a mere three short paragraphs on page fifty-nine, at the bottom of the page, no less. Hoover would go on to survive other dustups of various magnitude over the years, staying entrenched as the ever-more-powerful—and, depending on one's point of view, the most admired, despised, revered, or feared—FBI director for a total of nearly forty-eight years, serving under seventeen attorneys general and eight presidents of both parties, from Calvin Coolidge through most of Richard M. Nixon's first term.

Upon Hoover's death, however, Congress seized a greater measure of oversight and control of the bureau. The Crime Control Act of 1976 included language directing that henceforth nominees for appointment to the director's post be submitted by the president to the Senate for approval and limiting the term of office to ten years.

15

The Other Victim

All but forgotten in 1933 in the intense hullabaloo surrounding the chase, capture, sentencing, and incarceration of the Kellys was what was to become of the dazed fourteen-year-old Pauline Elizabeth Frye, Kathryn's daughter. What could the future hold for the forlorn daughter of a father whose whereabouts were long unknown and a mother, stepfather, and grandmother who'd just been sent off to prison for the rest of their lives? Well-kept secrets known by only a handful of people—Pauline herself not one of them—have now come to light with the discovery of some of Judge Vaught's old personal files by his granddaughter.

Left after the verdicts without a family or home, Pauline was for all intents and purposes a de facto orphan. Taken in by a sympathetic aunt in Asher, Oklahoma, who was far from well off, she eventually finished secondary school with good marks and was able to pull together enough money from various odd jobs to start normal college, looking toward a career as a schoolteacher. But money ran low and her dream appeared to be fading when, with excellent timing, in stepped Judge Vaught. Pauline had been corresponding with him ever since the trial about the chances of obtaining parole for her mother and grandmother.

One of his early responses to her was not encouraging. On July 27, 1937, he wrote:

I have no control over a judgment of this court after a term expires and any modification of the sentences of your grandmother and your mother will have to come from the President of the United States because he is the only one that has power to modify sentences after the term of court has expired and the defendant has entered upon the service of the sentence. My suggestion would be not to disturb this matter. I think after your grandmother and Mr. Shannon have served five years the Parole Board would consider perhaps an application of some character.

However, he then opened another door that allowed Pauline to continue her studies at East Central State Teachers College (renamed East Central University in 1974) in Ada, Oklahoma:

As to your going back to school this Fall. I have tried for a year to make some kind of an arrangement that would help you. I have one or two friends in the state who have made provisions for assisting worthy students in completing their college work, and, while I have not been able to get in touch with them, some months ago I did discuss it in a general way and I am satisfied that the matter could be worked out with them. Anyway, I called Dr. A. Lenscheid, president of the school at Ada, yesterday and discussed with him your work as a student and your standing in the school, and also the question of your expenses. He gave you a splendid recommendation; reported that you were an excellent student and that your personal conduct was above reproach.

He said that the college would furnish you room and board in their new dormitory for between $22 and $24 per month. I am making arrangements with him to furnish your room and board, buy your books and to pay your college fees connected with your work as a student. The only other expenses, which you would incur in addition to these, are for your clothes and personal expenses. I will arrange to pay you $50 on account for the clothes.

I do not care for any publicity to be given this matter. Nobody but you, your aunt, Dr. Lenscheid, and I will know anything about it. Dr. Lenscheid will send all of the bills directly to me and you will not be bothered about that at all.

On the same day, Vaught sent a letter, in an envelope marked "Confidential," to the school president, Adolph Lenscheid, authorizing him to

reserve for her a nice room at the dormitory, provide for her meals, provide her books and other necessary college expenses, for the year 1937 and 1938, and you can bill me for these items of expense and I will send you a check, promptly.

This arrangement will stand good for the next year providing Pauline's record as a student comes up to what you expect it should. I am leaving that matter entirely with you. I feel sorry for Pauline. She has suffered a severe handicap but I believe she is trying to do the best she can and I want to assist her.

This arrangement is strictly confidential. I am not seeking publicity, in fact, I do not want any publicity on account of it.

Taking the judge at his word, and believing as did the college president that Vaught himself was her benefactor, Pauline sent him a heartfelt handwritten note: "I had never before realized what a letter containing good news can do for you. Yesterday, when I read your letter I felt like, well, I just can't think of the words I want, but I'm sure you will understand just how much I do appreciate what you are doing for me. Thank you a thousand times, I am very gratefully yours."

Other exchanges of letters took place as Pauline went on to complete college. At one point, the judge emphasized to the young woman's aunt, "I am not making this as a loan and am not expecting her to repay it." Pauline continued to hope for freedom for Kathryn and Ora, but again, in a letter dated November 23, 1937, Vaught advised:

I do not want to discourage you in the least but, under the circumstances, feel that I should be perfectly frank with you. I think it would be a waste of time to make any kind of application for clemency for Mrs. Shannon at this time. I know how the Department feels about it and it is a matter over which I have absolutely no control but, knowing the attitude of the government in the matter, I think any effort to secure her release at this time would merely precipitate very vigorous protests or objections.

❖   ❖   ❖

These and other letters turned up in Judge Vaught's recently discovered private archives, and the family shared them with the author. Reading the letters, it is apparent that very few people knew of the financial arrangement, and they never disclosed it. But it can now be revealed that Vaught was merely the sympathetic go-between for an even more anonymous "angel." This fact is revealed, surprisingly, in an undated handwritten cover note attached to the collection of correspondence quoted above:

> The enclosed data has to do with Pauline Frye, daughter of Catherine Kelley [*sic*], convicted in this court for participation in Urschel kidnapping. Pauline was a student in Teachers College at Ada, and after her mother went to the penitentiary, all of Pauline's expenses were paid by *Mr. Urschel* but he did not want it known and hence the payments were made through me. [emphasis in the original]
> E.S.V.

Charles Urschel had one final word about this arrangement. In a note dated January 25, 1960, to Vaught's longtime secretary a month and a half after the judge's death, Urschel wrote, "As to your disposition of the file on Pauline Frye you may dispose of it in any way you choose as I would have no interest in having it. I am wondering just how happy Pauline is with her mother and grandmother out of prison."

Completely unaware of any of the above, the FBI's Hoover wrote about Pauline's mother in *Persons in Hiding* in 1938:

> In captivity she unwittingly performed one service for her daughter. She brought the girl, then about fourteen, into the courtroom, possibly with the idea that the child's presence might influence the jury. That failed utterly. I am hoping, however, that this maltreated girl, during the days in which she watched her mother convicted of a charge which brought about a sentence of life imprisonment, received a lesson which her mother had failed to give her—that crime is useless, filthy and futile.

16

What Happened to . . .

❖ ❖ ❖ ❖ ❖ ❖ ❖ ❖ ❖ ❖ ❖ ❖ ❖ ❖ ❖

Some seventy years after the fateful night of July 22, 1933, none of the principal players in the initial kidnapping drama is still alive, as far as can be ascertained. Where their paths led after that night, and after the trials, is recounted here as accurately as it has been possible to determine.

CHARLES FREDERICK URSCHEL

Arguably the shrewdest kidnap victim in American history, he and Berenice quietly slipped away from Oklahoma City to relocate in 1945 in San Antonio where he headed the Slick-Urschel Oil Company. They sold their house—designated the "Slick-Urschel Home" on a plaque placed in front by the Oklahoma City Historical Preservation and Landmark Commission—to former Oklahoma governor and later U.S. senator Robert S. Kerr, a freewheeling oilman/politician of the Tom Slick mode who headed Kerr-McGee Oil Industries. After their relocation, the Urschels largely continued their pattern of staying out of the public eye. They did exemplary charitable work, including serving as founding trustees and members of the board of governors of the Southwest Foundation for Research and Education. At age eighty after a lengthy illness, Charles Urschel died on September 26, 1970, four months after Berenice. Offered at an estate sale a few months after their deaths, Magnolia Hill, the magnificent house they had built in San Antonio, was filled with valuables they had collected in travels around the world (one trip was their honeymoon by sea to Europe after their private, unpublicized marriage in a St. Louis hotel)—rare objets d'art like antiques, wall coverings, porcelain, glassware, silverware, books, exotic plants, and paintings by old masters. The two-day sale brought in excess of $500,000, and the paintings sold later at a New York auction for more than $200,000. Continuing the family tradition of philanthropy, his son purchased and dedicated the Charles F. Urschel Memorial Pavilion at the Cancer Therapy and Research Foundation of South Texas.

BERENICE FRATES SLICK URSCHEL

Years after the kidnapping, she, along with other family members, made sizable donations to Tom Slick Jr.'s scientific research and education foundation, including $1,000,000 for a new building in 1959. Upon her death on May 30, 1970, she bequeathed "in excess of $2,500,000" to the foundation, according to newspaper accounts.

ERNEST EARL KIRKPATRICK

The wary but steadfast deliverer of the $200,000 ransom in Kansas City and the author of two small but informative "insider" books about his friend's abduction died of an apparent heart attack in April 1968 in Tulsa while on a business trip. He was eighty-six. Before aligning with Slick and Urschel, he'd been a newspaperman.

ROBERT GREEN ("BOSS") SHANNON

At his father's request, Kelly's younger son Bruce Barnes paid a visit to Paradise, Texas, in the early '50s, after which he made a sorrowful report: "I revealed the true conditions of the farm, house, outer buildings, straggly pecan orchards with unpicked crops, and Shannon's depressed frame of mind. . . . After twelve years in prison, he was a basket case." Boss kept the ranch going, to some degree, taking time off at least once, it is known, to bus to West Virginia for a visit with Ora and his stepdaughter. He died on Christmas Day 1956, at the age of seventy-nine. His grave is just a few feet from Kelly's in the small cemetery behind the white-painted cinderblock Church of Christ. It seemed to be the consensus around Wise County that Boss was an honest and hard-working farmer until marrying Ora and inheriting Kathryn. As a footnote to correct the erroneous "fact" repeated without exception in all other accounts the author found, Boss did not get his nickname because of any supposed political connections. In truth, it was his mother who for some unknown reason started calling him Boss when he was two years old, and the moniker stuck for life.

ORA LILLIAN COLEMAN BROOKS SHANNON

Like Kathryn, she never made it back to Paradise or Wise County. The government wouldn't give either of them permission to attend the services for Boss or George—but at Boss's crowded funeral there was a large spray of red roses on the casket with a ribbon saying simply "Husband." Hoover had adamantly continued to oppose granting her applications for clemency in 1936 and 1943, telling the Parole Board, "She actually participated in holding Urschel prisoner on the farm." Finally after two unexpected decades-plus on the outside, she died May 21, 1980, in Oklahoma City, at age ninety-one.

ALBERT LAWRENCE BATES

Learning of Kirkpatrick's first book about the kidnapping, Bates was given permission to write the author asking how he might go about obtaining a copy. Whether he ever did so isn't known. What is known is that he tired quickly of being visited by Urschel representatives and government agents seeking the missing ransom. As early as 1935, he spelled out his displeasure in a letter to the warden: "I am writing you in regards to two un-welcome visits I've had which have caused me considerable annoyance as well as apprehension. I realize that I am wearing a number now and haven't any choice in choosing my visitors, however, I endeavored to impress upon the first visitor that I have no desire to discuss any phase of my affairs now or in the future with the Dep't. of Investigation. I have never, since being in their custody, encouraged them to believe that I could or would divulge any information that would be of the slightest interest or benefit to them, nor has anything occurred since my arrival here to alter my attitude. . . . I would consider it a great favor to be permitted to serve my sentence in peace, I have plenty of troubles of my own without being molested with others and would appreciate very much if you will please enforce the order that you made known to me upon my arrival here Sept. 4th, that I would be allowed no visitors." Bates, apparently with no more callers, never got off the Rock, dying of chronic heart trouble on Independence Day, 1948. He was fifty-four, the same age as Kelly at the time of his death.

HARVEY JOHN BAILEY

When Bailey petitioned for parole from Alcatraz, his former government prosecutor Hyde, now in the private practice of law, sent a rather revealing letter to the then–U.S. attorney: "In view of the fact that he was not an actual kidnapper and could have had no part in the beginning of the original conspiracy, I am of the opinion that the ends of justice could well be met by ordering his release." Paroled from federal prison in 1962, Bailey was immediately rearrested by Kansas authorities who were still angry about the embarrassing eleven-man Memorial Day prison break in 1933 and the robbery sentence he'd left behind. That sentence was commuted by the governor in 1965, and Bailey lived in the YMCA in Joplin, Missouri, plying the new, respectable cabinetmaking trade he had learned in Alcatraz until he died at the age of ninety-one on March 1, 1979. In an interesting twist, Urschel and Kirkpatrick admitted knowing that Bailey had been framed and later strongly supported his parole. "Bailey had nothing to do with the Urschel kidnap case," Kirkpatrick wrote to the U.S. Board of Parole. "We all knew that. He was unlucky enough to be hiding at the Shannon farm." Perhaps to assuage their guilt at knowing Bailey was never involved in the kidnapping, the two of them arranged for Bailey's (subsidized) lodging at the YMCA and his job in Joplin.

WALTER R. JARRETT

The other (albeit brief) kidnap victim died at the age of sixty on February 16, 1947, in Midland, Texas, where he and his wife had moved nine years earlier.

ARMON CRAWFORD SHANNON

His probation was lifted in 1939 for good behavior. The father of six children, he died in 1968 at age fifty-seven. He is also buried in the Cottondale family plot, near his father and Kelly.

JOHN EDGAR HOOVER

Hoover died, unexpectedly, of "hypertensive cardiovascular disease" on May 2, 1972, at the age of seventy-seven. One of Hoover's most frequent and outspoken critics was the widely syndicated columnist Jack Anderson, whom Hoover vilified over the years of their torrid feud as "lower than the regurgitated filth of vultures" and "the lowest form of human being to walk the earth." Nevertheless, the nation owed Hoover—"the Old Bulldog"—homage for his accomplishments, said Anderson, who hastily rewrote his "Washington Merry-Go-Round" column the day after the director's death: "When he took over the FBI forty-nine years ago, it was loaded with hacks, misfits, drunks, and courthouse hangers-on. In a remarkably brief time he transformed it into a close-knit, effective organization with an esprit de corps exceeding that of the Marines. . . . Not a single FBI man ever tried to fix a case, defraud the taxpayer, or sell out his country." (Consider that record in light of recent bureau turncoats and traitors.) This dedicated public servant who rose from a clerk for the Library of Congress and a young Justice Department lawyer to the nation's top crime fighter would leave a legacy tough to follow—the country's premier law enforcement agency, world-renowned for its work. But today, even three decades after Hoover's death, he has his outspoken critics, some of whom would strip Hoover's name from the gigantic $126 million FBI headquarters on Pennsylvania Avenue in Washington. Half a million tourists every year stand in long lines outside the building to take the popular hour-long guided tour, which includes a "Gangster Era" diorama exhibit featuring life-size cutout models of desperadoes John Dillinger, Alvin Karpis, Bonnie and Clyde, "Pretty Boy" Floyd, "Baby Face" Nelson, Al Capone, and, of course, "Machine Gun" Kelly.

JUDGE EDGAR SULLINS VAUGHT

Widely esteemed, he was elected to the Oklahoma Hall of Fame in 1941, and the Oklahoma City University chapter of the Phi Alpha Delta Law Fraternity is named in his honor. He retired from the bench in 1956 and died on December 5, 1959, at the age of eighty-six.

THE ARNOLDS

Luther William Arnold, in his early forties at the time of the 1933 trials, relocated a number of times, reportedly dying around 1944 in southern California. Flossie Marie is believed to have died in 1963 at the age of eighty. Even after repeated directives from headquarters, Luther, Flossie, and Geraldine (who quite possibly may have taken a husband's surname) could not be traced, despite efforts by the entire cadre of FBI regional officers seeking them to get depositions or to appear at the reopened 1958 proceeding.

Author's Notes

❖   ❖   ❖   ❖   ❖   ❖   ❖

Following are bits of information about or related to the case, which are presented here rather than earlier so as not to interrupt the flow of the narrative.

The kidnappers first suggested Dr. Samuel Martin Gibson, pastor of the First Presbyterian Church in Oklahoma City, of which Urschel was a trustee, as the go-between. Gibson was away on vacation, however. Told by the kidnappers that they wanted someone away from all the "law" in Oklahoma City, Urschel then proposed the author's uncle, Ralph J. Pryor, who headed the Slick-Urschel operations in Kansas—known as Slick, Pryor and Lockhart. Urschel was unaware, though, that Pryor had departed for Washington on the Sunday morning of the kidnapping—having no knowledge of Urschel's predicament—for a meeting that prominent oilmen were having on Wednesday, July 26, with President Roosevelt to hammer out the industry's code of fair competition under the National Recovery Act. The angry kidnappers suspected Urschel's suggestion of the absent Pryor was a trick of some sort. Their inability to locate Pryor lengthened Urschel's captivity by a couple of days. Urschel certainly wouldn't have thought so while he was wondering whether he'd ever be released, but this delay turned out to be a blessing in disguise. Otherwise he probably would have been long gone from Paradise before the rainy Sunday that led to the major clue—the missing plane. Pryor, who died in 1968, told the author about these details in a number of conversations over the years and recounted various additional details about the crime. A maternal aunt of the author's, Mary Thomas of Lawrence, Kansas, also vividly remembered an exchange she heard as a teenager: "One time in Uncle Ralph's house in Wichita not long after the kidnapping, I heard him discussing it with 'Ursch.' Ralph said, 'Thank God I was gone when you gave them my name.' The two of them almost broke up laughing" and went into another room for a poker game.

Paradise, Texas, population still about three hundred, is on now-paved State Route 114 between Rhome and Decatur, the Wise County seat. Originally named Paradise Prairie because of the wildflowers surrounding the first settlement, it was shortened in the late 1800s. As observed by the author, the old Boss Shannon main house, well kept up, still stands although all the outbuildings have disappeared over time. Armon's weather-beaten old shack burned to the ground, reportedly some time in the 1970s. The well noted for its mineral-tasting water is now capped with cement.

Charles Urschel's World War I service began when he was inducted into the army in Philadelphia in September 1917 as a private first class. He spent time first in the Quartermaster Corps and then in the Field Artillery. He was honorably discharged at Camp Zachary Taylor, Kentucky, as a sergeant fifteen days after the Armistice of November 11, 1918, and accepted a commission in the Field Artillery Reserves. Like most U.S. veterans, he was awarded the World War Victory Medal, a handsome bronze medallion the size of the old, large silver dollars. The medallion bore the inscription "The Great War for Civilization" and the roster of the other allies: France, Italy, Serbia, Japan, Montenegro, Russia, Greece, Great Britain, Belgium, Brazil, Portugal, Rumania, and China.

The colorful Charles Colcord was the first chief of police when Oklahoma City was chartered in 1890. (Oklahoma would become the forty-sixth state in 1907.) In 1933, when he posted the rewards for the Kellys, he was lauded by the *Daily Oklahoman* as "the veteran peace officer and pioneer rancher, now a city capitalist . . . ready to return to the old vigilante days 'if such action is necessary to put fellows like Kelly, Pretty Boy Floyd, and other hoodlums where they can no longer prey upon society.'" When Colcord publicly offered to post the reward, Urschel told him privately that he would cover him for any financial loss. When Mr. and Mrs. Arnold later sued, seeking the reward on daughter Geraldine's behalf, they won a judgment of $4,000. Urschel (secretly) paid this.

Urschel was similarly generous in at least one other instance. Buried in the FBI archives is a letter to J. Edgar Hoover from a Fort Worth city detective—name still heavily blacked out after all these years, like many in the files—who said Urschel "paid me a very nice reward for services rendered."

Hoover's line about "the cowardice of this boastful Kelly" was the concluding sentence of a letter he wrote in 1944 to renowned *Baltimore Sun* columnist H. L. Mencken, who had quizzed the director about the "G-Man" origins. "G-Man was first popularized and applied to the Federal Bureau of Investigation following the apprehension of Machine-Gun Kelly," Hoover told Mencken. "If you will recall the case, Machine-Gun Kelly made numerous boasts that he would never be taken alive. Agents . . . were greeted by Machine-Gun Kelly, not with a machine gun, but Kelly standing in the corner with his hands in the air saying, 'Don't shoot, G-Man! Don't shoot!' "

Regarding how Hoover made over the FBI when he took command, one thing he developed was an annual Efficiency Rating Sheet. As described a few years after the kidnapping by Tom Tracy and Leon G. Turrou in *How to Be a G-Man*, there were ten points by which agents were judged:

Knowledge—How much he knows about his duties; his ability to use his mind in solving cases.

Judgment—Common sense; the ability to think clearly and sensibly.

Initiative—Whether he can pick up a job and do the right thing without having someone tell him every step.

Force—Going after his work with vigor and determination.

Industry—His application to his work; his health and energy.

Accuracy—Watching details; being thorough and careful.

Personal appearance—Neatness; keeping himself and his clothes clean; his personality; the impression he makes on other people.

Paper work—How he makes out reports, dictates, and puts facts together.

Attitude toward work—Loyalty to the service; attention to duty; dependability; acceptance of discipline.

Executive capacity—The ability to lead, direct, and control others in the proper performance of their duties.

Kelly's letter to Urschel from prison told only part of the story of the horrors of being penned up in Alcatraz, an always chilly and damp twenty-two acres of bleak rock outcropping on an island a mile and a half offshore from San Francisco. Each convict was confined alone in a cell roughly five feet by nine feet, with a seven-foot ceiling and a single twenty-watt light bulb. "Creepy" Karpis morbidly described in *On the Rock: Twenty-Five Years in Alcatraz* the place where he would exist (about the only word for it) for a quarter of a century:

The bunk hangs by chains from the wall and folds up against the wall when necessary. . . . The toilet is at the end of the bunk beside a small wash basin in the center of the back wall. . . . On the shelf I find the following items: a safety razor, an aluminum cup for drinking water, a second one with a cake of Williams shaving soap in it, a shaving brush, a mirror made of highly polished metal, a toothbrush, a container full of toothpowder, a bar of playmate soap, a comb, a pair of nail clippers, a sack of Stud smoking tobacco, a corncob pipe, a roll of toilet paper, a can of brown shoe polish, a green celluloid eye shade, a whisk broom for sweeping out the cell, and the rule book we were told to read.

If an acute case of advanced paranoia seemed to be afflicting the FBI over the 1958 release of Ora Shannon and Kathryn Kelly, it must have been aggravated considerably in 1962 when the eminent Washington criminal defense lawyer Edward Bennett Williams, who had never been involved, unexpectedly weighed in with an article in the widely circulated *Saturday Evening Post* containing excerpts from a book he had just written. Williams is remembered most for skillfully representing such unsavory clients as Teamster presidents David Beck and James R. Hoffa, New York congressman Adam Clayton Powell, Wisconsin senator Joseph McCarthy, and mobster Frank Costello. Williams was also an owner of the Baltimore Orioles and Washington Redskins. In this case, Williams picked up angrily on Kathryn Kelly's first trial as "a classic example of the need for fair discovery procedures. This story, perhaps as well as any I know, demonstrates why a major change is needed in pre-trial discovery procedures," he wrote in *One Man's Freedom*. The magazine excerpt is included in the Appendix.

Assistant U.S. Attorney George Camp remained convinced after the 1958 hearing that there had been ample reason to convict the two women in the first place. "I never believed," he told the author, "that the procedure invoked was one that would allow the court to take the action it did. There have been a lot of changes in what has developed as 'rights of the accused.' I would assume that there was adequate evidence in 1933 under the procedure in use at that time to sustain the conviction of the defendants involved. My point has always been that the proper procedure for any diminution of a sentence, after the appellate process was exhausted, was by the executive branch of government, not the judicial.

In other words, a President could have granted clemency, commuted a sentence or even granted a pardon, but the court system was improperly invoked in 1958."

Paul Cress, the lead U.S. attorney at the 1958 hearing, later served as a state associate district judge in his hometown of Perry, Oklahoma, where he died in November 1994.

Appendix: Documents

❖ ❖ ❖ ❖ ❖ ❖ ❖

For scholars and others interested in more in-depth information, full or relevant parts of texts of primary documents, articles, editorials, FBI memoranda, and correspondence relating to the case are presented here to help the reader gain a better understanding of the background of events.

THE LINDBERGH ACT, 1932

The Federal Kidnapping Act of June 27, 1932 (18 U.S. Code 1201(a)(b)), passed by Congress just a month after discovery of the Lindbergh child's body, read in part:

> That whoever shall knowingly transport or cause to be transported, or aid or abet in transporting, in interstate or foreign commerce, any person who shall have been unlawfully seized, confined, inveigled, decoyed, kidnapped, abducted, or carried away by any means whatsoever and held for ransom or reward shall, upon conviction, be punished by imprisonment in the penitentiary for such term of years as the court, in its discretion, shall determine: Provided, That the term "interstate or foreign commerce" shall include transportation from one State, Territory, or the District of Columbia to another State, Territory, or the District of Columbia, or to a foreign country; or from a foreign country to any State, Territory, or the District of Columbia: Provided further, That if two or more persons enter into an agreement, confederation, or conspiracy to violate the provisions of the foregoing act and do any overt act toward carrying out such agreement, confederation, or conspiracy such person or persons shall be punished in like manner as hereinbefore provided by this act.

THE PRESS "WITHDRAWS," JULY 27, 1933

When asked by the Urschel family to withdraw reporters from their stakeout at the house, the *Oklahoma Times* said in a two-column-wide box on page one headed "We Withdraw":

> The Oklahoma Publishing Co., not wishing to do anything which the Urschel family thinks might interfere with effecting the safe return of Charles F. Urschel, at 1 o'clock Thursday withdrew its reporters and photographers from near the Urschel home. There will be no more watching of the movements of the members of the family. The *Oklahoman* and *Times* will publish news which the family releases in formal statements, but will not do anything to interfere with access to or egress from the home.
>
> Our agreement with the family does not prevent our publishing other news of the kidnapping. We will continue to publish the facts of the story as we have in the past, except as stated. The Urschel family believes that our watching so closely may prevent a contact. We do not wish to interfere in any manner. The Oklahoma Publishing Co. has but one wish, and that is the safe return of Mr. Urschel. We hope that the withdrawal of our men from the neighborhood will speed his safe return.

KIRKPATRICK'S FEELINGS, DATE OF AUTHORSHIP UNCERTAIN

Ernest Kirkpatrick expressed his true thoughts about the kidnapping and his role in it in *Geese Flying South: A Collection of Poems*:

> I had left a letter to my wife to be delivered to her on Tuesday, if I had not returned. In it I told her I would most likely never return. I was carrying a fortune to deliver to gangsters in a city under the unspeakable Pendergast administration. I had learned from the underworld that the top price for murder in Kansas City at that time was $500.00. I dreaded the thought of being murdered by gangland without a chance to fight back. The long grueling hours were torture.
>
> At 4:00 in the morning I came to a decision. I made up my mind I would not worry. I would put my trust in God to take a hand in my behalf. Sitting on the bag of ransom money I composed the lines

of "Faith." At sundown, following telephone instructions from the gangsters, I walked down Linwood Boulevard and delivered the money under menacing machine guns. Back in my room at the Muehlebach Hotel I sat at the desk and finished the following poem, "Faith":

> If God in His infinite wisdom
> Takes care of the sparrows that fall,
> And tempers the wind to the shorn lamb,
> And loves little children and all.
>
> Then why should we weak grown-up mortals,
> With doubt and misgivings and fear,
> Shrink back lest our cause be unworthy
> As the end of our life span draws near?
>
> Ah, man with his power to reason,
> And his strange predilection to sin,
> Finds death a life problem to fathom,
> And life a death struggle to win.
>
> And each in his own little cycle,
> And each with his puny brain cells
> Spends life trying to vision a heaven,
> And praying to miss future hells.
>
> Little children, the lambs and the sparrows,
> In stormy old weather or fair,
> Live their lives with a faith without question—
> With a faith that suffices for prayer.

OKLAHOMA TIMES COLUMN, AUGUST 1, 1933

The *Oklahoma Times* column by Managing Editor Walter M. Harrison that ignited Arthur Seeligson's wrath appeared a day after Urschel's release:

> Now that Charles F. Urschel is safe at home, the big job begins. Get the kidnapers!
> We share the joy of the family at the safe return of the victim. We shall not criticize them for any of their activities, for they kept their

own counsel and did as they deemed best to restore the individual who meant so much to them.

But there is a larger interest, yours and mine, in the rising tide of outlawry, which must now be brought to the front and impressed indelibly upon the public mind, lest the holding of men, women, and children for ransom become as common as the violation of the ordinance against double parking.

Every agency of government must be swung into unremitting search for the men guilty of this crime. Until the gang is apprehended and given the limit of the law we shall feel that nothing has been done to compensate for this outrageous invasion of private rights.

The amount of the ransom is of no importance. It may have been $50,000 or it may have been $100,000. That is a private matter. Money means little to the wealthy. If the federal authorities know how the ransom was paid, know every step leading up to the release, we are willing to swallow the pique resulting from their duping us with half truths and misstatements when we were trying with every resource to cooperate, and go to the human limit to bring the public enemies to book.

Neither Mrs. Urschel nor Mr. Seeligson would say directly that they would go the limit in cooperating with the federal authorities. During the conference this morning in which the whole occurrence was discussed with newspapermen, the attitude was assumed by a questioner that the federal operatives did not know the inside of the case.

Lamar Seeligson, formerly prosecuting attorney of a Texas county, who in my judgment was the man who made the contact with the kidnapers and passed the money, reminded us that no one in the Urschel group had said that they were not cooperating with the federal men. That is true. It was an assumption. There were federal men on duty in the Urschel home at all times. If the federal knew about the first ransom note, if the federal was in quietly behind the negotiations and are now in a position to go full steam ahead toward a satisfactory denouement, we are satisfied.

But if the attitude of the Urschels is to withhold any shred of definite information on the method of handling the ransom, or of checkmating the effort now being made to locate the scene of Urschel's nine-day prison, they should change front immediately and turn every card for the common good. Urschel's safety is important, yes, but behind him stand your child and mine. We, the people, want protection from kidnappers. It cannot be secured by permitting the wealthy to pay the price demanded and then to cover up the tracks made by human jackals whose success will embolden them to crimes yet unconceived. . . .

SECOND NEWSPAPER COLUMN, AUGUST 2, 1933

A second Harrison column followed:

No one can prevent a flood of rumor and misstatement being broadcast with regard to the Urschel case.

Within an hour I heard that the family was embarrassed at the thought that they paid so little and that they were ashamed to publish the fact because they had paid more than $250,000 without haggling.

But the family need not be surprised at anything that is said or printed about the case. Walter Jarrett dissembled about his part in the kidnapping. Urschel himself has not been frank and complete in his stories. Arthur Seeligson thought it was quite all right to make definite misstatements to newspaper people who were attempting to cooperate.

If Urschel would tell all he knows the hideout where he was held prisoner could be located within 24 hours.

If Seeligson is cooperating to the limit of his ability the federal government will have all of the facts with regards to the handling of the money and has a dragnet out before this. If that sort of cooperation has been provided, what is the sense in not telling the public about it? The public has an interest in this case. Many a crime has been solved by broad publication of all surrounding circumstances.

THE SEELIGSON REPLY, AUGUST 3, 1933

Harrison, as asked, printed the concerns Seeligson spelled out in what appears to be a hastily written letter to the managing editor:

For nearly three years, ever since the death of Tom Slick, your papers have at different times given special prominence to various rumors, misstatements, and insinuations in regard to the Slick interests. We have become used to this, our friends know us for what we are. Apparently we cannot avoid what others want or are influenced to believe by some of the press.

The amount of the ransom paid for C. F. Urschel's release and the circumstances in connection therewith are purely personal matters, and no good, except to satisfy morbid curiosity and to give you a chance for additional headlines, can be accomplished by giving this information to you or the other papers.

You are correct in stating that during the progress of the negotiations I did not give the true information to the papers. Absolute secrecy was necessary to insure the safe return of Charlie Urschel and that was our first consideration. Past experiences have proven to us the inadvisability of giving you, or your papers, any information of a personal nature.

I feel that the Oklahoma papers, and yours, have been among the worse [sic] offenders, were responsible for the kidnapping of C. F. Urschel more than any other one factor. The sensational stories, misrepresentations and insinuations about the size of the estate that have been printed at various times during the past three years, together with all other personal matters involving the different members of the Slick and Urschel families which you have featured, and headlined at every opportunity, has so focused attention on both of these families as to make them one of the first targets for those in the kidnapping racket . . . .

Before your return, Mr. Bell [Edgar T. Bell, business manager of the publishing company] agreed to withdraw your reporters who were constantly on guard around the Urschel residence. We appreciated that cooperation on the part of your papers and have so stated on various occasions.

The so-called copyrighted articles which appeared in your papers were not written or signed by C. F. Urschel, and certainly an erroneous impression was created by your action in the way that article was handled. . . .

THE DISPUTED URSCHEL COLUMN, AUGUST 2, 1933

This is how the disputed account appeared, two columns in width, on page nine:

URSCHEL'S STORY
OF THE KIDNAPPING

"It Seems Like a Year, I Wouldn't Go Through It Again for Any-thing," Victim Says As He Recalls Long, Bumpy Ride At Night. Charles F. Urschel was held captive for nine days in a back woods bungalow with tape constantly over his eyes, somewhere the distance of a 12-hour motor car trip from Oklahoma City.

He never saw his kidnappers.

His wife, the former Mrs. T. B. Slick, paid without a quibble the entire amount of the ransom demanded by the machine gunners who seized Urschel from the sunporch of their home on July 22.

The ransom negotiations were conducted by Arthur Seeligson, attorney and co-trustee of the Slick estate, and Seeligson Tuesday refused either to divulge the amount of the ransom, how the release negotiations were conducted, or how the money was paid.

His own story of the wild ride to the hills, the experiences there, and the trip home, written especially for The Daily Oklahoman, follows:

BY CHARLES F. URSCHEL
(Copyright 1933, by the North American Newspaper Alliance and the Oklahoma Publishing Co.)

If my story is a little bit sketchy, blame it on the fact that I have slept scarcely at all for the last nine days. First of all, you simply can't appreciate how glad I am just to be alive and well. It has been a harrowing experience, probably even more terrible for my wife and family and close associates than for myself because I never felt that my abductors would harm me. I would not go through it again for anything in the world.

It seems like a year since we were playing bridge on our sun porch a week ago last Saturday night when two men entered with machine guns and demanded that my friend, Walter Jarrett, and I leave with them. Their faces were in the shadow at the time. All I could see was the menacing machine guns. I felt that they had me cold and that it was foolish to think of doing anything but obey their commands.

I remember a sort of empty feeling as I got up, gave one look at my wife and stepped outside as the man with the machine gun nearest me directed.

There was a quick ride over the pavement for a couple of miles to the point where the kidnappers told Jarrett to get out. Then they taped my eyes, put a big piece of tape over my forehead, and pushed me down into the bottom of the small sedan car in which we were driving. I think it was a Ford or a Chevrolet. One man with a machine gun rode in the seat above me. I was cramped up and as soon as we got on the dirt roads the bumps were terrible. I was not bound. The men told me that they did not want to hurt me, but that under no circumstances should I make a show of fight, else it would be too bad. They further expressed regret that they had to cramp me down in the bottom of the car, but said it was necessary because they might meet officers and there would be some shooting and they did not want me harmed.

We rode over dirt roads all night, I do not know in what direction. Sometime after daybreak—I could tell the difference between daylight and dark over my tape—they stopped and gave me a bottle of Coca-Cola. I did not get up or get out. We continued our ride until sometime in the afternoon, when we reached our destination, it was a backwoods cabin. By my movements about it, I learned that it was three rooms, a rude sort of place in, I should say, tenant farmer country or possibly foothill country. The equipment in the shack was very poor. The beds were cheap. I was tied up at night but given the freedom of my hands and legs in the daytime. There were guards at the shack in addition to the two men who took me away from my home. They seemed to be the principals in the case. The guards at the place where I was imprisoned did not know much about the case, in my judgment. They were decent, but not talkative. I do not remember them calling each other by their first names, nor do I remember the two principals referring to each other by first names. I never saw one of them directly and I could not identify them now.

On Wednesday, the tape was removed when I was permitted to

write a note in which I said exactly what my jailers directed me to write. The men turned their faces from me, however, and smartly kept me from getting a look at them. It was difficult for me to see after being so long in the dark. The only other time my eyes were untaped was Monday afternoon when I shaved myself.

I must have been a sorry looking sight with the beard I wore.

I did not get a change of clothing from them, although one of them decently loaned me a pair of pajamas to live in. They fed me regularly, although the fare was sorry, mostly canned goods and tomatoes and baked beans. The coffee was the kind a man often gets on camping trips without a cook. We had no fresh vegetables nor fresh meat, as there was no cooking, except coffee for early breakfast. I am satisfied that a store of provisions was laid in before we reached the place and that no contact was made for food after we arrived there. They were generous with cigars, but they were not my brand.

We were 14 hours in making the journey from Oklahoma City to our destination. The length of the trip in miles, of course, would be a wild estimate. I do not think we traveled any more than 40 miles an hour any of the time and much of the time we were slowed down to 15 or 20 miles. It may have been 300 miles and it may have been 500 miles away from Oklahoma City.

Under the circumstances I could not sleep. Every hour seemed a week long and every day was a month. I was very sore from the long ride knotted up in the bottom of the car and was physically uncomfortable for the first two or three days.

Of course I had a lot of time to think. When I dozed off occasionally, I would be the victim of the wildest sort of dreams. While awake, my mind naturally ran back to the folks at home.

I wondered what they were doing and how they were going about helping me. I knew that my affairs were in good hands and I got a great deal of satisfaction out of the thought that my wife and Arthur Seeligson were capable of handling any situation that might arise.

Although I lost track of time, they told me when it was Sunday and suggested that it was possible that I was going to be released on that day. When the hours passed and no move took place, my morale went very low. Sunday night was very, very long. I don't think I slept a wink. Monday things picked up around the shack.

There was a different tone to the voices and I felt that the end was near. When one of the fellows said, "Well, Mr. Urschel, we are going to give you a shave and clean you up for a trip to town," I knew that arrangements for my release had been effected. I wondered how much money they had secured. I felt sure that with business conditions as they are today and the oil business such as it is, my family and associates would have a great deal of difficulty raising any great sum of money.

We were 12 hours driving back to Oklahoma City. My eyes were taped again immediately after I finished shaving and I again was piled in the back of an automobile and bumped over endless country roads. North of Norman, just within sight of the lights of the town, I was released and told where I was and how to make my way from that point. I walked to a hamburger stand, called a taxi by telephone and was taken to my home on Seventeenth Street [*sic*] in Oklahoma City.

A man I never saw before answered the door and refused to let me in. Tired and near exhaustion as I was, I got a big laugh out of being refused admission to my own home. I went to the back door and as soon as some of the help was aroused, of course, the family began to show up and everything was rosy.

Although I do not care to discuss Mrs. Urschel's part in this affair in detail, I want to say that I believe that she is responsible for the quick and successful culmination of the negotiations with my abductors.

I do not know how much help I can be to the federal authorities. I shall be glad to be of whatever service I may. My present feeling is one of great joy at being restored to freedom and restored to my family. Naturally, I shudder at the thought of the things I have experienced and hope that no other man or woman or child may ever have to go through such an ordeal. I feel that everything the federal government can do to put an end to kidnapping in the United States is an imperative necessity.

HARRISON'S REBUTTAL, AUGUST 4, 1933

Harrison (who in his book twenty-one years later would say that "I have never ceased to admire the cold reason and careful conduct of Urschel while he was in the hands of his captors") could not let Seeligson's allegations about newspapers having actually contributed to Urschel's kidnapping go by, writing in his next column:

> Your charge that the newspapers are responsible for the kidnapping is too puerile to merit detailed discussion.
>
> If we have erred in publishing the estimated value of the Slick estate, it is because the estate itself never would place a figure upon it for publication. Governor [William H.] Murray, J. Berry King, the attorney general, and other public officials were quoted on the size of the estate. Their zeal in securing to the state a proper inheritance tax may have led them into exaggeration. If we were at fault in trying to report accurately this litigation, I apologize.
>
> There is great glamour and romance attached to the late Tom Slick, "The King of the Wildcatters," and members of his family.
>
> As one of the richest families in the Southwest, its members occupied a position at the peak for which they must pay the annoyances of public attention which come with fame and wealth. . . .
>
> If Mr. Urschel had telephoned the sheriff of Cleveland County Monday night when he was released, it is my conviction that his abductors never would have escaped. All dirt roads were impassable. The two concrete highways could have been barred within ten minutes. . . .
>
> Your admission that you did not give the true information to the papers must not have been a pleasant confession. Acknowledging your paramount interest in the safe return of Mr. Urschel, I cannot justify your blandly stating that no contact had been made as late as Saturday night, when the sole interest in our visit was to help you. It was not necessary for you to make a direct misstatement. . . .
>
> As to Mr. Urschel's signed story, I deny that any advantage was taken of Mr. Urschel. I did virtually all of the questioning of the victim on the morning after his return. Upon my arrival at the office, I reconstructed the narrative in the first person. I called Mrs. Urschel on the telephone and told her I was sending out the manuscript. I asked her to read it with Mr. Urschel and requested them jointly to correct, delete, and amend it as they pleased. . . .
>
> The story was revised by the Urschels, one paragraph omitted, another added, and returned to me. It was a fair and true report. Most of it was in Mr. Urchel's own language.

CONCLUSION OF NEWSPAPER FENCING, AUGUST 15, 1933

Finally, Harrison would use his front-page column, "The Tiny Times," to bring this public exchange of views to a conclusion:

> The capture of the Bailey gang eliminates the most vicious ring of criminals loose in the Southwest. The successful drive of the Department of Justice in this case will throw a scare into gangsters everywhere and reassure the people that our government can go places and do things when it gets its blood up.
>
> In light of subsequent events, we did the Urschel family an injustice in suggesting that they were not cooperating wholeheartedly with the government. In our joy at the outcome of this crime, we are happy to acknowledge our fault.
>
> In a radio address on a national hookup last night William Stanley, assistant to the attorney general, said the Urschel family was the first to respond to the request of the government that Washington be contacted immediately in the event of a kidnapping. Mr. Stanley said the Urschel family had Washington on the long distance telephone a short time after the two gunmen drove away with their victim and that throughout the hunt the associates of the victim gave the government complete cooperation. Mr. Stanley repeated the government's suggestion to the families of gang victims. He urged immediate action with the Department of Justice and stated that the family "should make no public statement until the proper time." In view of this suggestion, we drew the inference that Arthur Seeligson gave out false information to the newspapers attempting to cooperate with them in Oklahoma City, with the knowledge of the federal operatives. We also infer that it was with the advice of the federal operatives that the amount of the ransom and other unimportant details were omitted upon the return of Mr. Urschel.
>
> Apparently the Department of Justice is to be the judge of the "proper time" for a public statement. The grandest statement, of course, is the announcement that a crime has been cleared up and the criminals are in custody. Ahead of the actual cleanup, the government policy should be to release all information that will not jeopardize the hunt and to prohibit the giving out of any false and misleading information.

Newspaper cooperation is a logical arm of the national cooperation that is being sought to eliminate the racketeer. The efficient
Department of Justice can secure that cooperation without stint or
limit by playing fair and shooting square.

APPEAL BY KATHRYN KELLY, SEPTEMBER 20, 1933

Two days after the first trial got under way, Kathryn Kelly dispatched a
long letter to federal prosecutor Keenan from Chicago. Quite lengthy, it
was a rambling communication, first asserting that her mother and stepfather had nothing to do with the kidnapping and then proclaiming her
own innocence. As retyped in an FBI memorandum from Oklahoma City
to headquarters, which might account for the misspellings and gram-
matical errors, she went on:

I can prove to your satisfaction I had no part, or did not have any
knowledge, beforehand, of the Urshell [*sic*] kidnapping. I would step
into the electric chair now to save my loved ones, even undergoing a
trial with unfair people like you. I know their honesty and goodness,
and the two little girls need them at home, and the whole community
needs them, yet, Mr. Keenan, you are willing to let the Big Shots go,
and let the innocent suffer. Do you really, and truely [*sic*], believe you
are doing your duty by your country in prosecuting the Shannons?
Just between you and I, think it over, would their imprisonment stop
any crime? No, and if they were released they would go home, raise
their kiddies, plow their fields, and be assets in their community, and
be a help. They welcomed G.R.K. because he was my husband, but all
I am interested in Sir is my people. I love them more than the whole
world and I would have seen Mr. Kelly surrendered, regardless, if you
had really had the worlds [*sic*] sake at heart and interested in the criminal element enough to have released the innocent. . . .
Another thing, I want you to know I am not with Kelly and don't
intend to be, and I don't want any more "bum" raps, on me, as I
have a pretty good idea of what is going to happen right away, from
he and his associates, and if I have to be in jail to prove an alibi I will,
and I honestly don't believe they will be apprehended Mr. Keenan.
They have too many worldwide connections and why you are not

more interested in preventing a massacre then [*sic*] in aiding in prosecuting good citizens I do not know.

I could find 25 criminals for you inside of three days if you would trust me in the least. You should know I don't want to be on the "law." I've never been and I need to be with my father and baby. I've had an awful hard time in my life, regardless of what you think and I've tried to raise my baby to grow up a good woman, and after I knew Kelly's activities I could not break with him. My poor parents are already ruined from this undue publicity and Mr. Keenan, how you have the heart to imprison these innocent people, I can't understand. I know you can see that they are released. . . .

I want a chance for my parents and I to live in peace. I would love to discuss a lot of things with you, but you've put me in a position to where I can't—someone has got to be out to provide for those two little girls and until my parents are home with them its [*sic*] up to me to do it and if you will see they are released I will see you at once and the first thing will be the apprehension of Kelly and his two companions. . . . I want some of the guilty ones to suffer instead of the innocent. Please do something for my people, you can I know. You can talk to my attorney [name blacked out in FBI file] and if you want Kelly you'll have him if you'll release those people, and I will confer with you. Please I beg you, keep this letter secret or I'll be slaughtered.

Yours truly,

Kathryn C. Kelly

KELLY LETTER TO URSCHEL, APRIL 11, 1940

George Kelly's sometimes mournful, sometimes positive, sometimes humorous letter from Alcatraz to Charles Urschel, complete with typographical errors, reads as follows:

I hope I am not pulling a prize blunder (or should I say committing a "faux pas"?) in writing to you. I have two reasons for doing so: first, I wish some information; second, I want to appease my curiosity. In respect to the latter, it all came about this way: Several months ago I had a talk with Mr. J. V. Bennett [director of the U.S. Bureau of

Prisons for twenty-seven years]; in the course of our discussion, he mentioned that you had paid him a visit, and asked me if I ever wrote to you. Of course my answer was no. Another of his remarks was: "Mr. Urschel mentioned you and spoke well of you considering the circumstances"—or something to that effect. I have pondered over his remarks quite a bit, and often wondered if for some unknown reason you did wish to hear from me.

Now for the information that I desire. I believe that you are aware that both Mr. Shannon and I own farms in Wise County, Texas. Of course you know where the Shannon farm is located; mine adjoins it on the east. I understand that some oil company has struck oil in that vicinity, and at the present time is buying up leases close to the farm. Have you heard anything about this? As I seldom write anyone other than my wife it is almost impossible for me to get any information on the true conditions there. Situated as you are, you should have no trouble in getting the "low down" on what is going on. I would appreciate any information you might give me regarding the oil prospects in Wise County; especially, the prospects around the farm, which is four miles south of Paradise.

Now before I go further don't think I am merely writing this letter to try to get into your good graces. You can rest assured I will never ask you to do anything towards getting me out. Naturally I realize that your enmity could become a detriment in later years. So, to be truthful, I hope you do not feel too vindictive; although, I hardly think that you are a person of a malevolent disposition. After so many years, I must admit that I am rather ashamed of the grand stand play that I made in the courtroom—of course I am referring to what I said to you that day on leaving the courtroom. I was good and mad at the time. Need I of [sic] remind you of the enthusiasm of the days during my trial. You and your friends shared in it; seemed to revel in it. What produced it? The Department of Justice's love of the dramatic; the public's desire for a good free show; an accumulated spirited vitality which found no employment in the things of every day and so was ready to enjoy to the utmost anything out of the ordinary.

I feel that at times you wonder how I am standing up under my penal servitude, and what is my attitude of mind? It is natural that you should be infinitely curious. Incidentally, let me say that you've missed something in not having had the experience for yourself. No letters, no amount of talk, and, still more, no literary description in second-rate books—and books on crime cannot be second rate—could ever give you faintest idea of the reality.

No one can know what it's like to suffer from the sort of intellectual atrophy, the pernicious mental scurvy, that comes of long privation of all the things that make life real; because even the analogy of thirst can't possibly give you an inkling of what it's like to be tortured by the absence of everything that makes life worth living.

You must take everything I say as no more than a purely personal version. I no sooner write down a phrase than I want to scratch it out again as false, conventional, intolerably one-sided, as a wholly distorted view of facts.

Maybe you have asked yourself, "How can a man of even ordinary intelligence put up with this kind of life, day in, day out, week after week, month after month, year after year." To put it more mildly still, what is this life of mine like, you might wonder, and whence do I draw sufficient courage to endure it.

To begin with, these five words seem written in fire on the walls of my cell: "Nothing can be worth this." This—the kind of life I am leading. That is the final word of wisdom so far as crime is concerned. Everything else is mere fine writing.

You will say: "If you feel like that you must be a very weak person."

No, I'm rather a strong minded one—or so I think. I can only assume that a sort of pig-headed determination is all that I have to recommend me.

What helps me to carry on? Perhaps the thought that I might be worse off. You may laugh, but it's probably true. I might be in a worse place where there is brutality or even bestiality. I might be blind. I might even be dead.

I feel splendid and am in perfect physical trim. My one obsession is the climate of the island. I am constantly bothered with colds. My cell, made of steel and concrete, is always a trifle chilly; but I've even come to believe that [man] is so made that the presence of a small superficial irritation, provided the sensation is acute without being symptomatic of any serious trouble, is a definite aid to his mental equilibrium and serves to keep occupied the restless margin of his consciousness. He regards it, too, as a sort of ring of Polycrates, for I suspect that there is in all of us, always, an obscure sense of fate, inherited from numberless ancestral misfortunes, which whisper: "We are not sent into this world to live too happily. Where there's nothing to worry us, it's not natural, it's a bad sign." A little misfortune gives us the assurance that we are paying our "residence tax" so far as this world is concerned—not much to be sure, but enough to ensure us against the jealousy and the thunderbolts of Heaven.

I have found the secret of how to "do" easy time. I just let myself drift along; the tide of time picks me up and carries me with it. It will leave me high and dry precisely where it chooses and when it chooses; consequently, I have nothing to worry about.

But I must be fair. Being in prison has brought me one positive advantage. It could hardly do less. It's name is comradeship—a rough kindness of man to man; unselfishness; an absence, or a diminution, of the tendency to look ahead, at least very far ahead; a carelessness, though it is bred of despair; a clinging to life and the possible happiness it may offer at some future date.

A person in prison can't keep from being haunted by a vision of life as it used to be when it was real and lovely. At such times I pay, with a sense of delicious, overwhelming melancholy, my tributes to life as it once was. I don't really believe it can ever be like that again—but you can bet your last oil-well George won't loose [sic] any sleep over that.

How is your bridge game? Are you still vulnerable? I don't mean that as a dirty dig but you must admit you lost your bid on the night of July 22, 1933.

Ordinarily I am allowed to write only one page, but as this is a special letter, and as I will have to ask the warden for permission to mail it to you, I believe he will allow the three pages this one time. It is awfully hard for me to write a short letter; I get to rambling and seem unable to stop. I guess I am just long-winded.

I hope you will not consider my writing an impertinence, if you do, just tear this letter up and forget it. Of course, I should enjoy hearing from you anytime. With best wishes, I am

Very truly yours,
Geo. R. Kelly
Reg. No. 117

(Whether Urschel replied is not known.)

BATES, TOO, WRITES URSCHEL, JUNE 19, 1942

The letter Albert Bates posted to Urschel from prison is quoted here:

I have been informed that Mr. and Mrs. George Kelly and Mrs. Ora Shannon are under the impression that the recent denial of Mrs. Shannon's application for executive clemency was based upon the unrecovered portion of ransom money you paid to Kelly and me.

I, of course, feel terribly sorry for Mrs. Shannon; she is getting well up in years, in poor health, and after all, she took no active part in the crime—other than to carry out her husband's instructions to cook a dinner for you on Sunday while Kelly and I were absent.

For years I refused to discuss any phase of the case with the Agents of the F.B.I. I felt that inasmuch as I had been tried and convicted of an offense and sentenced to a penal institution that I was entitled to the same consideration accorded to others, consequently when I was isolated at Fort Leavenworth, I did not care to converse with Mr. Seeligson, or yourself, when you and he visited that institution, and besides, I did not want to jeopardize the life of a woman, my wife, who had almost innocently become involved in the case through possessing my personal effects. I feared that perhaps she, too, would get a life sentence if apprehended at that time while the whole country was in a turmoil over so many recent heinous crimes. My wife was arrested almost a year and a half after me. What occurred at her trial I have no knowledge of. I do not know how much money she could restore to you from the portion I received. All I know is what I read in the *World's Almanac* (1935) under date of December 8, 1934, that a total of only $126,000.00 had been recovered, which seemed to me to be an awful discrepancy. I have not corresponded with my wife, or any one else for that matter, so I am totally in the dark.

It is for this reason that I am writing to you; if you care to answer this it is possible that I can account for any shortage in the sum recovered from my share of $93,750.00.

I am sure, Mr. Urschel, that you will understand that I have no personal motive behind this. I expect to serve the rest of my life in this, or some other institution, for my crime. All I look forward to is to do my time as easy as I can; therefore I do not invite any visits

from the Bureau—not that I hold any ill will toward any of them as
men or officers—and they have respected my wishes to that extent.
My sole interest is to give you an accurate accounting of the money
I received from the venture.

    With best wishes I am
    Sincerely,
    Albert L. Bates
    Register No. 137A

SECOND BATES LETTER TO URSCHEL, SEPTEMBER 29, 1942

Bates penned another letter to Urschel in response to a letter from him
received earlier that month, a copy of which could not be found:

Your letter of September 10th was forwarded to me by Mr. James
V. Bennett, Director, Bureau of Prisons, and though there is little that
I can divulge about this case that isn't known, I can answer your
query in reference to the division of the ransom money.

After Kelly and I received the money from Mr. Kirkpatrick in
Kansas City we returned directly to the Shannon Ranch, arriving
there about 2 p.m., on Monday, July 31, 1933. We retired to the front
room of the house and divided the money in privacy. Kelly had a
"nut" (as we refer to an expense account in connection with any job)
of $11,500.00. I did not inquire what it was for simply because it was
customary for each individual of outfits like ours to keep a record
of his expenses on our various enterprises. I do know that we abandoned a new Buick of his on the night of July 29th about 2 or 3 miles
northeast of Luther, Okla., alongside the "Katy" tracks.

I received the sum of $94,250.00 for my "end," and when I left the
room to clean up a bit on the back porch I saw Bailey was still there,
although he had told me four days previous that his friends would
call for him not later than Saturday. I had warned him that the place
was "hot" on account of our past activities in Texas and our connections with detective friends, Messrs. Weatherford and Sweeney
of Ft. Worth. I was in a hurry to get the job over with so I did not
converse much with anyone. I gave Bailey $500.00 out of my pocket
and Kelly did likewise. I left the farm with $93,750.00. When we

released you at Norman, Kelly and I separated. I drove via Chickasha to Amarillo, thence to Denver. My wife was in Portland, Oregon, where I communicated with her, advising her to return to Denver immediately. I put $50,000.00 in a bag with surplus clothes, locked it, and left it with friends to keep until my wife called for it. I left instructions in a letter addressed to her in my postoffice box for her to rent an apartment upon arrival and to leave the address in that box. I had been under a tremendous strain for a week, on the go night and day, so I decided I'd have a little pleasure in Denver. I don't believe I spent over $1,000.00 during the three days I stayed there. I then went by plane to Minneapolis where I rejoined the Kellys as prearranged. I arrived there on August 5th. The following day the three of us drove to Mille Lake, a resort. Kelly told me he was leaving early the next day for Cleveland and in the event anything of importance occurred to wire him. I told him I brought $42,000.00 with me. The next day, at the Boulevards of Paris, a roadhouse, Jack Phifer (now deceased) got word via the grapevine that the "G" were concentrating in the Twin Cities. He learned that four of his crew had been arrested and held incommunicado. I warned Kelly by wire and left that night for Omaha and Denver.

When I was alone in the apartment my wife had rented I put $41,000.00 in the same bag with the $50,000.00. I probably spent about $2,000.00 all told and had $700.00 on me when I was arrested three days after returning to Denver. I told my wife when I left the apartment on the date of my arrest that there was over $90,000.00 in a locked bag in the clothes closet.

I did not authorize her to pay any money to anyone after my arrest with the exception of $200.00 to a trusty by whom I sent a message warning her to leave. She was not apprehended until 16 months after my arrest, and I, of course, do not have the slightest idea how much she spent or was bilked out of. She was never extravagant, but, I suppose, living as she had to for those 16 months she spent more than usual.

This explains about all so far as I know. In my honest opinion the Shannons did not, nor would not, accept any of that money. Kelly may have intended to give them some money later on after he exchanged it for other money. I know they refused time and time again to accept money from any of us. It would be purely a conjecture for me to say why "Boss" Shannon permitted us to take charge whenever we were inclined to do so—he just seemed to be fascinated with Kelly's line.

Respectfully,
Albert L. Bates

The memorandum that the Oklahoma City special-agent-in-charge dispatched to FBI headquarters in Washington pointing out the potential embarrassment to the bureau should the government reveal information concerning the handwriting testimony stated:

> Information concerning the testimony of handwriting expert D. C. Patterson, who appeared as a government witness during the trial of GEORGE and KATHRYN KELLY, was brought to the attention of the Bureau in order that these circumstances and their potential as a source of embarrassment to the Bureau might be fully evaluated and considered prior to the time that any action was taken by this office to inform the U.S. Attorney. PATTERSON was a private handwriting expert presumably hired by the U.S. Attorney at Oklahoma City. He is now deceased.
>
> As has been pointed out previously, it is KATHRYN KELLY's contention in her motion for vacation of sentence that she was denied the opportunity to engage the services of a handwriting expert to refute the Government's testimony that she had written certain ransom notes. Although the transcripts of the proceedings establish that there was no attempt by the Government to prove that KATHRYN KELLY or any other individual defendant wrote the ransom notes in this case, the transcript of the record of the second trial in 1933 does establish that she was identified by a Government witness, D. C. PATTERSON, as the writer of the two letters mailed from Chicago, Illinois, on 9/18/33 during the course of the first trial involving her mother, ORA SHANNON, and others.
>
> It should be borne in mind that a transcript of the second trial, which involved only GEORGE and KATHRYN KELLY, was not available at the time of the hearings on the motion in June, 1958, and it was

not then known exactly what handwriting testimony might have been used against these persons.

Should action be taken at this time to acquaint the U.S. Attorney with these circumstances, it is not improbable he might take the position that he was obligated to acknowledge to the court and the defendants at this time that the testimony of the government witness on this particular point of evidence was possibly based on an erroneous conclusion, even though it did not relate to actual *ransom notes* as alleged by KATHRYN KELLY in her motion. As was indicated in earlier communications to the Bureau, it was clearly brought out during the hearings in June, 1958, that the ransom notes were typewritten and that the Government had not sought to establish their origin through handwriting testimony in either of the 1933 trials.

The FBI file and the USA's [U.S. attorney's] file in this case do not indicate that the USA's office was ever made aware of the fact that the two letters mailed from Chicago on 9/18/33 had been submitted to the FBI Laboratory in 1933 for a handwriting examination or that the FBI Laboratory conclusion was contrary to that of PATTERSON. There is not any information indicating the USA's office was informed of the results of any examination other than that made by PATTERSON. To disclose the results of the earlier examination by the Bureau to the U.S. Attorney now, could be the basis of some embarrassment to the Bureau, and would probably result in a request from him for a re-examination to resolve any conflict.

As the Bureau is aware, the attorney for the defendants on 9/15/59 filed notice with the U.S. Supreme Court, appealing from the decision of the U.S. Circuit Court of Appeals, 10th District, on 7/27/59. By the latter decision, the matter was remanded to the District Court for further hearing on the motions to vacate sentence. Should the pending appeal result in a continuation of the hearings on the motion, it is entirely possible that this particular phase of the case might not be further pursued since it was covered by testimony offered prior to the time hearing was discontinued. On the other hand, should the counsel for the defendants reopen this phase of the case in the hearings in view of the information now shown by the transcript, it would appear that further handwriting examinations would be requested since Mr. PATTERSON is now deceased. On the basis of such re-examination, any error in Mr. PATTERSON's conclusions would be brought out and could thus be considered by the Court without raising any question regarding the possibility of any earlier examination by the Bureau.

In the event the pending appeal should result in a new trial, it would, of course, be the decision of the U.S. Attorney as to what items of evidence and testimony he desired to use. Should he elect to use the two letters in question, he would of necessity request further handwriting examinations in view of Mr. PATTERSON's death. Through such examinations, the U.S. Attorney would be aware of the conflict with the previous testimony and would not be in the position of having to disclose the conflict in open court or to inquire as to any earlier examination.

It will be noted that the motion as filed on behalf of KATHRYN KELLY reads in part as follows:

" . . . and therefore this phase of the case would not have gone to the jury virtually uncontested. The jury was of course, deceived and misled as to this aspect of the case and this was vital and fatal to the affiant."

As has been pointed out in earlier communications, the two letters mailed from Chicago had no direct connection with the original conspiracy to kidnap and hold the victim for ransom. The extent to which the introduction of these items against KATHRYN KELLY may have influenced the jurors cannot, of course, be determined. However, the Government can definitely establish that there was no evidence introduced in any trial to connect KATHRYN KELLY with the writing of the ransom notes.

Inasmuch as it is highly probable that if the question of handwriting is brought out in any further hearing or re-trial in this case, it will necessarily result in a reexamination of this evidence, thus revealing any erroneous conclusions in PATTERSON's examination, there would appear to be no useful purpose in advising the U.S. Attorney concerning this conflict of opinion, at least until such time as a decision is made regarding the appeal now pending before the U.S. Supreme Court.

Bureau advice requested.

ARTICLE BY EDWARD BENNETT WILLIAMS,
JUNE 16, 1962, AND FBI COMMENT

Criminal defense lawyer Edward Bennett Williams caught everyone by surprise when, having had no connection at all with the women's case, he came out with some brief but caustic comments about it in his book, *One Man's Freedom*. These were edited and excerpted in the widely circulated *Saturday Evening Post:*

> Evidence is a precious thing. It can be the key that frees the innocent and jails the guilty. Unfortunately it also can be blindly overlooked or willfully withheld. When that occurs, justice suffers. In one case with which I am familiar, a woman spent twenty-five years in prison, convicted in a trial in which evidence which might have freed her was withheld by the federal prosecution. The woman happened to be the wife of a notorious outlaw and kidnapper, George (Machine-gun) Kelly. But no matter who her husband was, she was entitled to a fair trial. She did not receive one. Even today the federal government continues to withhold the evidence in question.
>
> This evidence was kept from the jury that tried Kathryn Kelly. If the jury had known that the local handwriting expert was wrong, according to the FBI's own expert, and that Mrs. Kelly was undoubtedly telling the truth when she denied signing the letters, the verdict might have been different. This, of course, can be small consolation for twenty-five years in prison.
>
> But the most disturbing facet of the case is that this evidence was *not even disclosed in the 1958 hearing.* Instead, the government chose to keep the file closed and forget the case. This case therefore is a classic example of the need for a change in pretrial procedures to give the defense a fair opportunity to discover the evidence confronting it. If Mrs. Kelly had known in advance that a handwriting expert would testify, she might have obtained another expert to challenge his testimony. If she had known that the FBI's own expert had concluded after extensive analysis that she had not signed the letters, she could have called him as a witness. But the procedure of combat by surprise had dealt a lethal blow to her chance to defend herself.

This article brought an immediate, rather whiny, defensive internal staff note to Hoover of June 15, 1962: "In line with the article . . . written by Edward Bennett Williams, Washington, D.C., attorney and Bureau antagonist . . . this is to advise that we are reviewing extensive files at the Seat of Government and a search is being made at Oklahoma City. . . . Every effort is being made to determine how Williams became aware of the above information, including the identity of the FBI examiner. It should be noted in this regard that former Special Agent William C. Turner, who was assigned to the Oklahoma City Office during 1960 and 1961, has utilized the services of Williams' Washington law firm in connection with his unfounded claims against the Bureau and this is being taken into consideration as possibly Williams' "source of information."

KIRKPATRICK POEM ABOUT KELLY, C. 1958

Ernest Kirkpatrick, Urschel's friend and drop man, tried hard over the years to find the rest of the ransom bills. He journeyed to West Virginia in an unsuccessful visit to Kathryn and her mother, who knew nothing. Afterward he dropped in on Bates and Kelly at Alcatraz, with the same result. Kirkpatrick then wrote:

The experience of ransoming my friend from the gangsters was the inspiration for writing the poem "Faith." Some time later I had a conversation with one of these same gangsters in Alcatraz prison. The following poem, "Echoes from Alcatraz," relates in practically his own words, many of this gangster's experiences, and expresses his attitude and philosophy of life. It also expresses his miserable memories and remorseful reflections which create for him a living hell—the logical consequence of such a hellish life:

> I've robbed and I've raped and I've rutted;
> I've murdered and cheated and lied;
> I've lived by the sword and I've glutted;
> Oh God! How I wish I had died!
>
> I've thrown the death slugs from machine guns;
> I've stabbed with cold steel from the dark.
> I've held up poor beggars just for the fun
> In those years I deemed it a lark.

I sit day and night without pleasure;
A glance at the sun would be swell;
But the G-men have taken my measure,
And I'm already living in hell!

HOOVER "EXPLAINS" G-MAN "ORIGIN," JULY 1946

Over the years, J. Edgar Hoover continually embellished the "G-Men" tale. In 1946, he contributed "The Story of the Federal Bureau of Investigation" to the *Tennessee Law Review,* saying, in part:

> In the early morning hours of September 26, 1933, a small group of men surrounded a house in Memphis, Tennessee. In the house was George "Machine-Gun" Kelly, late of Leavenworth Penitentiary. He was wanted by the FBI for kidnapping. For two months, FBI Agents had trailed the gangster and his wife, Kathryn Kelly. Quickly the men of the FBI, accompanied by local law enforcement officers, closed in around the house, and entered.
>
> "We are Federal officers. . . . Come out with your hands up."
>
> "Machine-Gun" Kelly stood cowering in a corner. His heavy face twitched as he gazed at the men before him. Reaching trembling hands up towards the ceiling he whimpered, "Don't shoot, G-men; don't shoot!"

FBI MEMO ON TURNER BOOK, MARCH 12, 1970

When former agent William Turner's book containing previously secret memoranda concerning the handwriting revelations finally was published in 1970, it set off still more internal memo writing. A lengthy one went to Hoover's top assistant:

> Chapter III of referenced book begins with Turner's transfer to Oklahoma City and dwells upon his relationship with SAC [Special Agent in Charge] Wesley Grapp. Turner accuses Grapp of knowing about an FBI Laboratory handwriting examination report in the Urschel kidnapping case containing information contradictory to the testimony given against Kathryn Kelly by an outside (non-FBI) handwriting examiner (Reproduced in the Appendix at the back of the book are:

(1) a 1933 Laboratory report in which C. A. Appel concludes that the handwriting in question is not that of Kathryn Kelly, and (2) a letter from the Oklahoma City Office to the Bureau dated October 15, 1959, pertaining to this handwriting examination in the Urschel case).

The reference to Appel's handwriting examination is a rehash of information set forth in a 1962 "Saturday Evening Post" article by Edward Bennett Williams. Williams alleged the Federal Government willfully withheld evidence (meaning FBI Laboratory examiner Charles A. Appel's findings) in connection with the trial of Kathryn Kelly in 1933. This is not factual and full details concerning this matter are set forth in memoranda dated June 15 and 26, 1962 (attached). . . .

Insofar as the letters are concerned, it should be noted that Kathryn Kelly was charged with conspiracy to commit kidnapping, and there is nothing in the court record to show why the Government introduced these letters in the 1933 trial since they were mailed subsequent to the abduction and release of victim Urschel. . . .

In order to adequately prepare and assist the United States Attorney in the Government's defense of Kathryn Kelly's 1958 motion, our Oklahoma City Office advised the Bureau during 1959 that a review of the Urschel kidnapping file did not indicate whether the results of Appel's examination had been furnished to the United States Attorney at the time of the kidnapping trial in 1933. Oklahoma City requested Bureau advice as to whether the United States Attorney handling the appeal matter should then be informed of the existence of Appel's examination.

The Oklahoma City Office was subsequently instructed to closely follow Kathryn Kelly's appeal; and should it be determined that it will be brought before the court for a hearing, the Oklahoma City Office should immediately advise the Bureau, at which time consideration could then be given as to whether the results of the 1933 handwriting examination should be furnished to the United States Attorney handling the appeal. No action has been taken on this appeal, and the matter is still pending in the Oklahoma City Federal Court.

It was assumed in 1962 that SA Turner was the source of the material utilized by Edward Bennett Williams in his article appearing the the [*sic*] "Saturday Evening Post." While Turner had normal access to Bureau files, he was not assigned to any phase of this case.

Bibliography

BOOKS

Alix, Ernest Kahlar. *Ransom Kidnapping in America, 1874–1974*. Carbondale: Southern Illinois University Press, 1978.

Anderson, Jack, with Daryl Gibson. *Peace, War, and Politics: An Eyewitness Account*. New York: Tom Doherty Associates, 1999.

Audett, James Henry (Blackie). *Rap Sheet: My Life Story*. New York: William Sloane Associates, 1954. [Audett's three Alcatraz incarceration records give his Christian name as "Theodore."]

Barnes, Bruce. *Machine Gun Kelly—To Right a Wrong*. Perris, Calif.: Tipper Publications, 1991.

Barton, George. *Thrilling Triumphs of Crime Detection*. With a foreword by J. Edgar Hoover. Philadelphia: David McKay, 1937.

Beacher, Milton Daniel. *Alcatraz Island: Memoirs of a Rock Doc*. Lebanon, N.J.: Pelican Island Publishing, 2001.

Bennett, James V. *I Chose Prison*. New York: Alfred A. Knopf, 1970.

Bergreen, Laurence. *Capone—The Man and the Era*. New York: Simon and Schuster, 1994.

Breuer, William B. *J. Edgar Hoover and His G-Men*. Westport, Conn.: Praeger Publishers, 1995.

Clayton, Merle. *Union Station Massacre—The Shootout That Started the FBI's War on Crime*. Indianapolis: Bobbs-Merrill, 1975.

Colcord, Charles Francis. *The Autobiography of Charles Francis Colcord*. Tulsa, Okla.: privately printed, 1970.

Coleman, Loren. *Tom Slick: True Life Encounters in Cryptozoology*. Fresno, Calif.: Craven Street Books, 2002.

Comfort, Mildred Houghton. *J. Edgar Hoover: Modern Knight Errant*. Minneapolis: T. S. Denison, 1959.

Cook, Fred J. *The FBI Nobody Knows*. New York: Macmillan, 1964.

Cooper, Courtney Ryley. *Here's to Crime*. Boston: Little, Brown, 1937.

———. *Ten Thousand Public Enemies*. With a foreword by J. Edgar Hoover. Boston: Little, Brown, 1935.

Corey, Herbert. *Farewell, Mr. Gangster! America's War on Crime.* With a foreword by J. Edgar Hoover. New York: D. Appleton-Century, 1936.

Croy, Homer. *Last of the Great Outlaws—The Story of Cole Younger.* New York: Duell, Sloan and Pearce, 1956.

DeLoach, Cartha D. (Deke). *Hoover's FBI—The Inside Story by His Trusted Lieutenant.* Washington, D.C.: Regnery Publishing, 1995.

Demaris, Ovid. *The Director: An Oral Biography of J. Edgar Hoover.* New York: Harper's Magazine Press, 1975.

Denenberg, Barry. *The True Story of J. Edgar Hoover and the FBI.* New York: Scholastic, 1993.

Donner, Frank J. *The Age of Surveillance: The Aims and Methods of America's Political Intelligence System.* New York: Alfred A. Knopf, 1980.

Dunning, John. *Tune in Yesterday: The Ultimate Encyclopedia of Old-Time Radio.* Englewood Cliffs, N.J.: Prentice-Hall, 1976.

Edge, L. L. *Run the Cat Roads.* New York: Dembner Books, 1981.

Esslinger, Michael. *Alcatraz—A Definitive History of the Penitentiary Years, 1934–1963.* Dublin, Calif.: Ocean View Publishing, 2002.

Gentry, Curt. *J. Edgar Hoover: The Man and His Secrets.* New York: W. W. Norton, 1991.

Girardin, G. Russell, with William J. Helmer. *Dillinger—The Untold Story.* Bloomington: Indiana University Press, 1994.

Gish, Anthony. *American Bandits.* Girard, Kan.: Haldeman-Julius Publications, 1938.

———. *American Outlaws.* Cornwall, England: St. Ives, 1973.

Godwin, John. *Alcatraz: 1868–1963.* Garden City, N.Y.: Doubleday, 1963.

Goulart, Ron. *The Adventurous Decade.* New Rochelle, N.Y.: Arlington House Publishers, 1975.

———. *Line Up, Tough Guys.* Los Angeles: Sherbourne Press, 1966.

Haley, J. Evetts. *Robbing Banks Was My Business: The Story of J. Harvey Bailey—America's Most Successful Bank Robber.* Canyon, Tex.: Palo Duro Press, 1973.

Hamilton, Floyd. *Public Enemy Number One.* Dallas: Acclaimed Books, 1975.

Harlow, Rex. *Oklahoma Leaders.* Oklahoma City: Harlow Publishing, 1928.

Harrison, Walter Mumford. *Me and My Big Mouth.* Oklahoma City: Britton Printing, 1954.

Heaney, Frank, and Gay Machado. *Inside the Walls of Alcatraz.* Palo Alto, Calif.: Bull Publishing, 1987.

Helmer, William, and Rick Mattix. *Public Enemies—America's Criminal Past, 1919–1940.* New York: Checkmark Books, 1998.

Hoover, J. Edgar. *Persons in Hiding.* Boston: Little, Brown, 1938.

Hounschell, Jim. *Lawmen and Outlaws: 116 Years in Joplin's History.* Joplin, Mo.: Walsworth Publishing, in cooperation with Fraternal Order of Police Lodge No. 27, 1989.

Hynd, Alan. *The Giant Killers.* New York: Robert M. McBride, 1945.

———. *Great True Detective Mysteries.* New York: Grosset and Dunlap, 1968.

Inciardi, James A. *Careers in Crime*. Chicago: Rand McNally College
  Publishing, 1975.
Johnston, James A. *Alcatraz Island Prison and the Men Who Live There*. New
  York: Charles Scribner's Sons, 1949.
Karpis, Alvin, with Bill Trent. *The Alvin Karpis Story*. New York: Coward,
  McCann and Geoghegan, 1971.
Kirkpatrick, E. E. *Crimes' Paradise*. San Antonio, Tex.: Naylor, 1934.
———. *Voices from Alcatraz—The Authentic Inside Story of the Urschel Kidnap-
  ping*. San Antonio, Tex.: Naylor, 1947.
Livesey, Robert. *On the Rock: Twenty-five Years in Alcatraz—The Prison Story of
  Alvin Karpis*. New York: Beaufort Books, 1980.
Logan, James K., editor. *The Federal Courts of the Tenth Circuit*. Oklahoma City:
  U.S. Court of Appeals for the Tenth Circuit, 1992.
Look Magazine Editors. *The Story of the FBI: The Official Picture History of the
  Federal Bureau of Investigation*. New York: E. P. Dutton, 1954.
Louderback, Lew. *The Bad Ones—Gangsters of the '30s and Their Molls*.
  Greenwich, Conn.: Fawcett Publications, 1968.
Lowenthal, Max. *The Federal Bureau of Investigation*. New York: William Sloan
  Associates, 1950; Westport, Conn.: Greenwood Press, 1971.
Lysing, Henry. *Men against Crime*. New York: David Kemp, 1938.
McRill, Albert. *And Satan Came Also*. Oklahoma City: Britton Publishing,
  1955.
Messick, Hank. *John Edgar Hoover—An Inquiry into the Life and Times of John
  Edgar Hoover and His Relationships to the Continuing Partnership of Crime,
  Business, and Politics*. New York: David McKay, 1972.
Messick, Hank, and Burt Goldblatt. *Kidnapping: The Illustrated History*. New
  York: Dial Press, 1974.
Miles, Ray. *King of the Wildcatters: The Life and Times of Tom Slick*. College
  Station: Texas A&M University Press, 1996.
Milligan, Maurice M. *Missouri Waltz*. New York: Charles Scribner's Sons, 1948.
Nash, Jay Robert. *Bloodletters and Badmen*. Rev. ed. New York: M. Evans, 1995.
———. *Citizen Hoover: A Critical Study of the Life and Times of J. Edgar Hoover
  and His FBI*. Chicago: Nelson-Hall, 1972.
———. *Encyclopedia of World Crime*. Vol. 3. Wilmette, Ill.: CrimeBooks, 1990.
Odier, Pierre. *The Rock—A History of Alcatraz, the Fort/the Prison*. Eagle Rock,
  Calif.: L'Image Odier, 1982.
Owens, Ron. *Oklahoma Justice: The Oklahoma City Police—A Century of
  Gunfighters, Gangsters, and Terrorists*. Paducah, Ky.: Turner Publishing, 1995.
Paton, John. *Crime and Punishment*. Vol. 1. Freeport, N.Y.: Marshall Cavendish,
  1985.
Potter, Claire Bond. *War on Crime—Bandits, G-Men, and the Politics of Mass
  Culture*. New Brunswick, N.J.: Rutgers University Press, 1998.
Powers, Richard Gid. *G-Men—Hoover's FBI in American Popular Culture*.
  Carbondale: Southern Illinois University Press, 1983.

———. *Secrecy and Power: The Life of J. Edgar Hoover.* 1939. Reprint, New York: DaCapo Press, 1972.

Prassel, Frank Richard. *The Great American Outlaw—A Legacy of Fact and Fiction.* Norman: University of Oklahoma Press, 1993.

Purvis, Melvin H. *American Agent.* New York: Doran, 1936.

Quimby, Myron J. *The Devil's Emissaries.* Cranbury, N.J.: A. S. Barnes, 1970.

Reddig, William M. *Tom's Town: Kansas City and the Pendergast Legend.* Philadelphia: J. B. Lippincott, 1947; Columbia: University of Missouri Press, 1986.

Robins, Natalie S. *Alien Ink—The FBI's War on Freedom of Expression.* New York: William Morrow, 1992.

Ruth, David E. *Inventing the Public Enemy—The Gangster in American Culture, 1918–1934.* Chicago: University of Chicago Press, 1996.

Sifakis, Carl. *The Encyclopedia of American Crime.* New York: Smithmark Publishers, 1992.

Steinbeck, John. *The Grapes of Wrath.* New York: Viking Press, 1939.

Stewart, Roy P. *Born Grown: An Oklahoma City History.* Oklahoma City: Fidelity Bank, 1974.

Sullivan, William C., with Bill Brown. *The Bureau—My Thirty Years in Hoover's FBI.* New York: W. W. Norton, 1979.

Summers, Anthony. *Official and Confidential—The Secret Life of J. Edgar Hoover.* New York: G. P. Putnam's Sons, 1993.

Swisher, Carl Brent, editor. *Selected Papers of Homer Cummings.* New York: Charles Scribner's Sons, 1939; New York: DaCapo Press, 1972.

Theoharis, Athan. *J. Edgar Hoover, Sex, and Crime: An Historical Antidote.* Chicago: Ivan R. Dee, 1995.

Theoharis, Athan, and John Stuart Cox. *The Boss: J. Edgar Hoover and the Great American Inquisition.* Philadelphia: Temple University Press, 1988.

Theoharis, Athan, editor. *From the Secret Files of J. Edgar Hoover.* Chicago: Ivan R. Dee, 1991.

———, with Tony G. Poveda, Susan Rosenfield, and Richard Gid Powers. *The FBI: A Comprehensive Reference Guide.* Phoenix: Oryx Press, 1999; New York: Checkmark Books, 2000.

Toland, John. *The Dillinger Days.* New York: Random House, 1963; New York: DaCapo Press, 1995.

Tracy, Tom, and Leon G. Turrou. *How to Be a G-Man.* New York: Robert M. McBride, 1939.

Tully, Andrew. *The FBI's Most Famous Cases.* With an introduction and comments by J. Edgar Hoover. New York: William Morrow, 1965.

Turner, William W. *Hoover's FBI: The Men and the Myths.* New York: Dell, 1970. Reprint, New York: Thunder's Mouth Press, 1993.

Turrou, Leon G. *Where My Shadow Falls: Two Decades of Crime Detection.* Garden City, N.Y.: Doubleday, 1949.

Ungar, Sanford J. *FBI: An Uncensored Look behind the Walls.* Boston: Little, Brown, 1976.

Bibliography

Unger, Robert. *The Union Station Massacre—The Original Sin of J. Edgar Hoover's FBI*. Kansas City, Mo.: Andrews McMeel Publishing, 1997.

Vagtborg, Harold. *The Story of Southwest Research Center—A Private, Nonprofit, Scientific Research Adventure*. Austin: University of Texas Press, 1973.

Waller, George. *Kidnap—The Story of the Lindbergh Case*. New York: Dial Press, 1961.

Watters, Pat, and Stephen Gillers. *Investigating the FBI*. Garden City, N.Y.: Doubleday, 1973.

Whitehead, Don. *The FBI Story—A Report to the People*. With a foreword by J. Edgar Hoover. New York: Random House, 1956.

Williams, Edward Bennett. *One Man's Freedom*. New York: Atheneum, 1962.

Wilson, Donald Powell. *My Six Convicts: A Psychologist's Three Years in Fort Leavenworth*. New York: Rinehart, 1951.

ARTICLES, INTERNET

"The Adventures of Tom Slick," Robert Lubar, *Fortune*, July 1960.

"A Beautiful Heritage Hills Home: A Study in Mystery and Beauty," Debbie Anglin, *Norman Living*, May 2000.

"George 'Machine' Gun Kelly: Bank Robbing and Kidnapping Desperado," Allan May, Dark Horse Entertainment, The Crime Library (on Internet), 2000.

"George 'Machine Gun' Kelly et al.; Kidnaping of Charles F. Urschel," U.S. Department of Justice, Federal Bureau of Investigation (on Internet), 1935 (revised July 1989).

"Kidnaper Beware! How Uncle Sam's Detectives Smash Kidnap Gangs," Edwin Teale, *Reader's Digest*, May 1934, condensed from *Popular Science Monthly*, May 1934.

"Kidnaping of Charles F. Urschel," U.S. Department of Justice, Federal Bureau of Investigation (on Internet), 1935.

"Kidnapped!", Kent Frates, *Oklahoma Today*, January—February 2003.

"Machine Gun Kelly," Edgar E. Andrews, *Startling Detective Adventures*, January 1934.

"Machine Gun Kelly," Rick Mattix, Oklahombres, Inc., Oklahoma City (on Internet), 1996.

"Machine Gun Kelly—A Return to Paradise," Linda McGregor Scott, West Tennessee Historical Society Papers, vol. L, Memphis, 1996.

"Making the Twenties (and Thirties) Roar," Charles M. B. Smith, *The Sharpshooter*, July-August 1997, Oklahoma Rifle Association, Yukon.

"1933—J. Edgar Hoover Gets His First Woman," William W. Turner, *Scanlan's Monthly*, May 1970.

"1970—Kathryn Kelly in Peace and War," Stephen Schneck, *Scanlan's Monthly*, May 1970.

"A Short History of the Federal Bureau of Investigation," Federal Bureau of Investigation (FBI Internet home page), 1997.

"The Story of the Federal Bureau of Investigation," J. Edgar Hoover, *Tennessee Law Review*, vol. 19, no. 3, July 1946.

"The Unforgettables: Machine Gun Kelly," James Finnegan, *Master Detective*, April 1970.

"The Untold Mystery behind the Urschel Abduction Horror," Harrison Moreland, *True Detective Mysteries*, March, April, and May 1934.

"When Kidnapping Was America's Scourge," David Whitman, *U.S. News and World Report*, March 22, 1999.

"Your Money or Your Life: Strange New Rules in the Global Game of Kidnapping," Kevin Whitelaw, *U.S. News and World Report*, March 22, 1999.

FILMS, TELEVISION PROGRAMS, VIDEO

Crimes in Time ("What's in a Name?" episode), television documentary, executive producer Bram Roos, narrated by Tom Skerritt, A&E Home Video, the History Channel, 1997.

The FBI Story, motion picture starring James Stewart and Vera Miles, distributed by Warner Home Video (149 minutes), 1959.

Machine-Gun Kelly, motion picture starring Charles Bronson, distributed by Columbia Tri-Star Home Video (80 minutes), 1958.

Melvin Purvis G-Man, motion picture subsequently retitled *The Legend of Machine Gun Kelly* for television release, starring Dale Robertson, distributed by HBO-Canadian (76 minutes), 1974.

"The News Parade of 1933," Hearst Metrotone News, vol. 5, no. 226, newsreel distributed by Metro-Goldwyn-Mayer, 1933.

"Oil in Oklahoma—Tom Slick," a television documentary much of which is about the Urschel kidnapping, executive producer James C. Leake, written and narrated by Bob Gregory, first shown on KTUL-TV, Tulsa, 1981.

"You Can't Get Away with It—Behind the Scenes with the G-Men," introduction by J. Edgar Hoover and containing scenes of the Urschel trial, produced for the FBI by Universal Newsreel, narrated by Lowell Thomas, 1936.

MISCELLANEOUS

The author examined, and critically compared, numerous contemporary news reports and later historical feature articles from these other print media (more than a few, sadly, no longer in existence): Associated Press, *Britton (Okla.) North Star*, *Brownwood (Tex.) Bulletin*, *Chicago Tribune*, *Daily Oklahoman* and

Times, Dallas Morning News, Decatur (Tex.) News, Denton (Tex.) Record Chronicle, Denver Rocky Mountain News, Fort Worth Star-Telegram, Fostoria (Ohio) Daily Review-Times, International News Service, *Kansas City Times* and *Star, Kingfisher (Okla.) Times, New York Times, North San Antonio Times, Oklahoma Journal, Oklahoma News, San Antonio Express /News, San Antonio Light, Shawnee (Okla.) News-Star, Tulsa Daily World,* United Press, *Washington Evening Star, Washington Herald, Washington Post,* and *Wise County (Tex.) Messenger.* Information about the airlines serving the Oklahoma City area was obtained from *The Official Aviation Guide of the Airways,* Official Aviation Guide Co., Chicago, July 1933 edition. Information about the route of the train that the two couriers took to deliver the ransom came from *The Official Guide of the Railways and Steam Navigation Lines of the United States, Porto Rico, Canada, Mexico and Cuba,* National Railway Publication Co., New York, July 1933.

   In addition to obtaining transcripts of all three trials, the author also researched issues of the annual *Texas Almanac;* the *Chronicles of Oklahoma, vol. 37* (Winter 1959–1960); the "Thomas Baker Slick Papers, 1914–1973" at the University of Oklahoma Libraries; the weighty but still partially and ridiculously redacted record of the kidnapping case (No. 7-115) at FBI headquarters in Washington; files of the case maintained at the southwest region complex in Fort Worth of the National Archives and Records Administration (NARA); Kelly's criminal and prison records at the NARA offices in San Bruno, Calif.; the documentary motion picture files about the case at the NARA offices in College Park, Md.; the Oklahoma Historical Society; the Wise County Heritage Museum; the Encyclopedia Britannica; records of the Social Security Administration, the Department of Veterans Affairs, and the Bureau of the Census (including 1930 census information released in 2002); and numerous miscellaneous sources and leads from the Internet and elsewhere. Among the Slick papers was the unexpected wooden-bound book *Geese Flying South: A Collection of Poems* by Ernest E. Kirkpatrick, put together in 1953 by a Ben H. Moore. Additionally, numerous personal interviews and conversations were held with people conversant with various aspects of or about the case.

   Particularly interesting, and informative, was a huge, oversize scrapbook of newspaper clippings and photographs of the 1933 trials that was discovered in 2000 in a large sealed cardboard box in the basement of the Oklahoma Historical Society building. It was almost certainly put together by Judge Vaught. The author—the first person to examine it in half a century—pored over the seventy-eight pages containing roughly seven thousand fading, yellowed, crumbling clippings of various lengths from scores of newspapers carefully overlaid and folded one atop another, most supplied and dated by a commercial clipping service. Although only that, it was in effect a fascinating day-by-day journalistic chronicle of the two 1933 trials as people across the country were reading about them.

Index

❖   ❖   ❖   ❖   ❖   ❖   ❖